MW01073881

Praise for Jack Morris's

RUINED FOR LIFE

"Jack Morris was an extraordinary Jesuit who worked for peace until his death. I first met Jack in the 1990s, when we were both working with the Jesuit Refugee Service in East Africa - he in Uganda, me in Kenya. (In our very first conversation he gave me some mind-clearing advice about a difficult situation.) Jack's lifelong work for peace offers us a question: How do we put peace in the center of the church's thinking? Jack was the founder of the Jesuit Volunteer Corps movement, which has enabled thousands of college graduates to serve the poor, experience Christian community, deepen their prayer, and meet God in surprising new ways."

JAMES MARTIN, SJ, Editor at large, *America Magazine*; author of *The Jesuit Guide to (Almost) Everything*, and *Between Heaven and Mirth*

"Jack Morris was a Jesuit who had vision, but even more he put his ideas and inspirations into practice. His life story indicates just how much he did so. He was an inspiration to his fellow Jesuits as well as to countless others who knew him and collaborated with him."

MICHAEL L. COOK, SJ, author of *Trinitarian Christology – The Power That Sets Us Free;* Professor of Religious Studies, Gonzaga University

"Jack Morris was one of the unique voices for justice in the Society of Jesus and the Church, whether he was in Alaska, Uganda or a thousand other places where he spoke his heart. This book will be a gift for those who seek to understand and live out the inner life of faith as embraced by Morris."

GARY SMITH, SJ, author of *They Come Back Singing, Radical Compassion,* and *Street Journal;* minister to the poor in Sudanese refugee camps in Uganda and on the streets of Portland, Oregon

"Jack Morris's life from Sheridan, Oregon, to Copper Valley, Alaska, from Butte to Bethlehem, was no ordinary adventure. His enthusiasm always carried along dozens of people in his wake. Now, in his own clarion voice we hear the call to the depths of our own spirit to live the more authentic, more daring life of the Gospel of Jesus. Barbara Scharff has offered this further votive of love by offering up his memoir."

PATRICK HOWELL, SJ, Distinguished Professor, Institute of Catholic Thought and Culture, Seattle University

Ruined For Life

Ruined For Life

Jack Morris, SJ

with
Barbara Underwood Scharff

First Paperback Edition © 2016 Barbara Underwood Scharff
Kindle Edition © 2016 Barbara Underwood Scharff

ISBN-13: 9781519460912
ISBN-10: 1519460910

Cover Design by June Cooley
Front Cover Photo by William Lockyear
Back Cover Photo of Jack Morris, SJ, by Brad Reynolds, SJ

A significant portion of the proceeds from the sale of this book will support the on-going work of Jesuit Volunteers.

For my family, friends, peace pilgrims,
Jesuit Volunteers, and brother Jesuits
Who all formed the community of my heart.

Permissions

Editor's Note

JOHN "JACK" MORRIS, SJ, DIED before completing his book. His story, however, is told largely in his own words from beginning to end. I spent eight months interviewing him about his philosophy and life experiences. Before Jack's passing in September 2012, he placed in my care the half-finished project and asked me to complete it. I assembled, compiled, co-wrote, researched and edited the manuscript, drawing rich material from boxes of personal journals, letters, poetry, homilies, newsletters and news articles Jack entrusted to me. Several people who had accompanied Jack on parts of his journey corroborated the stories and are named in the acknowledgements. Some of the entries capturing the story of the Bethlehem Peace Pilgrimage were taken from newsletters and a communal journal to which Jack contributed many insights and observations. The quotes that start each chapter are Jack's words unless otherwise attributed.

Come now and travel the wide arc of Jack's life through his own consummate storytelling. You'll roam with him through his spacious Montana childhood, summer in the circus, the call of joining the Jesuits, and his challenging formation as a priest. He'll tell you how he developed the Jesuit Volunteer Corps movement, and how the crazy idea of the Bethlehem Peace Pilgrimage ignited him to walk almost seven-thousand miles with others from Bangor, Washington to the Holy Land. He shares what a tender grace it was to care for his dying mother, and his Jesuit Refugee

Service years in companionship with Sudanese refugees in northern Uganda. A pilgrim, philosopher, and gypsy at heart, he changed every soul he encountered by pointing the way to Christ's love and mercy. Jack has passed, but thankfully he passed on to us his poignant memories of a life lived on the frontiers of the heart.

Barbara Underwood Scharff

Table of Contents

CHAPTER 1

Exploring My Life–Why I Must Write

❖

"We shall not cease from exploration
And the end of all our exploring
Will be to arrive where we started
And know the place for the first time."[1]

— *T.S. ELIOT*

I WAS SEVEN WHEN I learned for the first time how babies got here. From that time, for many years, I carried in my subconscious a soft, persistent jealousy. Girls, I instinctively sensed, were lucky; boys had been cheated. The Creator made it this way and I wondered why. Never would I be able to experience what surely must be one of the most profound encounters of the divine universe in human flesh–giving birth. I was attracted to this female potentiality because it was so immense and clear. I wondered if any other influence could match it.

Later, I grasped the fact that this *instinct* to give birth is a precious gift that visits upon both sexes. It served as a primary guide through my childhood, young manhood, and into the fullness of my quest as a priest to walk in the steps of Jesus Christ. I knew that I, too, was invited to bring forth something full and fresh into the world, to surrender to the Holy Spirit and give birth to Christ in my life. I dare say the need to birth something new is a drive, a compulsion, a love quest at the center of human existence. No one can purchase happiness outside of it.

True birth, I now know, is linked to the adventure of love, the bringing forth of spirit, the emergence of one's own authenticity. We are invited to labor and bring something loving into the world that wouldn't have been created if we had not been born.

The creative impulse to write my story is mysterious, energizing, and intimidating. If I compare my life to a sunflower, then the individual leaves, petals, and seeds lie scattered along the paths I've walked. This memoir is a return journey to consciously pick up as many individual parts as I can, and from all I've retrieved, offer something of meaning and beauty for God. In doing so, I hope to warm myself and others at the fire of self-knowledge and understand my place and purpose for the first time.

I admit there is something of the shadow of death in all of this. Writing one's life and imagining others reading it, extends our personhood and relationships beyond the grave. I want to tell others that my life counted: I was, am, and will have been worth something. The life story of each one of us can be, at least for a small listening circle, like a hearth in the cold night. Come and sit. Listen and share.

T.S. Eliot reminds us to be explorers into old age. "We must be still and still moving/Into another intensity/For a further union, a deeper communion." [2] Aging steals away physical agility, quickness of body and mind. We move toward an inward center, yet still we long, dream, and demand depth. The primary adventure of old age ought to be this turning inward, away from outwardly superficial activities and concerns which, over the years, have attached themselves with a false importance.

Coupled with the urgencies of my Christian faith, is my identity as a Jesuit priest, with the prayer, meditation, worship, mindfulness, and call to action that a Jesuit life invites. It was a remarkable charge of dynamite set loose by Ignatius of Loyola, the founder of the Society of Jesus, who said that a good Jesuit always has one foot raised, ready for a journey.

As a Catholic priest, I followed Jesus, the one who poured himself out seeking to glorify the Father. His whole life was that single adventure into a deeper union, a further communion. He gave his all to accomplish it, and that's why we say he is the answer to the conundrum of life's journey.

Birth, death, and new life. It is true that my end is in my beginnings. I can only hand over to God what I genuinely possess. The "I" that I want to hand over isn't really mine until I am grasped by the primary purpose of old age, to have allowed the journey itself to fashion my life into some meaningful whole. I discover that it is not me, nor the small story of my brief time on this earth, which determines my explorations. Life has lived me far more than I have lived life.

CHAPTER 2

Beginnings

✤

"There are no weeds, folks.
We are all just a different species of flower."

I WAS BORN IN ANACONDA, Montana on October 22, 1927. My father was second generation Irish. My mother, Violet Agnes Murphy, was English, out of Liverpool on the last transatlantic ship before the Titanic disaster.

Granddad, John (Jack) Morris, landed in Philadelphia from Roscommon County, Ireland in 1875. He arrived in Butte, Montana in early 1883, and was hired to help build the foundation for a new smelter on Warm Springs Creek in Deer Lodge Valley. The adjacent town was named Anaconda after the mining company. Granddad died and was buried in Anaconda in 1924. Dad is buried in Phoenix, Arizona, and Ma lies at rest in Seattle, Washington. As I share this story, my older brother Pat, who worked for the State Department, lives in Washington, DC, and my younger brother Rob, a metallurgist and retired businessman in computer hardware, lives in San Diego, California. Like Abraham and Sarah of old, my forbearers set out in faith, not knowing where they would end up.

I look back on my boyhood in Anaconda with affection. Anaconda was "a boom town on the western frontier" as my brother Pat titles his book on the history of Anaconda. The town was twenty-five blocks long but only five or six blocks wide, rubbing up against mountains and lofty peaks on the south and west sides. Turning southeast, lay the vast Deer Lodge Valley, and to the east stretched open grassland for raising cattle. The land near town was unfit for crops due to smelter pollution. The mines in Butte drew hordes of new immigrants, as did the newly planned and created town of Anaconda, where the copper ore was smelted. Granddad, John James Morrisroe (he dropped the "roe"), one of the first city councilmen, had an early boarding house and saloon on Front Street which looked out onto the Butte-Anaconda-Pacific Railroad. Dad, also named John James, was later a one-term representative in the Montana State Legislature in the mid-1930s. He was not reelected, probably because his drinking and his ideas got in his way. But, yes, Anaconda was the Morris family nest.

Ma was a petite lassie of nineteen when she set sail from Liverpool, England on April 5, 1912. She and her younger brother, Finley, were raised in an orphanage, perhaps because her mother was an alcoholic. My Ma said to our family, "I saved every penny. I was determined to leave England and never return." Ma's ship, *Corsica,* just preceded the Titanic across the ocean. Only when her ship reached Halifax, Nova Scotia, were the passengers informed that five days earlier the mighty Titanic sank after hitting an iceberg.

Ma worked as a chamber maid three years each in Ottawa, Toronto and Montreal, then went down to New York City, to work as a salad chef at the McAlpine Hotel. In 1923, she took the boat to Palm Beach, Florida, where hotels catered to northerners escaping the winter chill.

My father had been roaming, playing minor league baseball, and working at West Point on the training staff. He boarded the same Florida bound ship as my mother. Ma told it this way, "I was seasick the whole trip and just wanted to be alone on deck to enjoy the sun's warmth. The blasted men kept pestering me. I told them to get lost, but this Morris fellow kept on. I didn't want to have anything to do with him, but we both ended up getting jobs at the Royal Poinciana Hotel in Palm Beach."

They had known one another only a short time when Morris got word that his own father, John James, was dying. He hurried back to Anaconda. From Florida, Ma went up to Chicago where she secured a job as a maid with a wealthy family. Violet and John carried on a correspondence which led to his marriage proposal. She was 30 years old, Dad was 36. Her yes, like every yes to marriage, changed her life.

She told us boys, "As I traveled on the train from Chicago to Deer Lodge to meet your father, I couldn't believe America was so wide. The train trip was long, but my heart was dreaming. As we crossed the country, we'd come to romantic towns with rolling hills, clear streams, and white churches. I'd say to myself, it will be just like that scene, or that, but when the train stopped in Butte, my heart dropped." Ma and the rugged, unkempt frontier met face to face. Twenty miles northeast of Anaconda, in Deer Lodge, Dad arranged for Father Landy to marry them in the parish house next to the church because Ma was not Catholic. There, with witnesses to the marriage, they were joined in holy matrimony in 1923. They caught the train the next day for Missoula, where they hopped a stage coach to take them on their honeymoon to Sleeping Child Hot Springs in the Bitterroot Valley.

The newlyweds moved into 1304 East Fifth Street in Anaconda. The dull brown house was built by Granddad John James in a new addition to Anaconda later called *Goosetown.* Thirteen blocks from the Main Street business district and impressive court house, our home sat across from the foundry, facing the Rocky Peak and the steep mountains yonder. Further on were two adjacent cemeteries, one for Catholics and the second for all others.

There were two cottonwood trees in front of our house. As a young tyke, I believed their churning branches caused the wind to blow through town. Across from our house was a large diagonal playground with tee-ter-totters and swings. A small stream oozing out of the foundry a block away bordered the park, and made for winter skating when the water iced over. Family homes were small, people poor, and children numerous. As kids, we watched the horse-drawn wagons—the ice man, the junk man, the milk man—all making their rounds. The AMC street car ran east on Third Street from the car barns on the west end of town. After passing Main Street, there were dozens of bars patronized by the men coming from and going to work. Several hundred men each paid five cents every working day to travel to and from the Washoe Smelter for their eight-hour shifts.

Anaconda took its name from Irish-born Marcus Daily's Anaconda copper mine in Butte. The site was chosen for its abundant supply of water essential for the washing and processing of ores. In time, Anaconda would claim the largest copper smelter in the world, with the tallest smokestack. Even now, all 585 feet of it stands tall, a lonely sentinel on smelter hill, the center of Anaconda's economy and yesterday's glory.

For the next thirty years of his working life, Dad labored on the Washoe Smelter of the Anaconda Copper Mining Company, changing shifts every two weeks. He and his fellow working men drank more than they should have. I recall the roundish aluminum lunch pails with two levels–sandwiches were stored in the lower level and tap beer in the upper. It took me years to realize that this was his weakness; it's how he numbed himself in his dreary sacrifice and love for his family. He had a serious intermittent drinking problem, which eventually saw the loss of family properties. He died at age 69 from silicosis, an occupational mining hazard.

As I look back, I marvel at how long it took me to grow up, to become aware of the love price he and Ma both paid to support and raise their boys, each special in their eyes. Dad's and Ma's hard work for their family was a kind of redemption by grit and determination.

Dad's all-consuming interest outside the mill and his family was the *International Mine, Mill and Smeltermen's Union*. Butte was Local #1. Dad spent a good deal of time in the union office. My hunch is that it was sometimes easier for Dad to stay away from home then to be with Ma. The Union Hall was a hangout for a certain clique, and Dad was in the thick of it. He talked on the radio at times, did one session as a state legislator, and initiated the Smeltermen's Credit Union. Dad's Irish blood ran hot, but it also ran for justice and the working man. He was a reader and he spoke his dreams. He gave Pat, Rob and me a vision of social and economic realities.

One night Dad didn't come home from his Union meeting in Butte. Ma fretted. The next morning, Ma said to my older brother, "Oh dear. Patrick, look at this." She had the morning paper. In the corner of the page was the story that Mr. John J. Morris of Anaconda was arrested for blocking traffic at the intersection of Park and Main Streets. He was jumping up and down on his own hat shouting, "This hat's not union made!" Apparently, Dad had resisted arrest.

My father was supremely concerned to see a better world. One snowy, January evening, he asked Ma to accompany him to an important election for the school board. Ma hated deep snow, and at less than five feet tall, sank far down. They'd had an argument about it and Dad won, so together they trudged the mile from our house through the cold, fresh night snow to the Hearst Library. Mom voted, and came home. Dad's candidate won by a single vote–hers. She was delighted.

Goosetown was the neighborhood where we lived–small, crowded, wood frame houses, with scads of children tumbling out of them who were Irish, Italian, Sicilian, Swedish, Norwegian, Greek, Croat, Serb, Finn and German. We learned about otherness. The teaming rich diversity taught us that there was more than one way to worship God, to cut salami, and to plant a garden. Old Mrs. Anderson taught us to say "tocksamiska" when she gave us an apple. "Dobra dawn, dobra utro" came from families who left Yugoslavia, and "hodja vad" from the Hungarians. And at Catholic Mass, where this great diversity became one, we heard "Dominus vobiscum," and replied, "Et cum spiritu tuo." Founded in the 1880s, the people of our town answered the welcoming words on the Statue of Liberty: "Give me your poor, your huddled masses." Sad to say, however, the small handful of Chinese and Blacks were excluded. It was only much later, when racial consciousness emerged, that I came to understand with regret how we all marginalized them with the poison of our prejudice.

On Sundays, Pat, Rob, Ma and I walked, sometimes together, often on our own, the five blocks to St. Peter's Church, where Father John Pirnat, from the Dalmatian Coast, was pastor. Someone once asked Ma why she became a Catholic. She answered, "Because I thought it would keep my damnable man from his damnable drink." Dad never went to Mass even though he was the first boy ever baptized at St. Paul's Catholic Church in 1888.[3]

Normally, Ma prepared meals for her three boys, while Dad's eating habits, like his working shifts, changed frequently. Ma fixed us bread with peanut butter *or* jelly sandwiches, never the unaffordable peanut butter *and* jelly. I used to wonder if Ma ever ate; she was such a wee woman. Dad ate meat but we boys seldom had it. I loved Thanksgiving and Christmas when all five of us would eat a turkey dinner together.

John James Morris, Violet Agnes Morris, brothers Pat, Rob and Jack.

Dad owned one suit. Ma possessed two dresses, one saved for Sunday Mass. Closets were small in those days. We three boys went to St. Peter's Catholic school where tuition was one dollar each child per month. Dad's paycheck was $23 a week. There were no frills. Pat, the oldest, heard Dad say to Ma that three or four years at St. Pete's was sufficient. Accordingly, each in turn, we transferred to the public system, where most of our friends attended. Ma always owed money: school, barber shop, coal company, grocery store–necessities often unfilled. Neither Dad nor Ma had a bank account until later. Like everyone else during the Great Depression, we were poor, but didn't know anything different.

Ma, like practically all other mothers in Anaconda, labored at home. Monday washing, Tuesday ironing, Wednesday bread-making, Thursday shopping, Friday cleaning, sewing, mending and whatever chores needed doing. I recall Ma knitting the most intricate yarn patterns until her eyes declined. When times were tough, she tried selling her pieces at Jacobson's dress shop on Commercial Street. Ma really lived for her boys and long suffered for us. She created a loving home and she was willing to do anything to make sure Pat, Rob and I grew up to be honest, truthful and good, capable of standing tall and walking straight.

Our family didn't have a car or a refrigerator when I was very young. I do remember we owned a radio, a large object with huge silver colored tubes in it. When I turned 8 years old, Dad bought an old Model T Ford for $35 with three different foot pedals and an emergency brake. Gas cost eleven cents per gallon. The five of us piled into the Model T with our mutt, Rex, standing with his head out the window. Dad drove the ten miles at the breakneck speed of thirty miles per hour to his unofficial mining claim on the rushing waters of Mill Creek. These excursions provided the best family togetherness we ever had. Ma put together the makings for mutton stew while Dad got his prospecting tools together. Pat loved to climb the slope above the stream. We brothers heaved and rolled big rocks, watching them gallop down the slope, plunging into the icy water below.

A mishap in his youth left Dad with sight in only one eye. As small children, each in turn, we would tiptoe into his bedroom while he slept, to glimpse the mystery of his glass eye staring up at us from his bureau. Thank God there was very little traffic on our outings because Dad tended to hog the middle of the road. We wondered if it was because he couldn't see perfectly. With Ma's warnings, Dad steadied his course. I remember a long car trip with the five of us to Flathead country near the Canadian border. I got my very first comic book and first hamburger on that trip. We putt-putted up hills, radiator steaming, brake bands grinding, and then raced dangerously down hills. Ma was so worried about Dad's driving, she put us all on the bus, leaving Dad to drive home to Anaconda alone.

Dad had high hopes to succeed as a gold miner. Prospecting meant digging, panning and hoping. Dad worked the prospector's tool, a sluice-box, and stooped on the edge of the stream with a pan to glean for the gold–bearing black sand caught in the sluice riffles. The eyes of Pat, Rob and I bugged with fascination as we gazed over Dad's shoulder at the bright thin streak of "colors" in the crease of his large gold pan. We learned to imitate his movements of the pan with our smaller kitchen pie pans. We watched him carefully uncork his little bottle of mercury (quicksilver), pour a small amount into the crease of the pan, then work it to pick up the specks of gold. Gold, like God, was where you found it! The culmination of the process was to retrieve the gold from the quicksilver. Over the fire, on a smooth iron lid, we'd cut a potato in half, dig out a dome, carefully dump the gold laden quicksilver onto the stove lid, and place the potato over it. With sufficient heat, the mercury evaporated into the potato, leaving an artificial nugget of pure gold setting there. I recall Ma once saying, "How nice it would be if he could get enough to send Patrick to college."

Neither of my parents finished high school, but over the years, we brothers achieved modest success in Anaconda's high school: Pat graduated in 1943, I graduated in 1946, and Rob in 1947. But instead of college, we went, one by one, to the military—Pat and Rob to the Army, and I to the Navy.

CHAPTER 3

Enchanted Boyhood

"How much we learned from the land we occupied."

MY BOYHOOD WAS A POWERFUL, abiding, and enchanted influence in my life. A sweet and gentle feeling arises as I conjure up scenes of childhood glory. I hear the hills, the wide open spaces, my neighborhood, my youthful haunts singing great songs. We roamed our surrounding hillsides free as the deer and elk. Time stood still as we played and dreamed away our days. It was never hard to get a group together for games, swimming or hiking. I don't recall ever being bored, though we had few toys or possessions. There was simplicity in harvesting berries, fishing for rainbow trout, hunting gophers, swimming, swinging, standing around fires after dark, or lying on the grass watching clouds. Each season had its mysteries and delights. I purr like an old tomcat and wonder at the sheer gift of it all.

Lefty, Gene and Robert, Art and Ray, Kesty, Ken, and I would all show up in front of Moyle's Garage where we stood around trying to catch the warmth of the July sun. We'd head for "the crick," our dam and diving board, which we had engineered ourselves. A mile upstream, in territory all their own, the Fourth Street gang had their dam. Neither group talked to the other. Our particular haven was a mile walk southeast of town, toward the Lost Creek hills. It was where we played follow-the-leader with crazy antics from the diving board, and gave pose to the "watermelon" and "pickle." In the former pose, we'd throw our hind ends heavenward; in the pickle, we'd showcase our front ends. Such laughter!

Building a fire was de rigueur, and how delicious its warmth felt after plunging several times into the frigid waters. We'd stand around the blaze innocently naked, laughing and jabbering for hours. No one ever fixed a lunch, except for the occasional raw potato pocketed from home to bury and roast in the hot coals. I remember my skin and hair smelled like smoke and flame.

In town, all mothers disciplined all children. But parents never came to our myriad exotic swimming holes–the Iron Mine, the Slaughter House, the Rock Crusher, the Warm Springs. Ma would say, "Take care of one another," so we did. On the southwest side of town was Washoe Park with a regular cement pool. With many swimmers there, including girls, you had to wear bathing trunks. We preferred the freedom of our boys' paradise. Girls? They were another species. Not until puberty did I wish for a sister to show me what a girl was all about.

The most exotic of these watery haunts was the Iron Mine. The pool there was perhaps ten by fifteen feet, with sheer sides. The opaque, rusted brown water was our hot spring and we reveled in it. It was a mile hike along the railroad yards, up through a narrow pass. We saw on one side the massive smelter complex with its loud, humming electrical power system, moving trains, whistles, and hulking buildings. On the other side of our walk loomed a mountain of flat-topped black slag, the residue from smelting. A railroad circled the outer edge of the heap, transporting smelting dumpings. Heavily polluted waters disgorged from the smelting process.

The smelter sat east of town. The north or east wind swept the acrid smoke horizontally off the stack, leaving a gray pall of arsenic to permeate the hills. Horses and cows went mad or just died within a radius of several miles. Wildlife was sparse. On the south hills wound an impressive flume like the Wall of China, a trough snaking its way from the west. The five foot by five foot troughs delivered rushing water twenty miles to the smelter works. Magically, this was covered with heavy planks–and was our smooth highway through the hills. We knew the location of every ladder to ascend and descend. We'd walk it, play games, shoot our sling-shots ("flippers") at birds, and here and there pull a plug from the side to shower and cool off or take a drink.

In the winter, mammoth icicles formed from the dripping water of the flume. We'd position ourselves precariously, strike the ice daggers with clubs, and thrill to the sight and thunderous sound as they plummeted twenty feet to shatter on the frozen ground below. Then we'd take off to ski, sled or romp in the snow. We'd clamp ice skates to our regular shoes, making sure not to lose the key to the skates.

I remember quarter inch frost in marvelous patterns on the windows of our house. My brothers and I could press a nickel into it, or take turns licking it. We'd huddle around the kitchen stove, worshiping the heat. The furnace was a big round beast down below which glowed and roared, sending warm drafts of hot air. We'd shovel coal and coke into it, haul sacks of coke on our sleds from the foundry area, and haul old telephone poles that we sawed or chopped to make kindling.

No matter the season, as soon as we got home from school, we changed to run outdoors, invent a game, and find buddies. Every boy carried a pocket knife. Memories abound of five or six of us sitting on the grass playing mumbledey-peg, knife baseball, or simply whittling. Other games were: erka-plerka, hats, Annie-over, chase, tag, weak horse, and marbles. Erka-plerka came from some ethnic background. If there were six boys, five sat in a row on a step with both feet on the ground. The sixth would pass along with a stick, tapping each of the ten feet with this rhyme–*erka-plerka, ploren-been, been-youn, kriben-shoelack-shay, shake-da-pilla, peistey-horney, goly, flacka-flacka*–touching successive shoes with each word. Whichever foot received *flacka* got firm, mean strikes–*flacka, flacka, flacka!* The owner of that foot pulled it back quickly to avoid the stick. That foot and all subsequent *flackas* were retired until there was a winning foot remaining. He became the next counter.

To be away from the house was to be free, so we never hung around our home. My companions and I were scavengers, carried our magnets with us on our romps, and found and sold every imaginable metal. In summer, we roamed the hills, flattened pennies and screws on the rail tracks, and generally ran around like Tom Sawyer and Huck Finn. In late summer, we'd fill our pockets with wild chokecherries that would crush and ooze. We were always on the alert to steal wild crab apples and currants, but they were more promise than worth the picking. Oregon grape berries were bitter but spilled a tantalizing color, and those awful, sour, Gooseberries made you wonder if the Indians hadn't starved in our territory decades ago. Surreptitiously, we chewed tobacco and smoked a local plant known as "Indian tobacco." How much we learned from the land we occupied.

My brother, Rob, was two years younger than me. His ambition at the early age of seven was to be an entrepreneur. With a buddy of his, he dragged a dead dog into our garage. He intended to "raise" maggots. Maggots sold for ten cents for as many as would fit in a Prince Albert tobacco can. Those cans were flat and could fit in a shirt or vest pocket. Our gallivanting took us to areas where garbage, refuse and junk were dumped helter-skelter. Often a pungent smell tempted us to explore a discarded carcass. We'd scoop up the fleshy mess, bring it to the garage and extract the maggots. One of us would filch a cup of cornmeal from the kitchen which served as a "bath" for the tiny worms. They emerged odorless and clean as pieces of carved ivory. We sold them to fishermen going to Georgetown or Silver Lake to ice fish. The men would place clean worms under their lower lips, like a chaw of tobacco, to keep them from freezing. That way worms were at their fingertips to re-bait their hooks. In our boyish innocence, we smelled nothing of our stinking, maggot hunting clothes, but Ma knew. Whether we stole cornmeal or matches, stood around fires, played hooky, or just weren't hungry at dinner, Ma read our minds and knew exactly what we boys were doing.

When my brothers and I successively turned 16 years old, we were each allowed to get jobs. The war was on and many men were gone. I worked at the smelter on the mason gang, jackhammering furnace bottoms, with fiery furnaces expelling great heat. I also worked in the zinc leach plant, in the converters where twenty-five ton ladles passed precariously above my head. Sometimes when asked why I became a priest, I responded that anything was better than working on a smelter! But the parents in our town couldn't get away from the gases and the dust. Over a lifetime, they succumbed to silicosis, which, along with cigarettes, killed many, including my Dad.

I remember a photo from the late summer of 1944, when I was going into my junior year. The image displayed seven, smiling, bald boys. In that era, a bald head was unheard of. For some unknown reason, we'd gotten ourselves locked into a dare to begin school with buzz cuts. There was much hesitancy all around, but I broke the inertia by climbing under the clippers first. Our mothers had a fit. Though the war was going on, and every one of us in that photo would, in due time, take our turn in the military, we lived in a state of innocence.

CHAPTER 4

My Interior World

"God's love runs within us like great streaming rivers."

MY EARLIEST MEMORIES, VAGUE AND tangled, revealed a glimmering awareness more hidden than manifest of something beyond, deeper, and more penetrating than the stuff-and-things of the world that confined me. I sensed I belonged to a realm more real and lasting than this material domain.

By temperament, some people are more spiritual or religious than others. It's also clear to me that this intuited sense is something given long before it is chosen. For me, I was compelled to follow an urging arising from deep within. I heard whispers that there was more to human existence than simply what the mind and my physical senses told me. The poet William Wordsworth alluded to this:

"Our birth is but a sleep and a forgetting:
The Soul that rises with us, our life's Star,
Hath had elsewhere its setting,
And cometh from afar:
Not in entire forgetfulness,
And not in utter nakedness,
But trailing clouds of glory do we come
From God, who is our home..."[4]

Once I joined six older boys in a swimming hole. I hung onto a large rock because the water was over my head. I didn't know how to swim. I lost my grip on the boulder and drifted down. I found myself on the bottom of the watery hole fascinated by a kind of slow motion movie about my life. The next thing I knew, I was being grabbed and lifted up by Gilbert McMullin, who rescued me. It seems I might have been drowning, but something so peaceful and serene had entered my being. That watery, wondrous experience came back to me in a comforting way many times in my life. It was all so strange that I never shared it with my parents or friends, but I believe it contributed to my intuition of another realm.

In my boyhood wanderings, my friends and I came upon a dead dog or cat several times. We would perform a strange ritual: we spit on the dead animal and said, "Dead dog, don't come to my supper." Where this came from, I have no idea. Very early, in an inchoate way, I was unsettled by the mystery of life and death.

I had a primitive interest in blood. It was a sign of life and a signal of death. The times when I accidentally cut myself intrigued me by the color and taste. When I was 9 years old, I trapped gophers. Once, I sawed off the head of a gopher carcass with my pocket knife to watch the dark blood ooze. As a priest for fifty years, almost every day at Mass, I have celebrated the ancient story of blood all the way back to Abel with these words, "This is the blood of the new and the everlasting covenant; it will be shed for you and for all for the forgiveness of sin." With each celebration, I was caught up in the same strange mystery that tugged me. Is there a connection between my boyhood fascination with blood and my being a priest, who each morning partakes in a mysterious ritual that speaks of the blood of the new covenant, the blood of Christ? Joseph Campbell, the modern herald of the power of myth in our lives, thinks we inherit primordial memories and patterns of mind that slumber within us. Is there a connection between my boyhood questions and the insights of Carl Jung about the subconscious, and of Campbell about the power of myth? Are we called to listen to those impulses which rise up early and unbidden?

I recall when a neighborhood man committed suicide up the gulch from our house. We boys went to see where he'd done it. I returned alone, drawn inward by the finality. My awareness of death floated vaguely in my psyche. But the reality struck home when I was 10 years old and called to be a pallbearer for a neighborhood friend. With the help of two men, we boys felt the burden of death in carrying the heavy coffin containing the body.

I found solace in the small holy cards we were given at Catholic school, as common to us as poker cards in a local bar. I carried around one image depicting two children playing close to a cliff; an attentive guardian angel with bright wings hovered to protect and save them. From some deep need in the privacy of my inner life, I embraced that metaphor, and felt watched over. How could I go to my parents, or anyone at such an early age, with questions about the mystery that summoned me from a place beyond the world I could see and touch?

At St. Peter's grade school near our home, the nuns wore black. Ma told me it was because they were grieving the death of Jesus. I remember Sister Mary Jordan read Bible and saintly stories to us. One story caught my wandering mind, that of the boy Tarsisius. He lived in the dangerous time of the early Church when Christians were persecuted. That meant they couldn't bring the Eucharist to men in prison. Tarsisius, appearing young and unsuspecting, volunteered to carry the secretly hidden, sacred hosts to the prison. On one occasion, some ruffians stopped him and wanted to know what he was hiding. Tarsisius refused to surrender his treasure. He was killed, a martyr for Jesus. I admired this young hero of the faith. His deed touched off something in me. It was my earliest inspiration that my life might have a purpose, and that something from within was tugging on me.

CHAPTER 5

Leaving Home

✦

"God writes straight with crooked lines."

— OLD PORTUGUESE SAYING

MY OLDER BROTHER PAT WENT to war in 1943. He participated in the December, 1944 Battle of the Bulge, where he was declared "missing in action." A brooding silence came over Ma and the rest of us for months. Was my brother dead? Could he be alive? Would we ever see him again? On Easter Sunday, 1945, Ma, Rob and I turned into our driveway after returning from Mass. We found a telegram delivered from the War Department. Ma was too terrified to open it. She handed it to me to read. Pat was alive! What a resurrection gift.

Even though World War II was almost over, I left home my senior year of high school and enlisted in the U.S. Navy in February, 1946. Home was cherished, but we were taught that growing up required the maturity to fly the nest. If there was any fuss in leaving, I don't remember it. Five of us in our high school class passed tests for admittance into the Navy Air Corps training program, which carried the promise of a full four year university education. I was 18 years old, having spent two years as a first grader. In school, I couldn't quite escape my dreaming long enough to attend seriously to academics, but, yes, I did eventually receive my diploma as a bona fide graduate of Anaconda High School.

In March, the five of us classmates chugged by train to Denver, and made our way to the University of Colorado in Boulder. Our Navy unit had taken over a girls' dormitory where we were assigned rooms. We got in line to receive our Navy blues, endured inspections, and did some early morning marching, but in general we were regular students. The student body was largely female due to the war. At gatherings, the coeds eyed the uniforms and competed to ask us to dance. It stoked our vanity.

Studies were another matter. We all entered the engineering track, pushed toward becoming top gun pilots. Having taken no science classes in my past, I did poorly, particularly in physics. Looking back, I enjoyed the uphill climb of trying to get good grades. Toward the end of our first quarter, I caught a cold virus that settled into my kidneys. I was diagnosed with acute nephritis and sent to the huge Fitzsimmons Army Hospital in Denver, bulging with wounded combat soldiers. After six weeks, I was transferred to the Navy hospital at Norman, Oklahoma, and then relocated to Milledgeville, Tennessee, where I spent the remainder of my Navy career. In February, 1947, after fourteen months in the Navy, I received a discharge "at the convenience of the government."

There's a time honored Portuguese adage that "God writes straight with crooked lines." In retrospect, that bent-nail Navy experience was formative. I look back on it amazed at how our hidden God guides us through the zigs and zags. I graduated from high school, never having read a book from cover to cover. Neither Ma nor Dad had much schooling, although Dad read everything that passed his way. Both parents wanted us to study and succeed but neither knew how to help us become students. University was a dream beyond the means of Anaconda's largely immigrant population. For many, getting a steady job at the smelter, the foundry, or railroad, and raising a family, was the extent of their hopes. Ma, a dislocated immigrant, saw the limitations of the town. She encouraged us to dream, and get out of Anaconda.

In that hospital stay of nine months, I learned to delight in the written word. Once each week, the library cart was wheeled into the ward. I remember telling one of my companions that I didn't know what to choose. He told me he liked an author, Rafael Sabatini. I followed his lead, and was especially moved by the story of *The Strolling Saint* who I felt was living out my own unformulated hopes and longings. For the first time, I began to pay close attention to my interior life. Like that young protagonist, I too was wandering, searching and aching. My query for a good book put me in touch with my inner self. I also began to attend Mass during the week.

One other great gift issued from that crooked-nail year in the Navy. Upon discharge in March, 1947, I was entitled to the G.I. Bill, a free ride to college due to the largesse and advanced thinking of Uncle Sam. With my discharge papers in my pocket, I visited my brother Pat, now attending Georgetown University in Washington, DC. I stayed a month with him and his boarding house crowd. He said, "Come on back with me. Don't go to school at home; you'll end up with the drinking crowd at Missoula or Bozeman." I temporarily returned to Anaconda, got a job on the smelter paying less than eight dollars a day, and worked until I could begin the summer term at Georgetown University's School of Foreign Service. In late June, I hitchhiked across the country to begin university studies.

With a spirit of risk, I enrolled in Georgetown University in the summer of 1947. I was a hick from remote Anaconda, a town of nine-thousand, coming to the east coast. Georgetown University, with its impressive Gothic, granite buildings, intimidated me. I took up residence with my brother Pat and his friends at Mary Royal's boarding house. The swampy summer heat and the traffic noises below us were appalling. Like Pat, I enrolled in Father Edmund Walsh's respected School of Foreign Service.

After a few semesters of studies at Georgetown, I was happy to see the days lengthen and summer roll around once more. I needed a break. Pat graduated and headed off for Cuernavaca, Mexico to study Spanish and immerse himself in the Hispanic culture. Looking back, I realized that while I was determined to be a student, I really wasn't fully engaged. At age 21, I didn't know who I was, or what I wanted from school or life.

New England, that legendary center of learning and the cradle of America's earliest beginnings, beckoned me. I used my thumb, hitching rides up through Baltimore, New Jersey and points north. I found myself in Providence, Rhode Island, looking as I went for any kind of a job.

CHAPTER 6

Circus Summer

"Bless every city, town and street that I have known."

RINGLING BROTHERS BARNUM BAILEY CIRCUS–The Largest Show on Earth just arrived in Providence, the summer of 1948.

The Show was moving up through New England, then to Chicago, and all the way to the west coast. I didn't have any plans, but something in me quickened. I imagined myself traveling with the circus all the way to Salt Lake City, then leaving to briefly return home to Anaconda. I wandered down to the railroad yard, located the manager's tent, and signed on as a roustabout, a manual laborer, for $12 a week. That supplied me room and board and a ticket for a shared bunk. Next, I was led to the third track and entered the stale and harsh air of sleeping car number 112 where I would later have to climb in with a total stranger. I slept with my clothes on the whole time I traveled and never did eyeball my bunk mate. Parking my little suitcase near the bunk, I leaped into work.

I was thrust into the spectacular event of raising the Big Top: the unfurling of long ropes, unfolding of tons of canvas, and hauling of poles. With four others, I rhythmically swung a sledge hammer to drive in scores of stakes. My ears were bombarded with a cacophony of sounds–men barking orders, elephants trumpeting and snorting while lifting heavy poles, horses neighing, and the staccato of driven stakes. Above it all boomed the voice of the yard boss with his megaphone: Heave! Heave! Heave! Ropes tensed, heels dug into the earth, muscles bulged. Scores of men, with four or five elephants, accomplished the impossible. They lifted the towering Big Top two-hundred feet into the air. How spellbinding! Bystanders from Providence looked on open mouthed. I overheard one say, "I come to watch the raising and lowering of the Big Top each year. That's the real show."

An hour before midnight, the evening show finished and the crowds dispersed. No one paid attention to me that first night as I gawked in disbelief at the unadvertised, free and amazing second show—the noisy, boisterous disassembling of the circus. Garish lights flashed, crisscrossing like swords. Men atop elephants cast huge shadows, and guy lines were loosed. Tons of canvas were lowered and rolled. We loaded railroad cars, and amidst a chorus of goading and shouting, young men vied with one another to run as high up the deflating canvas as possible.

Artists, clowns, acrobats, dancers, trainers, lions and tigers, along with more than one-hundred horses were caught in their own disassembling routines. As the tasks were finished and the mad activity subsided, I noticed small circles of roustabouts sitting along the railroad tracks casting dice, drinking, playing cards, and smoking until the signal that it was time to move on. Piercing whistles sounded, announcing that it was time for the fully loaded train cars to clank on to the next town where *The Show* would once more unfold and bedazzle. That was the circus—always moving on.

After midnight the first night, I climbed into my bunk and closed my eyes before my bunkmate arrived. Tired as I was, I scarcely slept. Whistles blew at every town as the circus train snaked through the night, trembling over the tracks forty miles northward for another one-night stand. Two long trains hauled four-hundred men and women, eleven elephants, one-hundred horses, nine lions and tigers, twenty dogs, and tons of canvas and props. The performers had superior quarters to the two score crew of roustabouts like me.

At sunrise, the train halted. We were shouted awake for one purpose, to get the Big-Top up and ready before the afternoon town parade and evening performance. I followed the men to a tent with long tables. Tantalizing piles of eggs, bacon, hotcakes, coffee, and bread lay before us. Many of the roustabouts were drifters, drinkers, and short term workers, but the circus was a decent way to get a couple days of good grub and free transportation. I gravitated to three other naïve college men like myself. They'd traveled up from Georgia with the circus for several weeks, but were ready to leave. With earnings of only $20 a week, it wasn't easy to save money. We laughed together as we shared observations of this peculiar world, casting judgment on the motley crew of tough, hard drinking, cursing, and sometimes threatening companions. After breakfast, I was assigned to work a three-man sledge crew to drive stakes all around the four-acre Big-Top site.

By the second night, I better sized up circus life. Animated shouting arose as more than 125 ropes were loosed and the Big-Top was lowered. One of the rousties on crew lowering the gigantic mast of the center pole, mistakenly stood in the twist of the main rope. Like a mean coiled snake, the rope caught him and flung him some twenty feet. He was a flying rag doll. The poor guy bled profusely and groaned. Rushed to the train, he was administered a bottle of hard gin to doctor the pain until the manager could check on a doctor at the next stop. The incident brought out a lot of meanness among the laborers. I'd worked on the railroad before, and at a smelter, but I'd never encountered such an ugly concentration of harsh, cruel words from men.

When we reached Maine, I jumped off at Portland. It was time to bid goodbye to circus life. In Portland, I got hired on the pier at Old Orchard Beach as a clerk and gopher at a confectionary stand. I discovered a hole-in-the-wall summer rental for myself and made some friends. Where sea, sky and land meet, wonder breaks through. I had some good times.

As summer drew to a close, my impetuous nature got triggered again. One day, I passed a bicycle shop in town and curiously glanced in at their back room piled with wheels, frames and pedals. I asked the proprietor how much it would cost to put a bike together from old parts. He paused, and then blurted out, $12. "Come back in two hours and it'll be ready." Ten days later, this lad, who never owned a bicycle in his youth, was on the highway peddling a one-speed to Washington DC. I carried only the clothes on my back, an army blanket and a toothbrush. The stars were my domed roof as I slept in graveyards, churchyards, corn patches, and potato fields all the way south.

CHAPTER 7

Meeting Maureen

"God set me up, duped, and seduced me.
It was a bait and switch."

As a child, I perceived in girls something special. I wanted something unnamed that they had, and I longed to understand them. I felt a kinship between girls and my guardian angel, but in that era, play was segregated by gender. Ma had driven home restraints because she had brought with her to America her English Puritanism. In our home, it was as if girls had no existence. However, before finishing high school, I wished for a sister who could tell me what it was like to live in her skin. I speculated that what made the most sense for my future was to marry a fine woman and raise a dozen children.

I met Maureen Casey in the spring of 1948. She had made a bus trip with her graduating class to see the nation's capital. My brother Pat was working as a tour guide for a bus company. He came home from work one afternoon announcing that he and I were going on a double date with two delightful women from a Brooklyn Catholic high school.

Maureen was 17 years old, and I was 21. I don't recall one blessed detail about what we did during the three hours of that first date. I do remember that she was petite, blond, with the softest, smoothest features, and almond eyes, full of confident joy and laughter. We exchanged addresses and wrote. I visited her several times.

Maureen's beauty seized my imagination. When I fell in love with her, I saw the world anew. She was the rising sun that cast light upon the landscape of my life.

Looking back, I recognize the plaintive longing of a young heart with a wound. To say that I was lonely scarcely touches the pervasive ache that was within me. Oh, I had friends, played sports, hiked and fished in the mountains, and laughed with the guys. I dated a few girls while in high school, and I felt a freedom and delight in my childhood, but on a deeper level beyond reach of my mind or senses, something mysterious haunted me, and I was incapable of fully enjoying life. It seemed there must be a more compelling way of living with more substance and depth.

In hindsight, I also perceived something deeper within myself, a conviction that life had purpose and that I was being asked to face reality and soldier on. I was raised Catholic and was taught in Catholic school that God was real, and so was his anger at those who disobeyed. I grew up thinking it best to stay below His radar, to avoid being noticed. I wanted to like the nuns and the priest too, but they were so busy, and I was invisible. It took me long years to recognize that I was a sensitive child, alert but afraid. I was also a dreamer who didn't understand or belong to the hard, tussled world around me. Females, it seemed to my awakening psyche, possessed a key to a more gentle truth. I wonder if that isn't what underlies the Catholic devotion to Mary?

I'd always admired my brother, Pat. During high school, he was class and student body president, and winner of awards. He reveled in his bellhop job at the Montana Hotel on Main Street. Now, here in Washington, DC, his love for learning, jazz, partying, and avid reading of the *Washington Post*, challenged me. From DC, he went to Mexico for a couple of years, then on to the University of Peru to get a master's degree in history and culture which led to a job with the United States Embassy. While in Mexico, he wrote an excited letter, suggesting that I come down to buy and develop property with him in Acapulco. But nothing in me quickened. I tried to imitate his style, but it didn't turn my lights on. Maureen did. I knew that meeting Maureen and our mutual falling in love, was the single most thrilling event of my life up to that point. My freeing from some cramped prison began with her response to my longings.

Maureen lived in a working class neighborhood in Brooklyn. Both her parents were Irish. They thought I was a fine man for Maureen because when I visited, I'd go with her family to morning Mass a few blocks away. I only came to see her a handful of times. When together, we exchanged hard delicious kisses, but our romance was mostly tender letters, longings, and gladness for the interior unfolding of the mystery of love.

Often, especially after I'd seen her, the thought would steal into my mind: if God could fashion such an exotic, compelling creature as woman, then God really knew His business. God, I began to see, was all of the wonderful feelings, and more. I was greedy for it all. What Maureen had was of God, and this God was charged with compelling beauty and excitement.

To compound the power of the mystery, Maureen bought me a book at Christmas that stoked a new fire. It was titled, *Theology and Sanity* by Frank Sheed.[5] First published in 1946, within a year it was a best seller. Lay people like Frank Sheed, Jacques and Marisa Maritan, and E. Gilson, were bringing theology down from the clouds. The book sent me reeling. It set loose the "hound of heaven," baying and pursuing me down a labyrinth of my unhinged mind and heart. Without knowing it, I was experiencing God through my awakened love for Maureen. God set me up, duped, and seduced me. What was coming was a bait and switch.

Maureen and I talked of the future, of marriage, of a big family we'd care for and nurture. This was what it was all about—life giving life, on and on. I would pursue a degree in theology. We would marry and raise children while I shared my epiphany and taught people about this awesome God who was love itself. Looking back, I realized that only through these new truths did the true Jack Morris begin to awaken. I recognized for the first time the beauty, wonder and delight of the world around me.

I discovered there was no university in the United States where a lay person could get a degree in theology. Both in seminaries and Catholic universities, only philosophy counted. If I couldn't get a degree in theology, I'd go up to Toronto and study at the renowned Medieval Institute and get a doctorate in philosophy. This could be another way to my goal of teaching others about God. Yet, my Catholic upbringing was a far cry from joyful, energetic, spirit-inspired evangelization. The God who I'd learned about in Catholic school wasn't charismatic and didn't particularly appreciate feelings.

In the midst of these unfolding questions and desires, a further complication intruded. One quiet evening while studying, a sly thought, yes, a thought "wise as a serpent," seemed to enter my room and slither into my consciousness. It suggested in a veiled manner that perhaps I ought to become a priest. I tried to beat back the importuning "creature," but it kept making unannounced appearances, communicating its disruptive message. How should I handle this agitation, this stirring to consider the priesthood?

In the ethnically diverse, very Catholic environment of Anaconda, it was an accepted fact that God called some to be priests and sisters. Some of my friends were moving in that direction. But it never entered *my* mind or *my* heart to consider such a thing for myself. Ma had been Anglican. She converted to Catholicism when she married Dad. She saw to our Catholic upbringing, but it never entered her mind that one of her three boys should become a priest.

My love for Maureen stirred my desires, but the Sheed book dredged up the deeper strata of my Catholic faith. Damnation was one such layer. I found myself worrying about my father. As an adult, he never went to Mass. As a boy, he'd attended Masses but said he had enough of them saved up to last a lifetime. The serpentine, bargaining voice seemed to suggest that I could save my father if I sacrificed my love for Maureen to become a priest. I rebelled against this motivation, but I was now caught between two opposing forces. I'd visit Maureen, returning to school glowing with the promise of perfect love fulfilled, pouring over my heart like honey. Then, through some gap in my soul, my unwanted spiritual tempter would appear, and the battle raged once more. I watched my dream castle of bliss in marriage and family collapse before the unwanted tide of becoming a priest.

This desire for marriage and family ran deep. My attraction to a woman was a highly idealized and satisfying pattern that I thought defined adulthood. The new business of priesthood was an unfamiliar and strange house in which I felt totally awkward. No, it was really a frontal assault on all the joy and security I had come to hope for. Who gave the protagonists permission to wage war inside of me?

Maureen and I wrote about this ironic dilemma. Was it possible that my encounter with the beauty of a woman was actually pointing me toward God and the celibate life? I decided I needed to get away to a neutral zone. Only much later did I equate my story with that of the Biblical Jacob who crossed the Jabok River to be alone. Just Jacob and a mysterious heavenly being, wrestled. That wrestling changed his name and his whole life, just as the wrestling would change my call and destiny. We are, as the New Testament tells us, children of Israel when we imitate Jacob and wrestle with reality, with the mystery of our own calling and existence.

The year was over at Georgetown, so I closed my suitcase of few belongings, and made my way up to Brooklyn. Maureen was working, but we arranged lunch together. I kissed her a deep, wistful goodbye, and boarded the Greyhound bus for the long haul to Anaconda, Montana. I wondered whether I'd ever see her again. I only knew that she and author Sheed had put my life on a new path. My quest now was to my own truth, however that manifested. I knew that nothing else mattered.

CHAPTER 8

Joining the Jesuits

✤

"I instinctively knew I had to decrease and let Christ increase."

THE JESUITS I CONSULTED AT Georgetown suggested I consider Regis College in Denver. Taking their advice, I began Regis (now Regis University) in the fall of 1949. I took a room with an elderly landlady, just two blocks off campus. I wanted to be alone so I could wrestle with this whole business of vocation. I attended Mass each day, and in the evening, before bed, I'd kneel, hold my arms out, and pray the rosary. I asked God for guidance. This fight, this contest was flaring in me like a wind on hot coals.

I decided to put aside the regular course; I wanted to choose my own courses, responding to what appealed to me. One of the best classes I took highlighting the writings of Cardinal John Henry Newman, focused on the role of the laity, the conscience, and an ecumenical view of the world. Philosophy and a course in Shakespeare also turned me on. It seemed as if for the first time, college studies had purpose and meaning. I stayed pretty much to myself but I still felt happy even though I was balancing on the cusp. I was a man with feet in two rowboats.

The most significant event of my year at Regis happened during the Christmas break. I drove with an older student to Butte, and then Anaconda. He planned to get a few shifts in the mines over Christmas. After the holidays, in a howling snow storm on the return trip, we made our way to Kemmerer, Wyoming. It was dark when we found a small hotel room for $4, and we went immediately to bed. The next morning was

New Year's Day. I rose early and headed off for Mass, noticing that a thief had broken into our car. My luggage, my one suit, books, camera–pretty much everything I owned–was gone. I continued on to church, reviewing my thoughts for the poor, benighted thief. He clearly didn't grasp the basic truth that stealing was wrong, that I was his brother, and he mine. I offered my Mass experience for him, and my anger turned into forgiveness. Something profound–something unconditional–actually began to stir in me. I thought it might be a sign from God to give up all my earthly possessions and take a vow of poverty.

A couple days later, I wrote to Maureen: "Sweet Maureen, I'm not going to write for a full month (which seemed like a self-inflicted life sentence), and then I'll give you my final answer whether I'll join the Jesuits or whether the two of us continue our journey toward marriage." She could see what I was struggling with, but what was she to conclude, looking through the lens of all my previous romantic letters?

Before the month was up, something powerful happened within me. The swirling conflict of my mind came to rest. A great calm overtook me. My senses seemed sharp and clear. I moved about within myself, no longer in my head, but within my heart. I noticed a quiet joy and surety. I knew without the slightest doubt what I had to do. The long, demanding wrestling match was over. I had come home to myself and knew what life called me to do. In seeking to be true to my deepest self, I was putting on Christ. Like John the Baptist, I instinctively knew I had to decrease and let Christ increase.

Maureen wept when she got my letter saying the dice had been thrown, and she had lost. A plaintive response came by return mail. I wrote a long letter and waited. She again responded. Apparently, the spirit of God had visited her, too. She was at peace, and saw God's hand in all this. We continued writing letters for the next several months. They were warm and serene, but the romance had cooled.

The year 1950 brought a mild summer to the Rocky Mountains. At age 23, I'd closed the door on that wide open freedom of my youth to follow a mysterious call that I found so irresistible, it turned my life upside down. I traveled away from the love of a woman I thought would lead me to my heart's desire, and instead veered into an unknown future.

My own family's reception toward my news of joining the Jesuits was troubling. It confused Ma. Dad's attitude was best expressed by his words to me: "Why the hell you want to waste your life like that?" His disappointment didn't dissuade me.

Needing a haircut before leaving Anaconda for the Jesuit Novitiate in Oregon, I dropped in on an old boyhood friend, Fred Petrovich, now a barber on Main Street. We hadn't seen one another since we'd gone off to military service. As I eased into his chair, he asked what was new. I told him I was going off to join the Jesuits. He stepped back and let out a howl so loud it awakened waiting customers, and embarrassed me. "You? You are joining the Jesuits?" He guffawed. Fred and I had been pranksters, dare devils, and done a little stealing in our youth together. I'd earned the reputation of a wild guy, "Blackie–crazy Jack." How could I be headed to the Jesuits?

Four friends drove me the twenty-five miles to the Northern Pacific station in Butte to catch the train that would transport me across the Rockies and on to Portland. Outside my assigned railcar, I bumped into Steve McMahon, destined as I was for St. Francis Xavier Novitiate. He heard my old buddies say their goodbyes to me as "Blackie" and the nickname carried into the Jesuits.

I was on my way to the Jesuit Novitiate in the hills above Sheridan, fifty miles south of Portland, to begin a whole new life. I was madly in love with Jesus, and I wanted to prove my love. I yearned to become a saint, to die for Christ, to become a celebrity for God. I had given up everything, or so I thought.

CHAPTER 9

Jesuit Formation Begins

"And there is a part which is still in shadow. A community is not made up only of the converted. It is made up of all the elements in us which need to be transformed, purified and pruned."[6]

— JEAN VANIER

DURING THOSE YEARS OF JESUIT formation from 1950 to 1962, we scarcely accomplished anything of importance in strictly human terms. But we were at work wrestling with several "mysteries:" how to wear a black, ankle length cassock and climb stairs; how to respond to ancient Latin prayers; how to gear our lives to the ubiquitous bells calling us from one exercise to another, bidding us to meals and recreation? I met Bill Davis during this time and we became lifelong friends. We knew we were not so subtly being shaped by community. Through long periods of silence and a rigid daily routine that began before dawn, we asked—who am I, and who is Jesus the Christ? To put it more colloquially, what's life all about anyway?

The overall aim and purpose of the long formation was holiness. Through prayer and studies, we were being equipped for one of the many Jesuit works. From the get-go, my heart was set on serving in the Arctic, called by Pius X, the most difficult of all missions. In my untamed conceit, I couldn't see much beyond my own potential greatness, my own daring, adventuresome accomplishments. In retrospect, I remember it took Thomas Merton years to be able to say, "What can we gain by sailing to the moon if we are not able to cross the abyss that separates us from ourselves?"[7] The aim of formation was precisely this, to separate the false self from the true self. I was so full of myself, both blind and deaf, that I didn't know I was on a disaster course. But how else was I to learn?

There are many Jesuit saints and martyrs. The halls of our novitiate were lined with their images and exploits. Their spirits spoke to me and filled me with excitement; I sensed this was what being a Jesuit meant. The stories of three youthful saints, Stanislaus Kostka, John Berkmans and Aloysius Gonzaga, especially resonated. The beauty and discipline of their response to the Jesuit vocation was compelling. They too had prayed the favorite prayer of St. Ignatius of Loyola: "Dearest Lord, teach me to be generous; teach me to serve You as You deserve; to give and not to count the cost, to fight and not heed the wounds, to toil and not seek for rest, to labor and not to ask for reward save that of knowing I am doing Your will." Stanislaus was of Polish nobility. He heard of the Jesuits but his father wanted none of that foolishness. One early morning, Stan slipped away and walked the five-hundred miles to Rome to join the novitiate. He was a Jesuit a mere ten months before he died, and became a canonized saint. If he could do it, why couldn't I? My heart ached to measure up. Everything in me was focused on one thing–to become a saint!

But when that ten-month mark of my two-year "novitiate" formation came, I was a walking mess. Plagued with stomach ulcers and almost constant headaches, I joined three or four others who were on "special order," unable to deal with this mysterious reality, this invisible God I so wanted to please. I just couldn't fit in to the regimentation. Studies sometimes seemed deadly. At times, I seriously thought I was losing my mind. I tried sharing my inner confusion with the Novice Master. He tried to guide me, but my inner noise was so cacophonous, I couldn't understand him. I talked, he talked, but we passed one another like two rafts in the fog. In my private prayer, I'd tell God: "You called me, you upset my life, and I fought you all the way. I didn't want to be a priest. Through Maureen, you duped me. If I go mad, it's in your hands. It's your problem, not mine." This railing against God hardly soothed my cracked and parched soul.

I carried in my heart a dread as repulsive as rotting fish—that I would be sent home, told to leave, that I wasn't cut out for this kind of life. In those early months, this person or that person would suddenly be gone—no communication as to why. It was frightening. I'd run to chapel or to my room and, in desperate anxiety, plead with God to let me stay. I was certain I'd been called to be here. In fact, a bold inner resolve rose up in me—if they told me to go, I would simply refuse to leave the property. Come rain or cold winds, I'd fast, pray and stay! Strange as it may sound, in spite of all my inner confusion, I was where I intended to be. On the deepest level, I felt a compelling rightness. I was absolutely certain that it was God who had unraveled my former dream. There would be no turning back. God had wooed me onto the path to a bigger love.

My fretful angst, confusion, fears, and determination made sense only in the light of my first long wrestling match with God. Yes, he had won, and paradoxically so had I. Like Moses, happy with a wife and shepherding his flocks, I too had been led beyond to a burning bush and told I was on sacred ground. I had experienced and been deeply touched by the mystery at the center of the universe, the stunning mystery we name God. But I was so caught up in willing my own individual way in the opaque light of that experience, that nothing we were doing in the novitiate seemed to make sense, except the sufferings of Jesus. The novitiate routine had us praying several times each day, trying to saturate our lives in Christ, our crucified Lord. The words of St. Paul thrilled me; they rang true, not to my mind but to that deep inner well where one's whole being is a quiet pool. Jesus was, I saw clearly, all knowledge, wisdom and understanding. He was the truth, the way, and life itself. It was for him, to be with him, that I was here. I didn't understand that my confusion, my inner turmoil was the merciful God trying to shake me up and catapult me beyond the lens of my pitifully self-centered ego. Only years later could I see that I was being born again. Every woman who gives birth could have told me how much pain the ordeal caused.

To this day, I'm moved emotionally by St. Paul's words: "For his sake I have accepted the loss of all things and I consider them so much rubbish, that I may gain Christ, and be found in him, not having any righteousness of my own based on the law but that which comes through faith in Christ."[8] But I was a frog and didn't know it, nor that I needed to humble myself to receive the transformative "kiss" of His love. So, all tied up in knots, I stumbled on. I would *will* my way to perfection and sainthood. The ego is a ravenous beast, feeding on whatever comes within range. It turned my prayer, my penance, and every discipline of the novitiate into a self-enhancing elevator lift.

Two years sped by, and it was with a sense of surrender and gratitude that I knelt with twenty-five other men to recite my vows to live and die in the Society of Jesus. The day was August 14, 1952. To celebrate, we all climbed into the cattle truck and drove two hours on twisting roads to the Jesuit retreat house on the Oregon Coast. We anticipated four full days of glorious freedom from the rigid routine of that foreboding, institutional Sheridan building.

Through the two years that followed, while I was in the "juniorate" for classical studies, I grappled with the three mighty beasts intended to strengthen us—the call to holiness, living in community life, and the rigor to learn Latin. As well as Latin, we studied Greek and ancient history, and did our praying and readings. I'll always remember the long walks, as well as solitary birdwatching by day, and stargazing at night. It was my sanity. Through everything, I suffered daily headaches and soothed my ulcer with gulps of a sickening medicine called ampha-jel. What a relief that final drive down the hill from the novitiate-juniorate building. At last, four long concentrated formation years had come to an end.

It was 1954, and we were all given leave of five days to visit home before checking in to Mount St. Michael, located on a high hill on the outskirts of Spokane, Washington. I received my bus ticket to Anaconda, Montana. Glad to be going home, I felt insecure and uptight about everything. I seemed stuck, somewhere in the birth canal of development. I lacked any interior freedom, and yet felt firm in the knowledge that this was God's will for me.

CHAPTER 10

Mount St. Michael

"But now we are released from the law, dead to what held us captive,
so that we may serve in the newness of the spirit
and not under the obsolete letter." [9]

— ST. PAUL

ONCE MORE, I FOUND MYSELF on a winding road, climbing to a promontory. This time, I looked out on Spokane and asked: why these isolated mountain fortresses? Wasn't St. Ignatius a man who boldly engaged the world? Weren't his headquarters right in the heart of Rome? *The Mount*, as we dubbed our mountain stronghold, was the house of philosophy for both the Oregon and California Jesuit provinces. We were more than 150 men, and would spend three academic years here. Some few who had previously taken philosophy found their way into the social sciences to attend courses at Gonzaga University, to which *the Mount* was academically attached. This was the beginning of my trek to achieve a master's degree in economics. My thesis focused on a socio-economic analysis of all Catholic parishes in the United States who hosted credit unions.[10]

The novitiate-juniorate mentality still clung to me. Rigid, uptight and terribly preoccupied with getting holy, I failed to appreciate the wonders and beauty of community. I couldn't respect the lighter side of life, and was stern in my judgments.

Of course, it was through my fellow Jesuits, in all their marvelous diversity, that God desperately struggled to instruct me. I had ears, but heard not. I was an example of what Paul meant when he said the letter kills; it is the spirit that gives life. I was determined to keep all the rules. Hadn't we been taught, "You keep the rules and the rules will keep you." Through these years, I utilized a spiritual director. I went faithfully every two weeks to lay out my inner life, to find reassurance as I tried to make sense out of our strange ways. I felt grateful for each and every chance to express what went on within me, but I was caught in some dark night of the soul. My confusion draped over me like a hungry lion. Tense and anxious, I ventured to my director's door, but couldn't knock. The deepest aspects of my inner life had risen up within, but I panicked, not knowing how to put into words my confusing emotions. I returned to my room, knelt in prayer, and went back. But again I was defeated at his door. I was unable to get beyond my shame of being who I was.

I hiked the hills. I kept bees. I did work projects. I gazed at the constellations, but did not easily enter into the very legitimate and healthy life that beckoned. Life seemed too serious to be playing games. I continually judged others harshly without ever being aware of this basic sin in myself. During these years, I couldn't understand that I was not a fit instrument. I was unaware that the Lord was laboring mightily to heal me of my blindness and conceit. I was a lonely, renegade Montana stallion, galloping blindly. God was trying to saddle me up to guide me to the true blue horizons where all mountains meet the sky. My false-self defied all; my true-self languished in the prison I'd brought with me into Jesuit formation. I had never digested those liberating words of Jesus, "And you will know the truth, and the truth will set you free,"[11] nor those other words, "I came into this world for judgment, so that those who do not see might see, and those who do see might become blind."[12] Before I could see, I had to have my blinders exposed.

The first glimmers of new sight appeared when Jack Evoy, SJ, returned to Gonzaga University from doctoral studies in modern psychology in 1955. From Gonzaga, he came up to *the Mount* for our segregated course. Part of the conventional curriculum consisted of philosophical psychology, the study of will, intellect, imagination and memory. But it was a tired, dry curriculum, floating up in the heavens of a safe and pristine abstraction. Father Evoy's arrival was like a long awaited downpour of glorious rain in the desert, allowing me to inhale and exhale the fresh air. For the first time, I began to glimpse the contours of my true-self. Father Evoy talked about the dynamics of personal growth, the weight of parental influences, the existence of the subconscious, and of how all this determines the way we define our God and life itself. His course proved the high point of my three years of philosophy at Mount St. Michael.

My intuitive nature told me: yes, yes, this is what we all need. I wanted to ask to go on into advanced studies of psychology. My instincts were strong since these seminary years had wounded and crippled me. My own feeling system had been compressed by a powerful morality system. But I lacked confidence, and was afraid to broach the subject—it might point the finger at my own shameful neurosis, my Irish madness. I continued to go birdwatching by day, and follow the moon by night. I stumbled along in the therapy of nature.

One saving feature of those years was the presence of the Jesuit Brothers. I look back to them with gratitude and affection. The brothers took the same vows, but their vocation led them into manual and practical work. They were cooks, shoemakers, farmers, accountants, janitors, buyers. They were unassuming, down-to-earth, friendly and helpful. I recall Brother Riley, with his Irish brogue, daily setting tables for 150 of us, talking to himself or praying. And there was Brother Winkler in the laundry. Every day I'd find him at his peddle sewing machine, repairing shorts, shirts or socks to make our clothes endure. In the main, the priests seemed apart, dwelling in their heads, terribly formal. In contrast, the brothers lived a gentle spirituality of the heart. Whenever I dropped into chapel, there'd be a brother quietly praying. Their witness was like a glad refrain in a song, subtly pointing toward hope. The old regime held on: although the brothers probably could read, the rule demanded that they gather each day to be "read to" by one of the scholastics, those bound for priesthood. Their rank kept them from talking with the scholastics. We were of that era when the archaic rules, generations old, slowly began to fade away along with the instruments of physical penance. We seminarians came and went in three years; the brothers stayed, some for thirty years or more in the same humble duties.

I departed in late spring for Port Townsend, Washington, to make my annual eight day retreat. My emotions, as usual, were intense and eager, but tempered by little self-knowledge. I longed to get out of my own "personal monastery." I told myself, if I risked falling apart, so be it. I would need to be the grapes crushed. Only then, could I be made into wine. I asked only to see and do God's will as Jesus had done.

During that retreat, a repeated longing for the far north, for the Alaska missions brewed up in me. My motivation was not only to be with the people, but to go to the very edge of life, the place of greatest demand and suffering. I could reduce that desire for Alaska–the toughest of all missions–to my narrow, yet sincere desire, to aim for the hardest and the highest, the greater glory, *Ad Majorem Dei Gloriam.*

CHAPTER 11

My Father Dies

"God sees all, knows all and forgives all."

— *Agnes Violet Morris*

The far north was to be. It was June, 1957, and in two weeks, I would fly
to Alaska. I'd been corresponding with my wayward father who had gone
to find one of the fabled Lost Dutchman's mines in the mountains north
of Sacramento. He'd gotten snowed in, caught a severe cold, and ultimately
retreated to the sun of Phoenix where he took up residence in a boarding
house.

Ah, the allure of gold! It had been with him for years. All striving in
fallen nature is for glory or gold—was there all that much separating my
quest for glory from my father's dream of gold? For the Irish soul, it's about
the tortured, heart scalding, never satisfied dreaming.

I wrote a postcard: "Dear Dad, I'm soon on my way to Alaska where
I'll be teaching for the next two or three years. I want to keep in contact
with you. I haven't heard from you in a while, and I worry. Please write."
He was 69 years old at the time; I was 29. He and Ma had separated due to
his drinking and gambling. She was living in Butte with Rob, my young-
est brother. Dad's health was problematic. Less than a week from the date
I was scheduled to fly north, I received a brief note from Phoenix. The
cleaning woman at the rooming house where my father boarded, found my

42

postcard. She sat down and wrote, "Your father is in the hospital, dying. You had better do something." She signed the note, Maria.

Luckily, there was a Jesuit house in Phoenix where we had a high school and parish. I phoned, and got in touch with John Becker, SJ. He searched and found Dad, transferred him to a Catholic hospital, anointed him, and phoned me. I got permission to delay my departure for Alaska. I arrived in Phoenix, visited Dad, and phoned Ma, who flew out to join us. I rented a small house close to the hospital where I stayed ten days, visiting Dad each day. Cancer of the lungs had him on the ropes.

I tracked down the Phoenix doctor who had cared for my father, to inquire about medical costs. He said, "Sit down. I want to tell you something. Your father came to me a few months ago. I saw him two or three times. He was full of yarns of the early days. His condition worsened; he was eating mostly popcorn on a bad stomach with a hernia that was beyond operation. I was called to visit him at this boarding house. It was right on the route I took to walk home. I was trying to break myself of stopping for drinks in a local bar. I decided I'd visit John instead, knowing he'd spin some interesting yarn about railroading, the mining country, and Indians." He looked at me and said, "I'm not of your faith, Jack, but like you, I'm a human being. I always keep three or four patients on my free list. Your father was one of them. You don't owe me anything."

Next, I went to the head sister of the Catholic hospital. Dad had been there for almost three months. She smiled, telling me there was no bill. I couldn't believe the love, the good fortune, the benevolence of how things worked out—the postcard from the cleaning lady that arrived before I had departed for Alaska, Father Becker's finding and anointing Dad, the compassionate doctor, the free board and room at the Jesuit residence, and now this astounding hospital generosity.

With a sad heart, I said my goodbyes, then departed Arizona to fly to Alaska. Ma stayed behind in Phoenix and visited Dad daily.

Three days after landing in Alaska, I drove two hundred miles to Copper Valley School. It was the beginning of the two most eventful, powerful and enlightening years of my formation. To once again drive was exhilarating, but to be alone in the endless, ever changing grandeur along the highway awakened each fiber of my being. I felt free and alive.

James "Jake" Spils, SJ, was superior of Copper Valley. One day he came to me with news that my father had crossed over. He died on my Ma's birthday. Father Spils asked if I wanted to fly to Phoenix for the funeral. I told him I didn't need to. My two brothers would take care of the funeral. Years later I connected my stance to Jesus' words to the disciple who requested leave to return home to bury his father. Jesus said, "Follow me, and let the dead bury their dead."[13] No, I told myself, I needn't go. Rob and his wife, Norma, drove up from Mexico, brother Pat flew in from Washington, DC. I knew they were there for Ma.

I went over to the chapel, knelt in prayer, and asked for God's mercy. It was Dad's drinking and total absence from church life that, along with Maureen, were part of God's strategy for getting me into the Jesuits. Whether good or bad, I didn't know, but I never shed a tear at news of my father's death, even though I held a genuine affection for him. I felt some fundamental trust in the mystery of life, which included God's omniscient love. Strange as it may seem, I grieved more properly for Dad when Ma, some thirty years hence, crossed over. By then, I knew that God's mercy was within all his works. Or as Ma used to put it, "God sees all, knows all, and forgives all.

CHAPTER 12

The Far North

"Life happens on the frontiers of the heart."

THAT YEARNING FOR THE WILDS of Alaska lodged in my heart from my Navy hospital days. Perhaps beneath my prolonged confinement was the mysterious movement of a benevolent, guiding hand. Ten years later, I was in this mysterious Land of the Midnight Sun where the Church was building mission schools.

The early work of the Catholic Church in the far north of Alaska began on the Yukon River in 1888, where Jesuits, Sisters of St. Ann, and children of all ages, including many orphans from various native villages, lived, studied and worked at Holy Cross Mission. Jesuit missionaries also set up a school for Yup-ik Eskimo children at St. Mary's on the north bank of the Andreafsky River, five miles from its confluence with the Yukon River. From the beginnings of these missions, scores of St. Ann sisters and Jesuit brothers and priests did a lot of heavy lifting, teaching, caring for children, and quiet prayer.

The winters brought temperatures of minus fifty degrees. Survival challenged every human resource. Summers were short, which meant hard, long work hours to turn the soil, plant, tan hides, repair buildings, catch and dry salmon and eel, pick berries and gather driftwood for stoves for the houses, school and church building. Absolute necessities–nails, wire, shovels, hoes, dried fruit, flour, seeds and altar wine–came by steamer once or twice a year after the river ice melted. The mission had its own saw mill requiring felling, hauling and handling of timbers of all sizes. It survived rushes for gold, as well as typhoid, cholera, influenza, diphtheria and whooping cough epidemics. Death rates generally among the natives were high due to the harsh life. There was never enough money.

Sternwheelers on the way up to the Yukon gold fields stopped at the Holy Cross settlement, a haven of civilization in the wilderness. The outpost consisted of several large buildings, a recognizable church, schoolrooms and cultivated gardens. Disembarking, sternwheeler passengers met the locals. Many wrote home about this mission where, over the years, hundreds of native children found refuge, home and education. Holy Cross was known to many as the Catholic orphanage on the Yukon.

The coming of the whites, with new diseases and problematic habits, added to the complex challenges of life. The corrosive influences that had damaged the integrated communities of the Native Americans in the lower forty-eight states were now affecting the natives on this farthest frontier. Alaska was still a territory, but on the fast track to statehood. There were no native high schools north of Sitka. Public high schools awaited statehood, which didn't happen until January 1, 1958.

The Jesuits had chosen to "companion" with the Eskimo, Indian and Aleut people since the late 1880s. Copper Valley was the second post-World War II Jesuit project in Alaska to help the natives grapple with the intense pressures from the white man's world, stemming in part from geopolitical changes. The U.S. saw Russia as a sleeping bear at Alaska's back door. In early 1943, not long after Pearl Harbor, the Japanese had surprise-landed troops to occupy two outer Aleutian Islands, Attu and Kiska, prompting a U.S. military invasion into native lands, with many casualties on both sides. All this was kept secret from the American people. Military might poured into Alaska—air and army bases, the establishment of National Guard units in numerous native villages, and the early warning "Dew Line" system that picked up every possible murmur from Russia. This vast defense effort brought white faces and white ways into native villages. New jobs and more money surfaced than the natives had ever seen, accompanied by radios, air travel, manufactured clothing, demon liquor, and confusion.

John "Jack" Buchanan, SJ, charismatic, energetic, and fresh out of Jesuit formation, was assigned "to work the Alcan Highway" from the border of Canada into Alaska. His parish assignment consisted of 74,000 square miles with seventeen native villages and a growing white population along the new arterial. He built four chapels since being ordained in 1949 located at North Way, Tok Junction, Big Delta and Glennallen, where he envisioned Copper Valley mission school for indigenous and Caucasian youth.[14] Fr. Buchanan's dream took shape. In 1952, a government land grant was passed by Congress to give the Jesuits the needed acres in Glennallen, at the confluence of the Copper and Tazlina Rivers. A story in a periodical years later, tells how the penniless Buchanan soon became known as the "Pack-Rat Priest," so skilled was he in scrounging money and materials for his project to brighten the futures of native boys and girls. Often hauling building materials alone up the Alaska Highway, he once covered 5,600 miles in two weeks. His big truck that plied the highway was a gift of his friend, Bing Crosby. A monster D-7 tractor was donated from Caterpillar. He begged cement from Permanente, steel from Bethlehem, a salvaged Air Force landing mat, wire, paint, roofing, and glass. The first building, a wooden structure shaped like a T, was occupied in 1955. A year later, responding to a call from the Bishop of Northern Alaska, Jesuit scholastics Bill Dibb, SJ, and Tom Gallagher, SJ, came to help develop Copper Valley School.

Buchanan's new school was a true "happening of the Spirit" about halfway up the highway between Anchorage and Fairbanks. Copper Valley School was an effort to continue the original work of Holy Cross after that mission shut down in 1956. Called "Operation Snowbird," twenty-six students, St. Ann sisters, Tom Gallagher, and Brother John Hess, SJ, packed up their bags from the Holy Cross site and traveled by small bush planes and a DC-4 arranged by Alaska Airlines to land at the Gulkana airstrip, twelve miles from Copper Valley School. Albert Gyllenhammer, just discharged from the Air Force, was designated the chief purchaser and expeditor for the Copper Valley School project. Gill, as he was called, drove the bus to pick up the children and adults flying in from Holy Cross. Many children had never been on a plane or a bus, and they were completely silent. As the story goes, Gill pulled the bus to the side of the road, told the children that he was a mean old man and that only music made him nice. So from the airstrip to Copper Valley, the children sang their hearts out.

The superior, Father Spils, also played a large role at Copper Valley. Spils had completed a five year effort to construct St. Mary's mission school, when he was collared to help in the construction of Copper Valley School. Spils served as chief engineer at Copper Valley, and persuaded a group of engineering students from Gonzaga University to help with the building. Among the group were Dick Spils, and Tom and Larry Reisenauer. Michael Lyschinsky, carpenter, served as Fr. Spils' assistant. Others came up for summer construction work in 1957 and 1958. But building supplies were scarce, and sometimes months would go by between receiving donated nuts and the donated bolts that went with them.

A lively Sister of St. Ann, Mary George Edmond, SSA, got permission from Bishop Gleeson to use lay volunteers. This was a revolutionary idea for its time. Sister Edmond, toughened by years at Holy Cross mission and very convincing, persuaded a group of lay college women from Massachusetts to come to Alaska and serve as the founding faculty at the new Copper Valley School. Sister Edmond's fundraising and her 1955 winnings on "Strike It Rich," a television quiz show, generated funds that she gave to Fr. Buchanan who used it to pay the workmen building the school. That check literally saved the project. Sr. Edmond also brought a donation of $1500 earmarked to purchase an organ.

With the help of five St. Ann Sisters, the lay east coast women[15] joined a brigade of others to create a brand new school, making the most of secondhand government surplus: desks, books, pots and pans, five gallon cans of surplus pink paint, copper tubing, heavy timbers, picks, shovels, nails, battered motors and engines. They survived, cooking what they caught and hunted in the wild. Sister Mary Ida Brasseur remembered barbecuing fifteen beavers, and smiled at the requests for seconds "of that delicious pork."

Here I was at Copper Valley School, after two years in the novitiate, two years of undergraduate studies at Sheridan, Oregon, and three years of philosophy at Mount St. Michael in Spokane. What I witnessed was a

marvelous, holy happening, suffused with a kind of vaguely ordered acceptance of the inevitability of disorder. Tom Gallagher, a year ahead of me
in novitiate and studies, was the only familiar face. Kind and steady in his
ways, Tom was solace to my confused heart and mind, a guiding angel to
me that first year. I met Francis "Frank" Fallert, SJ, school principal, and
76-year-old Brother Hess, as durable as an old shoe, and as gentle as the
first light of dawn. I met the Sisters of St. Ann, the indispensable work-
horse companions of the Jesuits, as well as the marvelous volunteers.

Hunting dinner for the Alaskan school children, 1958.

My assigned job was to teach Latin, math, sociology and English.
Fortunately, a student of mine named Pat Snow had a proficiency in math
which I lacked. I also became caretaker, parent and guide to the fourteen grade school boys when Father Tom moved across to another classroom with the high school boys. My responsibilities ran day and night,

and somehow the boys survived my untrained ministrations. I had never worked with children before. Years later, I repented of my inflexibility and discipline, but I sought to care for them and learn as I went along. I would wake them, have them clean up and make their beds, and keep them busy all day long. As soon as the classroom day was done, we started chores that ranged from carpentry, construction, hauling coal, and cleaning dormitories and classrooms. I made sure they had some time for play each day.

Copper Valley School, Alaska.

The quarters for volunteers, both workers and teachers, was at one end of the impractical, star shaped school building. Nearby was the residence of five Sisters led by French-Canadian Sister Alice LeGault, who guided all the girls, most of whom had been together at Holy Cross. Sister Alice was a loving mother-hen to all. Tom confided after introducing me to her, "Before becoming a nun, she was a Communist!" I liked her generous spirit immediately.

The first west coast volunteers arrived at Copper Valley in 1958. Joanne Manfred, Judy Casey and six others from Gonzaga University were persuaded by Fr. Buchanan to teach at the mission school. Joanne served as a secretary of the school, as well as teacher and bookkeeper. To reach Copper Valley, the volunteers traveled the unimproved Alcan Highway for five days, sleeping only one night along the route.

The dreams and persistence of Fr. Buchanan and Fr. Spils, the inspiration of Sr. Mary George Edmond to invite lay volunteers, the exuberant hard work of the early volunteers, and their combined vision of service and companionship with the native people, made Copper Valley School a joyful place from the beginning.

CHAPTER 13

Memories from Copper Valley

"This is the kingdom of God...the kingdom of danger and of risk,
of eternal beginning and of eternal becoming,
of opened spirit and of deep realization,
the kingdom of holy insecurity." [16]

— *Martin Buber*

Copper Valley School was built on a former flood plain, dense with aspen and birch. With the first frosts in mid-August, we lived in an illuminated world of silver filament. Winter, of course, came early. By late September, the temperatures hung below freezing. Sleet and snow covered the earth. The naked trees made me shiver.

One raven-black night in November, the temperature dropped precipitously. Driving, I could hardly see the road through the dense, falling snow. I panicked as I realized I didn't have enough gas to get me home, and how lonely the road was ahead. It wasn't long until sputter, sputter, and the engine died. Cold and afraid, I bundled up in my seat. I told myself not to venture out hiking. As the hours slipped by, I wondered if this was the end for me. My bones felt frozen. Thoughts of home, my parents, my brothers, my loved ones, took over. I struggled to turn my fright into prayer, but I must have nodded off. Suddenly, I awoke and realized it was after midnight. I couldn't remember where I was, but I heard a grinding noise bearing down on me. I saw a faint light. In a few minutes, I left my car, hailed a big logging truck and climbed into the warm cab. I had never been so in need. Relief and thanksgiving permeated my being.

The last task most school days, after praying with the boys and settling them down to sleep, was to quietly bundle up, find my flashlight, and head out to the root house cellar that housed a massive twenty-thousand gallon water tank. My job was to walk the hundred fifty-yard path and light the stove to bring sufficient warmth to keep our vegetables from freezing. Periodically, the boys would help by sorting through the winter supply of potatoes, carrots, cabbage and turnips, throwing the spoiled ones outside, tempting moose to come around. One night, three of the great beasts greeted me. I immediately retreated to find my camera, and on my return, I moved in quietly. Quizzically, they turned their bulky heads my way, their inelegant rumps facing the building. My flash blinded all of us. Thundering confusion ensued as the three stunned beasts tore through the trees in panic. Goose bumps sprouted over my whole body as they stampeded by and I realized that my foolishness could have gotten me trampled. But I'd taken a splendid picture–fiery red moose eyes staring me down.

Because of the severe winter cold, life became more confined to our network of buildings. The trusty generator thumped through the night. I knew the temperature had plunged when the pounding of the generator near my window ceased. I'd haul myself out of bed, bundle up, and with the blazing flame of a blowtorch, go outside to thaw the fuel line and warm the fuel tank. My reward one night was the awesome, utterly silent spectacle of the Aurora Borealis. Whipping, lashing and shimmering movements of color splashed across the heavens. The tantalizing, heavenly dance of these images moved through a seven year cycle, from bright to more subdued. What I witnessed must have been the pinnacle of their glory. Brilliant colors of green, blue, orange, yellow, white and purple swayed like folds of massive curtains across the sky, and then abruptly disappeared. Against the inky atmosphere, the drama streaked from a far horizon like a vast kite tail, zigzagging, and splitting down the middle, the splices retreating to the horizons to disappear. At other times, the spectacle blazed overhead like the interior wires of a huge birdcage, with streams of colored light extending to all points of the compass, disappearing and then reappearing. I was transfixed. Only the bitter cold drove me indoors to warmth and sleep.

Through the challenging process of teaching a full load of subjects I'd never taught before, and performing parenting duties for the boys, I was, by God's kindly graces, led out of the straight jacket of the Jesuit law and order formation program of the previous seven years. During those formation years, my zeal for holiness, to give my all, was total. I viewed holiness, not in terms of love or community, but as the center of my own sanctification, my individualistic quest to bond with God by keeping the rules perfectly. I bought the literal whole of what I believed we were taught. This literalism was imbedded in me, I believe, from a certain rigid, Puritan strain from my mother. I was a fundamentalist, or in novitiate terms, "a hair-shirt." With regrets looking back, I recall the time Tom Pleas came to me, much in need, during "magnum silenca," right after night prayers in common. I was the sub-beadle, in charge of incidental supplies. Tom had cut his finger and came to me for a Band Aid. Because it was the designated time for strict silence, I shook my head and refused him. Rules were rules! I thought I was being righteous, enforcing self-sacrifice, and gradually working my way to sainthood.

Yet I, too, had unmet needs. Early on in Alaska, I went to Fr. Fallert, wanting to know when I could see him for spiritual direction. Frank looked at me and said, "I don't have time for that. Just do your work and things will work out." He got up and walked out, leaving me in my confusion. Frank was a busy, tireless and generous man, but his refusal left me stunned. What could be more important than guidance in holiness? However, Fr. Spils, hailing from a farm family in eastern Washington, confused me even more, but in a very different way. He seemed to live outside of all the rules we'd been taught, yet in my gut, I recognized his integrity. He possessed such easy joy and humor. He was genuinely graced, but I couldn't acknowledge it.

Native German, Brother Hess, also awakened something sleeping within me by his human, down-to-earth manner. Immigrating to the United States after serving in the Kaiser's army, he spent several decades at Holy Cross mission. He told me, "It was late June when we sailed into Valdez harbor. Ahead lay my destination–trekking two hundred miles north to Fairbanks." With a wide smile, he said, "Today folks marvel at such a journey, but you just put one foot in front of another." Hess puttered about doing odd jobs, and like most brothers, showed us youngsters an authentic element of religious life, gently finding God's beauty in the practical tasks and realities of the day.

An earthshaking moment occurred during my second and final spring at Copper Valley. I was out at the furnace house by myself, working on a motor. The tips of purple and white crocuses pushed up through the melting snow as the temperature hovered just above freezing. Hardy snow birds had returned. One has to live through a long, hard Alaskan winter to know how one's soul longs for the relief of warmth and light. I felt alive and glad as I silently worked. All at once, to my own consternation, I started weeping profusely. I looked around, dumbfounded, hoping no one had caught me like this with my guard down. It was a penetrating warming, unclenching of a fist, a loosening of a stranglehold in me.

Years later, I was forced to explore what brought on this strange, sobbing episode in Alaska. My rumination brought back a memory of me as a novice seven years earlier, going in to see William Elliot, SJ, our excellent master of novices. I had mumbled to him about my experience of not fitting in, of feeling constricted and estranged. I told him I was losing confidence and was withdrawing, that so many fears and insecurities assaulted me. He listened and said something I don't remember. I left his office feeling sad, worried that he hadn't understood me.

I looked back at the absurdity of the situation of Fr. Elliot serving as the sole guru for some fifty needy novices. We lined up to see him once every two weeks. I had felt alone, my struggles blended into the endless current of troubled novices that he encountered. Because the challenges of religious life were real and had to be accepted, he had no real companionship or comfort to offer in the face of my misery. In fact, it struck me somewhere in my rumination of Copper Valley that not long after I met with Elliot, I was directed to join three others on "special novitiate order." We were excused from the common order of studies and prayer and were given some breathing room. How good it felt to sleep in beyond the 5 a.m. rising. Elliot had known that I was having prolonged headaches and ulcers. He had understood what I needed, after all. I realized somewhere in my tears and confusion that, while on one level I was depressed as a novice, and later depressed while working in Alaska's harsh winter, on a much deeper level I believed God was trying to get through to me. I saw my struggles as part of my own intimate suffering, but also as part of being sought after by God.

I eventually came to see simplicity in my transformation as well. What had triggered my spontaneous sobbing was the warmth of the returning spring, the sun gradually fighting back the cold, the icicles beginning to thaw and drip. My own tears flowed from the melody and invitation of spring, God's renewing invitation to life.

Years later, I discovered the poem *Gypsy Music* by Sister Lou Ella Hickman, IWBS, and I realized it perfectly captured the feeling I experienced that day in Alaska as spring thawed my frigid heart:

> *"God is a gypsy who plays her violin*
> *at the gate of my heart.*
> *Hidden in the high thin notes*
> *of her wild music*
> *is her longing for love.*
> *She plays her rhapsody*
> *until the tears come…*
> *longing, longing to be invited in."*[17]

Finally, I saw in myself the person from John's gospel, Nicodemus, who came to Jesus in the night. Like Nicodemus, I was searching, groping, responding to something deeper within, beyond the mind, beyond the rule of law that I had been so rigidly keeping. Jesus tells Nicodemus that unless he is born again, from above, he would not find his way to the kingdom to which he had dedicated his life. That visit of mine with the master of novices seven years before was a kind of *conception*, making my Jesuit life more real. The sobbing episode was *birth-pangs*. From that time on, I believed the further words from John's gospel applied to me: "The wind blows where it wills, and you can hear the sound it makes, but you do not know where it comes from or where it goes; so it is with everyone who is born of the Spirit."[18] The wind came that spring day under God's glorious sun, ending a dreadfully long winter. It took those seven years for me to trust the wind, to loosen my grip, to lose my life in order to find my deeper self. Since then, I have often felt that I didn't know where I was going, but it didn't matter. My conversion of heart–that surprise sobbing incident and that gift of a whole new way of seeing reality and myself–trumped all the other blessings of my two fulfilling years at Copper Valley School.

Only later did I see with the clear eyes of hindsight, that another significant event was unfolding in Alaska at the same time–the work of lay volunteers. It was an amazing seed that had taken root and was growing. Today it is known across Catholic America as the Jesuit Volunteer Corps movement.

CHAPTER 14

Toronto and Theology

"Ecumenical Councils, whenever they are assembled,
are a solemn celebration of the union of Christ and His Church,
and hence lead to the universal radiation of truth..."[19]

— *POPE JOHN XXIII*

I MADE MY WAY TO yet another Regis College, the Jesuit School of Theology at University of Toronto, Canada in the fall of 1959, after completing my teaching period that Jesuits call "regency." I was 32 years old. On the way, I visited Maureen who was married with three children. Her family was bursting with life.

Regis sat on the edge of Toronto's industrial parks. Beyond our quarters lay a vast, bleak railroad yard, cutting us off from the shores of Lake Ontario. Four years of theological studies lay ahead. These years were to be the pinnacle of our preparations to become men of the Church. Ten of us from the Oregon Province joined four others who had initiated our presence with the Canadian Jesuits the previous year. The student body was diverse: English and French Canadians, Cubans, Spaniards, Belgians and now Oregonians.

After the freedom of my years teaching and moving around, I was entering a somewhat unwelcome confinement. Attending class and pounding the books were required. We reentered a mentality mired in yesterday rather than tomorrow. There were strict rules and patterns of submission:

we couldn't leave the premises without wearing the Roman collar and a proper black clerical hat; we had to humbly ask the procurator for street car tickets. At least we had a four story, chocolate factory in the next building. We'd whistle, and the working girls would throw us chocolates, an indulgence for which we were reprimanded.

The seminary had grown up around an old mansion perched in grand prestige on the shores of the great lake. There was a rumor that a former owner had built a secret room so his mistress could clandestinely live with him; the mistress committed suicide in the room, and ever since had haunted the college. I believe it had been willed to a religious congregation of women, the Sisters of St. Joseph, decades before. The sisters added living quarters as well as a chapel. Ten-foot, heavy, double oak doors with burnished, brass handles opened onto a cavernous tunnel of pews facing a distant altar. The Jesuits came into possession of the property past its glory days. Layers of soot darkened ornate ceilings, and the hardwood chapel floor had partially rotted out due to wet and cold. All wore outdoor coats to Mass. Mike Walsh, a fellow Oregonian, used to go up to communion wearing gloves, provocatively holding them before his chin as the rector distributed communion. We prayed in common and in quiet meditation in our rooms, and looked forward to ordination, and a return to the real world.

During those years, we studied all aspects of the Catholic faith. Moral theology manuals covered virtues and vices, sin, good and evil. The study of Dogmatics explored the Trinity, the Incarnation, heaven and hell. We studied Church history, canon law, and the Catholic Church itself. There was the "long" probing course taught in Latin for the bright, and the "short" course in English for the strugglers.

Those of us in theological studies entered into privileged seats of one of the great unfolding dramas of the Catholic Church. The unassuming John XXIII had been pope about ninety days when on January 25, 1959, he exploded an historical bomb in the Vatican. He planned to convene a great council of the whole Church—the first since Vatican I, less than ninety years earlier. The stunning news captivated the world media. One Lutheran source commented that perhaps the "sleeping giant was awakening." This would be the 21st Ecumenical Council since the beginnings of the Church, summoning bishops from around the world to prayerfully read the signs of the times. The cultural consequences of the Second Vatican Council would reverberate throughout the Catholic world and beyond.

Years later, the renowned theologian, Karl Rahner, SJ, commented that this was the first time the Roman Catholic Church genuinely celebrated its global nature, its universality. Time and the world had moved far since Vatican Council I. Laying heavily over the political powers of both West and East, as well as the very soul of the Church, were the still open wounds of World War II, Nazi Germany's grim slaughter of millions of Jews and other victims. There had been the appalling devastation of the Stalin era. Economic and technological progress on land and sea, had shrunk the globe. A new Asian Catholic Church was emerging. Pope John felt and saw the need for reform, renewal, and a reshaping of the ancient doctrines, as well as new strategies of evangelization and engagement with the secular world.

In a positive and optimistic speech inaugurating Vatican II, the 83-year-old Pope chided the many prophets of gloom among cardinals and bishops whose attitude was to let sleeping dogs slumber. John wanted an awakening. He spoke of the world's need for the medicine of mercy and healing, and for the Church to release and radiate a universal truth. The Pope's call for such a council rang around the world. In Toronto, I felt we had a ringside seat on the unfolding drama.

On October 11, 1962, after almost four years of exhaustive preparation, the council finally opened what became the greatest reform of the Church for hundreds of years. Seminarians across the world, with many of their professors, felt keenly the disjointedness between what they perceived of the world and the narrow concerns of the Roman Catholic theological syllabus. Long suppressed by tired, pinched, and worn out understanding of Catholic Church dogma, hierarchy and morality, the Church faced a new beginning.

The astounding truths Vatican II promulgated fit hand-in-glove with what transpired in my own heart at Copper Valley School. While there, I felt my own spirituality had gotten beyond law, rules and regulations, and entered into the freedom of the Spirit. That movement was now happening to the whole Church. I had been painfully born again in the wilderness of far off Alaska, and knew that what was unfolding with Pope John was real, authentic knowing–beyond the mind. The change would herald a long, painful birth. My heart sang when I read Pope John's words chiding some of his fellow prelates: "We feel we must disagree with those prophets of gloom, who are always forecasting disaster, as though the end of the world were at hand. In the present order of things, Divine Providence is leading us to a new order of human relations....And everything, even human differences, leads to the greater good of the Church."[20]

The Council proceedings were a trumpet call to boldness and engagement with the world. They transformed students and professors. An unfamiliar, happy excitement percolated throughout Regis College–in our classes, in the journals we read, in the feelings we had about our coming ordination. The Holy Spirit was doing her transformative work.

CHAPTER 15

Ordination and First Assignment

"All that I have I have received, Great God, bless the world."

DUE TO THE LONG COURSE of Jesuit training, the Jesuit Order ordained its men at the end of the third year in a four year theology program. We all went home, only to return for our final year of theology. But we returned as priests of the Roman Catholic Church, linking us back through the centuries to that humble meal we speak of as The Last Supper. With enthusiasm, we were now ministers of the Word in the book and in the bread. We sought out parishes near and far, wishing we could encounter evil spirits so that we could cast them out.

For many years, I had struggled painfully with perfectionism and legalism. But when ordination time came, my capitulation resonated from a longing deep within. I was ready to surrender to God.

Twenty-two of us were ordained at St. Aloysius' Church in Spokane, Washington on June 16, 1962. The following week, we each separately celebrated our first Solemn Mass with family and friends. June 24 saw me in Anaconda for my first public Mass celebrated in old St. Paul's Church where I had first worshipped as a youth.

Perhaps it's strange, even narcissistic, but what sums up the ordination event for me, with all its excitement and cathartic release, is the prayer that I put on my ordination card. On the front was to be our priestly image, and on the back a prayer of our own choosing. The new Jack, reborn in Copper

Father Jack Morris is ordained.

Valley, saw no reason to link my image with someone else's prayer. This prayer came to me on the eve of my ordination:

Mighty God, Father of all
Bless every person I have met
Every face I have seen
Every voice I have heard
Especially those most dear
Bless every city, town
And street that I have known
Every sight I have seen
Every object I have touched

In some mysterious way
These have all fashioned my life
All that I have I have received
Great God, bless the world.

The prayer brought into focus the substance and spirit of what I had been seeking when I joined the Jesuits in 1950. It still rings true and sounds clear in my heart. Somewhere in the 1970s, I amended the prayer by adding to "Mighty God, Father of all," the words "Compassionate God, Mother of all."

Jack and his mother celebrate Ordination.

After a summer assignment in Harlem, New York City, I returned to Toronto, where I landed a counseling job at Catholic Charities. I spent each Thursday counseling youth and was a priestly presence in the agency. I felt happily alive, perhaps as I'd rarely been before.

As newly ordained priests, each of us celebrated morning Mass in private chapels. The unaccustomed wine made for lively breakfast conversation. We often went out to help at weekend Masses near and far, and to hear hours of confessions at Catholic schools. We were enchanted by the unexpected wonders of priesthood, and the deference of the people towards us.

Before we knew it, spring had come, and with it, the end of our four years of theology at Regis College. I had received my assignment to return to Alaska, and expected that I'd spend my priestly career in what Pope Pius X had called the most difficult of all missions, the Arctic. In fact, I'd requested that mission because it seemed for me a way to give my all.

I felt some gravel in my britches when in 1963, I learned that my assignment was a predominantly Caucasian Monroe High School in Fairbanks, Alaska. This was not what I wanted for myself. I hadn't anticipated being a teacher ever again. I wanted to be "in the bush" with the Indians on the Yukon or with the Eskimos in small villages on the vast Yukon Delta. But here I was, an ordinary teacher at Monroe High in Fairbanks. As a seminarian, I had taught for two years at Copper Valley School, and I admit I learned to enjoy it, but teaching didn't fuel my heart. However, my upbringing told me that whatever you're given to do, dig in, and you'll discover gold.

One golden memory of my assignment in Fairbanks was standing next to the open door of my classroom before first period in the early morning. Youthful laughter, bright smiles, cheery conversation carried down the hallway, and the stomping of cold feet that accompanied the swinging of school doors, made me smile. Such a parade of young beauty, wonder and hope.

What I missed was diversity–not one native Alaskan among our 250 students. But I'll never forget Alice. She was the one and only Black student. I taught sociology, and asked Alice if she'd mind telling the class what it felt like to be the only "colored" girl in school. Her description of the loneliness was met with discomfort and stunned silence. Out of this moment, I watched as new sympathies and connections were born.

A good part of a Jesuit's ability to adjust depends on the vow of obedience, on the belief that one's Jesuit superior reveals God's will for the individual subject at that time. Objections, it was taught, come from the head; obedience, being of the heart, overrides.

On some level, I now see that my quest for holiness in Alaska at the time was largely self-centered. My ego wanted to go where it was most difficult, where I could challenge the darkness to give my life to the Father—still to become a saint. If I'd been sent to an isolated village, I may have felt heroic, but my ego would not have been challenged as it was by doing a humble, ordinary job, and living in Jesuit community. Back then, I thought I knew what was best for me. I didn't have a clue how God's desire differed from my own. My kind of God was still too small.

CHAPTER 16

Jesuit Volunteer Corps Movement Is Born

✠

"When you dream alone, it is only a dream.
When we dream together, it's the beginning of a reality."[21]

— *DOM HELDER CAMARA*

THE MOST SIGNIFICANT MOMENT IN my two years at Monroe High occurred in the early spring of 1964. George Boileau, SJ, fellow Montanan and affable superior of the Alaska Missions, came into my office and dropped twenty manila files on my desk with applications from lay Catholics to help our ministries in Alaska. He said, "It's all yours."

What took place that moment had its origins in my heart six or seven years earlier while I was at Copper Valley School with five Jesuits, five Sisters of St. Ann, Fr. Spils's motley construction crew, the children, and a new, vibrant force–a dozen lay volunteers. Most of the volunteers from Massachusetts and Gonzaga University were young and fresh out of college, but there were a few older men and women as well as two native men on Fr. Spils's crew. There was something about the volunteers' exuberance and generosity, their freedom and camaraderie that made me jealous. As volunteers, they received less than $20 a month, a roof over their heads, all they could eat, but alas, no insurance coverage. They taught elementary or high school, worked in the kitchen, laundry, offices, carpentry or maintenance shops and played with the children. Often in the evenings, their bright laughter sounded above the constant thump of the school's mammoth generator. They added something I'd never before witnessed–lay men and women doing mission work. I instinctively knew this was real and of the Spirit.

While I was away in Toronto doing four years of theology (1959 to 1963), I heard that the number of Alaska volunteers and the placements where they served, had increased. Several were teaching in Fairbanks, Dillingham, and Nulato. They had indeed become a new force in the Jesuit mission work of Alaska. I realized that what the great Vatican II Council had set in motion was happening here on the frontiers of the American Catholic Church: the laity was important. It had a priestly role to play in animating our mission projects.

After several of the Alaska volunteers returned from Copper Valley to Gonzaga University in 1959, they gave some definition to the volunteer movement. They named it LAMB, Lay Apostles Mission Board, and it was about doing the corporal works of mercy. I remember Buchanan's mission statement: "As long as you did to one of these my least brethren, you did to *Me*." Joseph Conwell, SJ, and Armand Nigro, SJ, helped LAMB create an application form that Bishop Gleeson approved. All requests for volunteers came to Spokane and screening took place from there. From the lower forty-eight states, the group, led by student Mickey Byrnes, sent boxes of apples to the mission school. They made trips to Yellowstone where they shot elk and sent the meat up to Copper Valley by freight. They were a great support group.

When Boileau dropped those files on my desk that day in Fairbanks, I took up the challenge of putting order into a spirited rag-tag volunteer happening. It seemed clear that this was the future. I felt a call to ride the wave, to take it on, and give it form and structure.

Father Boileau and I considered the power of the laity, the baptismal call for all believers, as well as the problems of this emerging reality. Bishop Gleeson was getting very old. While he loved overseeing the volunteer program, its demands exceeded his energy. Some of these untrained, adventurous volunteers were getting hurt, even sent home. It was evident to me that these raw volunteers were tender, uninitiated and lacked guidance. They were generous but lacked wisdom. I told Boileau that I'd be glad to orchestrate and shape the program—some forty new volunteers each year. My certainty of the rightness of this program energized, directed and delighted me. There I was, being asked to play a key role in the unfolding of tomorrow's Church. I had a new job that would turn out to preoccupy me for the next thirty years. In fact, what in time came to be named the Jesuit Volunteer Corps, brought me from spiritual adolescence to adulthood.

From my time at Copper Valley and Fairbanks, I saw new volunteers trickle in, and immediately dive into a full work schedule of largely unanticipated challenges. The harsh, confining, arctic climate was rough. It took until Christmas for the volunteers to really know Jesuit and Sisters of Providence ministries, and to know one another, having been thrown into their housing and work placements. Jesuits individually reached out and were available for counseling, but the lack of a formulated program left many volunteers untethered. In the Fairbanks' "pink palace" house were ten volunteers, housed in eight bedrooms. While amazed at their joy and motivation, we Jesuits were sometimes humbled from wondering if and why our own long Jesuit formation gave us greater solicitude and importance.

Starting in 1964, I acted as the first director of what grew out of LAMB to become the Jesuit Volunteer Corps. My first obligation was to structure an orientation program. I knew it must psychologically prepare the volunteers for the experience of mission before they arrived at their site. How best to orient young Christian laity to serve as an extension of the mission of Jesus Christ? I didn't have a clue, but I knew the spirit of Vatican II was an essential ingredient. I envisioned these young volunteers acting in the role as "mini-Jesuits" who needed formation in ministry. Vatican II spoke of the priesthood of the laity, of their call to participate in the upwelling of the social order, of their becoming sanctifiers. I felt a need to create a substantive orientation to prepare them to go out into the world, encounter its broken people, face reality, give back life, imagine God's point of view in their work, and do something great beyond themselves. I wanted to prepare them for living in community, to accept that everyone has a shadow, to learn to suspend judgment of one another, to forgive and let some things go. I hoped to offer them tools to resolve problems together, make peace, reconcile, live with integrity, and pray together.

In my free time, I began developing presentations to address these needs. I wondered whether those who had volunteered would be willing to arrive earlier for an orientation. I grappled with how to build a program that was real enough to actually prepare them for their work. At the end of the school year, I told Boileau I needed to go outside my own resources, to Gonzaga University, to see about getting a locus for the program and to ask select Jesuits to give presentations. What about prayer, sharing, money, and everything under the sun? I was clueless about how to pay for the program. I'd not handled money since I entered the Jesuits. Boileau handed me five hundred dollar bills to cover the program. Gonzaga University gave us free use of one of their small halls. Vince Beuzer, SJ, Willie Schoenberg, SJ, and Joe Conwell, SJ, gave presentations, gratis.

I was a complete tenderfoot bursting with questions. What was the goal? How should the program proceed? What might be its components? I wrote to each of the new volunteers, surprised that three-quarters of these recruits were eager for the extra preparation time I called Orientation. They arrived at Gonzaga University in Spokane for the first Orientation program for volunteers in August of 1964. With twenty-four volunteers in a classroom, I asked them to tell the group what friends thought of their joining this lay volunteer movement in Alaska. Many of their friends thought it truly bizarre. Now, Orientation had purpose.

We were heralds of a new force within Church life–the volunteering of young and older lay men and women, shoulder to shoulder with sisters, brothers and priests. For six days we explored, listened and shared, transforming us into a genuine community of joy and gladness. The new volunteers heard about new dimensions of Church life, especially *the priest-hood of the laity*–that they had their own unique and free role to play in establishing the reign of God, and rediscovering the place of the Holy Spirit within the Church and their personal lives. These bright souls learned about the unfolding of the Jesuit missions in Alaska from a hundred years earlier. In two days, they relaxed enough to share their fears, doubts, anxieties, and their hopes. The movement of the Spirit was felt most keenly in our daily Eucharist. I saw eyes meet, and faces light up around our small Eucharistic circle.

I got wind of a new Roman Catholic movement called *Cursillo*, founded in Majorca, Spain by a group of lay people in 1944, while they refined a technique to train pilgrimage leaders. The *Cursillo* focused on showing Christian lay people how to become effective leaders over the course of a three-day weekend. It consisted of fifteen talks, some given by priests and some by lay people. The emphasis of the weekend was to ask participants to take what they learned back into the world, on what they call the "fourth day." The method stressed personal spiritual development, accelerated by a weekly (now monthly) group reunion after the weekend.

I learned that at the conclusion of the *Cursillo* course of prayer and study, each participant was presented with a cross. I wanted to adopt this symbolic tradition, but wrestled with the cultural realities—would these young people see it as hokey, strange, and embarrassing? At our final Mass, we held a commitment ceremony. I presented each of the volunteers with a six-inch, brushed bronze cross. After we saw the volunteers off to the Spokane airport to continue their journey to Alaska, volunteers Joe Ford and Tim Walsh, and I drove the 1,500 miles of the unpaved Alcan Highway together. On the third morning of our drive, Joe said, "I didn't sleep so well, my cross was digging into my side." We laughed, but I was touched that the cross meant enough to be worn day and night. What was true for all of them, was that they were moved by this commitment ceremony. Again, the wisdom of the Church: the soul and the human psyche need ritual and concrete symbols. I don't know who was more thrilled for this Orientation program, the young volunteers or me.

Before I knew it, my second year as a teacher at Monroe High had started. The bright, happy faces and laughter of students from day one guaranteed it would be a good year. I knew the students now, and I was happier in my vocation. Half of the Jesuit Volunteers were staying on for a second year. For two of them, this was a third year. For the school, it was a huge bargain—ten idealistic, generous, hard-working staff who gave all this for room and board, a small stipend per month, and a ticket home at the end of their commitment. By now, they were an established force in the Fairbanks Catholic Church, doing more than maintenance and secretarial work. They were also teaching at both elementary and high school levels. Without knowing it, these volunteers were positive role models for the school, the parish, and the wider community. Their presence spoke volumes to parents and parishioners–being Catholic was about serving others. Their commitment was known throughout the wider community as a witness to the power of the Holy Spirit operating through the laity. They were hallowing the name of God alongside priests and sisters.

My short, Fairbanks stint proved a time of priestly growth and maturing. One cannot teach, work with, and interact with youth, dedicated sisters, and Jesuit Volunteers without being awakened to the splendor and beauty of being human and alive. To this day, awe comes to me when I think back on those two years at Monroe High in Fairbanks, and the earlier two year period at Copper Valley School with largely native children. I learned so much simply because I was doing what my vocation as a young Jesuit taught me–what you are assigned to is God's will for now. However, even though I embraced my assignment, I was sure that I was not being led to become a lifetime teacher. But what I was being led to, I did not know.

CHAPTER 17

Tertianship

*"I had such an intense longing to grasp and possess holiness
that its pursuit became my greatest sin."*

AFTER THIRTEEN YEARS AND A taste of the apostolic nature of Jesuit life,
I could see the completion of formation ahead. With twenty other men, I
traveled to Port Townsend, Washington in 1965 to start tertianship, the
culminating period of interior formation lasting nine months. It offered
another opportunity, as in the novitiate, to descend from head to heart, and,
as Mother Teresa reminded us, to put all things together and make something beautiful for God. Ultimately, it was about humility, as we attempted
to see all of our studies and apostolic works from God's point of view, and
to allow one's self to be encountered by the mystery of the universe.

This final formation process began with a thirty-day retreat, just as my
Jesuit career began when I first left family, personal career and hopes of
marriage behind, to enter the Jesuit novitiate. I felt in my bones a need to
spend time on the inner journey, to discover how I could more adequately
give my life to God as did our illustrious Jesuit saints. From the very beginning, I realized my Jesuit life was more about the interior world than the
outer one, yet here I was, almost fourteen years later, still an unlettered
novice in matters of wisdom and spirituality. What did sanctity mean?
How could I surrender fully to God's will? How would I lose my life to
find life? Why was it so difficult to rein in my small self and tame the
unbridled spirits within?

I entered tertianship, conflicted of mind. St. Paul expressed my conundrum: "The willing is ready at hand, but doing the good is not. For I do not do the good I want, but I do the evil I do not want."[22] From the time I sacrificed my love of Maureen and marriage, I was driven by the seriousness of the quest to become holy, but I was aware of the wide chasm that separated where I stood from where God's Spirit dwelled.

In fact, from the dramatic experience of severing Maureen from my intimate life until entering tertianship, I had such an intense longing to grasp and possess holiness that its unyielding pursuit became my greatest sin. I didn't recognize that this passion had placed me squarely in the shoes of the Pharisees. Simone Weil saw rightly when she warned that all beliefs, including religious ones, risk idolatry.[23] I've heard it said that religious people will tend to worship glory or God. Under the guise of total surrender, was I really seeking God, or just my own petty glory and personal deification? Isn't that the burden noted in the Epistle of Peter, where we are called to vigilance? "Be sober and vigilant. Your opponent the devil is prowling around like a roaring lion looking for someone to devour."[24] Every decision we make is on the cusp between worship and idolatry, between humility and pride. Tertianship offered one more chance for self-scrutiny, a time to plumb my depths and listen to God's call for me.

What does a Jesuit do in the thirty-day retreat of silent meditation, contemplation and prayer, the culminating experience of his long Jesuit formation? Although I made this retreat with others, I, like Jacob of old, climbed into the wrestling ring alone, to wrestle all through the long night with a mysterious adversary. Jacob, we know, was wounded, yet refused to surrender until he received the blessing he climbed into the ring to obtain. He received it in a new name. Ultimately, the Jesuit is in the dark, yet the contest takes place under the bright dome light of his Catholic and Jesuit tradition. The adversary calls his whole being into question, all his years of formation and his deformation, his strengths and weaknesses, his successes and gifts, and his failures and conceits. The mysterious adversary is sly and hard hitting, delivering wounding blows. Again, like Jacob, a Jesuit must not give up even though "the dawn is coming," if he is to receive the longed for blessing sought before the retreat began. St. Ignatius tells us that we must know what grace we crave before entering into prayer. The craving might be for clarity about whether one should continue to be a Jesuit, or as simple as wanting to attain purity of heart. Some of the men fasted, some spent long hours in quiet, others went on long walks, sifting through the wisdom of the scriptures laid out by the tertian "master." Jesuit styles of prayer are as varied as the number of Jesuits. But the real purpose of tertianship was to "cross the abyss" of our egos.

During tertianship, my inward journey was joined with a practical task of running the lay volunteer program. Before tertianship ended, I was handed a new, unexpected, and decidedly undesirable assignment–to go to Portland, Oregon, to be assistant to Joe Conyard, SJ, in the Jesuit Seminary and Mission Bureau, and to rub elbows with the provincial and his small staff.

Office work and begging money spelled misery for me. I desired an Alaskan village to be with the native people. At that time, I was completely inept, caught between ego and surrender, unpracticed in honest dialogue with a superior about an assignment. No one asked what I thought. Obedience had taught us, if you don't like it, lump it. In retrospect, what guided me through this uncomfortable time was trust in God's long plan. It was what Simone Weil might conjecture–God is in the real, whether that is a crushing stone or nourishing bread.

CHAPTER 18

Ruined For Life

"Come and labor on the frontiers of the Church!"

THE OREGON PROVINCIAL HEADQUARTERS OF 1966 was an elegant, baronial, Scottish mansion that drew the eyes of passersby. The old edifice stood grandly on the corner of Nineteenth and Hoyt Streets in northwest Portland. The Seminary and Mission Bureau, plus living quarters for several of us, occupied the adjacent two old frame houses. We had our meals, and required recreation periods after both dinner and supper in the provincial house. I judged the mansion pretentious, a contradiction to our Jesuit vow of poverty. The formality and decorum of the place didn't jibe with my own attraction to informality and simplicity. I even had my own new car, but, as when I entered the novitiate, I was psychologically caged and didn't really fit in. I didn't feel at home as I'd felt in the spacious, simple, generous environment of Copper Valley.

As assistant to the director, routine office work occupied my days. Three women augmented the staff and I composed letters of thanks to those who materially supported our work. I knew administration wasn't my forte or my desire. Was the best way to love God to let go of self and just do my job? Yet didn't God want me to be discerning? God's greater glory seemed to be about change, movement, questioning, and experimenting. How in these times that demanded authenticity, could I be anything except questioning?

Central to my senses of passion and responsibility, was the Jesuit Volunteer task Fr. Boileau had handed over to me in the spring of 1964. It needed much more care and feeding. For the past two years from Fairbanks and in tertianship, I had set in motion the Orientation program for the new Jesuit Volunteers. I'd not only begun to establish ongoing relationships with the new volunteers through letters, but had become excited by what I saw of the power and possibilities of these young lay people. My interest in the laity derived partly from the unfolding story of Vatican Council II, but primarily from our very baptismal call to put shoulders to the wheel of changing the world, to build community, and spark a revolution of the Holy Spirit.

I stole time from the endless tasks of the Seminary and Mission Bureau to develop the lay volunteer program from my office in Portland. The program had won my heart, even though I scarcely knew what I was trying to accomplish. I was not free enough personally to ask for help. Conyard, my boss, saw me as the point man for news and programs to help the Alaska missions. He also began talking about the possibility of international volunteers starting in Zambia, the mission our province had taken on.[25]

By the time my first year in Portland was over, my confidence was growing. Jesuit Volunteers had been going to Alaska for a full ten years. The literature spoke of Alaska Volunteers, and Lay Men and Women in Alaska, but the program lacked an exciting, enticing name. I put out a colorful flyer with the psychedelic script of the era. The insight of Mary Webber, of Portland, helped me see the name I suggested, "Jesuit Volunteers," was stodgy. She said, "It sounds like an old women's hospital program. How about adding "Corps?" She and I did just that, and it became the much more vital Jesuit Volunteer Corps. *(See history of JVC and JVC Northwest.)* [26]

I began to market the program as "Older than the Peace Corps, twice as tough, and ten times more rewarding–give up one year of a money-making job, come, and labor on the frontiers of the Church." I begged advertising space in several Catholic weeklies across the country and I began formalized recruitment for the Jesuit Volunteer Corps. "Give a year of service, make a world of difference!"

Missioning celebration for new Jesuit Volunteers.

I was quite aware of the growing need for more volunteers in Alaska as well as to support the mission of our men on the Native American reservations, but no one knew about this Jesuit Volunteer program. I began to recruit for the program that Joe Obersinner, SJ, ran at Omak, Washington, incorporating a mission outside of Alaska. I assembled a traveling show to recruit students at Catholic colleges and Newman centers, and to visit all the placement sites. With no budget, I charged the mission office for my travel since the volunteers helped the Jesuit missions. It seemed clear to me the Holy Spirit was moving the Church in this direction.

I believe the JVC movement sprouted, flourished, and continues to do so, because of two implanted energy sources. The first component is that JVC was born on a tough, wild, northwestern frontier of America. The Jesuits and Sisters of St. Ann for well over one-hundred years had honed and lived a spirituality of hard work, laughter and gratitude at Holy Cross Mission on the banks of the Yukon River. The leadership of Fr. Buchanan and Sr. Edmond brought this spirit to what became Copper Valley School in 1956 when Edmond invited the first women volunteers to teach and fortify a twelve-grade school in the Alaska wilderness. Those early days were wild and free and full of adventure. It began the tradition of "ruined for life," yes, ruined by responding to the Gospel call. It was a lifelong invitation to compassion. Once a volunteer, never again in your life could you ignore the plight of people living on the margins. JVC was a frontier movement, literally and figuratively. Frontiers demand risk, cooperation and resilience. In return, they give back grit, laughter and new confidence. I hope JVC never forgets its origins on the northwestern front lines. These challenging words from the Jesuits sum it up: "Jesuits are never content with the status quo, the known, the tried, the already existing. For us, frontiers and boundaries are not obstacles or ends, but new challenges to be faced…ours is holy boldness."[27]

The second source of identity and energy that makes all the difference for the JVC movement is the name Jesuit. It stands for so many values and attitudes, but above all, it stands for Jesus—the truth, the way and the life, and the source of all wisdom and knowledge. And He came for one purpose, that his joy would be in us and our joy complete. That, it seems to me, is the very soul of the Jesuit Volunteer Corps movement.

Twelve years after the JVC flower began blossoming, I wrote an article in 1968, *"The Laity Have Become the Church"* for the Jesuit magazine. Nineteen volunteers were now with John Morse, SJ,[28] and Joseph Obersinner, SJ, running St. Mary's Mission School at Omak, Washington. Father Obersinner told me, "You might not believe it, but the volunteers run the whole place—teachers, secretary, prefects, kitchen, and laundry workers. They get great satisfaction knowing that without them, the place would fold."

In Alaska, by this time, sixty-seven volunteers served in eight locations. Bishop Gleeson said, "This is the only area of the American Church where volunteers outnumber priests. They've become an absolute necessity." Volunteers at Copper Valley numbered eighteen; at St. Mary's on the lower Yukon, fourteen; in Fairbanks, thirteen. Ye gods, I thought, something marvelous was happening! Our JVC movement brochure echoed the hope of it all, "We'll get you there, work you hard, pay you a small monthly stipend, build you a unique adventure, and get you back home." The pamphlet went on to say, "Problems of racism, peace and poverty will never be solved until more people take concrete steps and become personally involved. Becoming a volunteer is one small step toward justice and peace." It was a whole new way of looking at Church and evangelization, as well as formation of the laity to serve the poor. It was about the People of God taking responsibility on the rough, unsophisticated outer edge of a bureaucratic Church.

Memories of the rich, fruitful, intergenerational friendships between Jesuits, nuns and JVs set me singing. So many Jesuits commented to me over the years about the gift that JVs were to them personally. In those days, every JV had daily contact with the Jesuits and the Sisters. It was familial, spiritual, and genuine. Those early relationships shaped the ethos of the JVC movement and its core values of social justice, community, simple living and spirituality. It wasn't easy; community life could be brutal. And the psychological "dangers" of self-discovery were real as reflected in a slogan on the wall of a community house: "It is easier to fight for one's principles than to live up to them." Like missionaries before them, the JVs discovered their service and companionship was not about some disconnected piety, but was simply the grit and satisfaction of getting out there, in the name of Christ, to work together in community to help and be with those in need.

Orientation week for Jesuit Volunteers Corps Northwest.

My prayer for the volunteers persists: "O Lord, may all who participate as Jesuit Volunteers be humble while being proud, sober yet silly, always willing to wash the feet of others, knowing it is far better to serve than to do anything else. Let them be ruined for life."

The Jesuit Volunteer Corps movement was a sheer gift of the Holy Spirit. That spirit always comes as a surprise, lifting us beyond where we are, showing us that we can "turn water into wine," and even rise from despair to life. What a joy to have been in the company of so many stunning, marvelous, generous, laughing, hard-working, genuine Christians. Like 99 percent of the former Jesuit Volunteers in America and around the world, I was profoundly grateful for having been drawn into the movement. May the dance go on and on.

Jesuit Volunteer Corps Northwest, Camp Adams, Oregon.

Here's a letter I wrote to all JVs:

Dear JVs,

Hello to you all. It's February and the days are lengthening, buds are budding, the sun moves higher and stays longer...but let's get to you, who are laboring to be ruined for life, laboring in the vineyard of the Lord. Yes, the brilliant silver moon of your JV year reached its apogee and is now waning. Six more months. Is it possible?

The moon's first light, when you said YES to the JVC movement, got brighter as you left home. Ever more round light came with Orientation, the funny people you discovered you were to live with, a new job in a new place, a brand-new adventure. And what laughter you've continually had by the light of that silvery moon. Know it or not, you're being ruined for life.

I'd like to suggest that while the waxing of your JV moon is most likely more exciting than what you look forward to, as you peer down to next August and shutting off the light of your volunteer moon, the waning in some ways, has more to offer. It's a real fruit-cake if you want it to be. Or, if you like, the first half of your year finds fruition mainly during the final half. It would be a shame if you were to think that the best of your JVC year is now over. Let me clarify.

I suggest you have a community meeting on the "waxing of your JVC moon": return to the day you left home for JVC, speak of your fears, your excitements. What did you think about one another when you first met, and how about your living situation, your jobs and bosses? What of your many adventures in your new environment? What has been the best of these months? What have you found the most wonderful? And flip the coin—the most challenging? (I know you could spend a whole meeting recalling the crazy cooking schemes of each community member!)

Did you know that the person you appreciate the least is the one who has the greatest treasure and wisdom for you to grow? Growth stems from differences; differences are plant food for the soul.

To get the most out of this second half, I suggest that you privately review your relationship with each person in the house. Be grateful, be surprised, be sad, make amends, reconcile, risk saying "I goofed, I'm sorry, forgive me, please." Why? Because how you relate to others can tell you more about yourself than the nerd you see through the smoky lens.

Also, it's a good time to ask how your community prayer is going. If you've dropped the ball, pick it up; if it's like a dead dog in the living room, then breathe new life into it. Even if you simply sit together with a candle, in silence, that can be a top-flight prayer.

Well, you've got six months to reflect, remember, and resolve. And to work on your interior prayer...put all things to prayer. I know many voices are singing their siren song for you to follow. You have my prayers. Let the Spirit lead you into the desert where God always makes love—trust and surrender.

Let me end with an Alaskan story. It was 1964 and I went with a priest, Fr. Fallert, on a short hike on remote Nelson Island to examine a cairn of rocks the natives had built long ago. We saw a native boy about 12-years-old sitting on a bluff overlooking a choppy sea. He paid no attention to us, and he was still there forty minutes later on our return walk. Fallert asked me if I knew what the boy was doing. I nodded. Fallert continued, "He's listening to the wind. The elders teach their children to listen to the wind; it will tell them who they are." I think the second half of the JVC year, as the moon wanes, is about listening. The wind, of course, is the Spirit.

Love and peace,
Fr. Jack

CHAPTER 19

Roundtable

"At present we see indistinctly, as in a mirror, but then face to face.
At present I know partially, then I shall know fully,
as I am fully known."[29]

— ST. PAUL

IN 1970, KEN GALBRAITH, SJ, appointed me to be part of the new provincial's "cabinet," in charge of Social Ministries and Parishes.[30] At that
time, Bill Davis, SJ, returned from the New York Jesuit Mission office to
take on my former mission bureau office job, and the JVC portfolio. With
Bill, and former volunteer Denny Duffell, acting as co-directors of JVC,
the organization really expanded, gaining over two-hundred volunteers.
Bill and Denny accomplished a lot, enlarging my own vision of placing
volunteers in Alaska and in Native American missions. Placements moved
beyond helping Jesuits and Catholic institutions, to serving the poor in
various jobs. Bill and Denny extended the reach of the Jesuit Volunteer
Corps to Portland, Seattle, Spokane, Tacoma, Oakland, El Paso, Chicago,
and more, both nationally, and in Zambia and Guam. It was about a loving
year of service that saw itself in a spiritual context, as well as in the transformation of volunteers to become agents of social change.

I kept asking the question: what do volunteers do after leaving the
Jesuit Volunteer Corps program? Can we carry on community? How do
we stay connected?[31] How can the Holy Spirit guide us? How might a new

effort infuse the Society of Jesus and the wider Catholic Church? It was part of my continuing dream to give birth to a network of communities, a federation of small local communities, all united in a common philosophy and purpose. I envisioned developing a healthy relationship between privacy and community, between inner growth and outward involvement, communities of young and old, strong and weak, married, single, celibate, the well and the infirm. I wanted to live out the beatitudes of Christ in community, to know fully and to be fully known.

This idea of starting new communities that could contribute to birthing a new Church stuck in my craw. My heart told me that the core of renewal depended on building community. My knowledge about bringing this intuition to fruition was partial and imperfect. I only knew what I saw bubbling up here and there in the new freedoms of the post Vatican II Church, and from my experience with the Jesuit Volunteer Corps movement.

In 1972, Bill and I recruited Larry Gooley, SJ to become fulltime director of JVC. Larry accomplished great things. He organized the office, finished pulling together a board of directors, incorporated as an Oregon nonprofit, articulated our four values, created the application form and procedure, and began fundraising. That same year, about fourteen Jesuit Volunteers lived in a house on NW Hoyt across the street from the Jesuit Provincial House in Portland. I visited often. Later in 1972, six former volunteers established a community called Johnson House. I began talking to these folks, wanting the JV experience to leave a deep imprint on everything that followed in their lives. Together, we grew excited about starting an on-going community. With that inspiration, several former JVC volunteers–Denny Duffel, Joe Rastatter, Pam Piering, Charlie and Charlene Collora and their baby Andy, JoAnne McGinnis, Dionetta Hudzinski, Gloria DeGaetano–and I, established a post Jesuit Volunteer community in Seattle.

In the summer of 1973, we moved into a large house in a dilapidated neighborhood on the corner of Sixteenth and Union in Seattle that Catholic Charities owned and had used as a group house. Catholic Charities planned to sell the house to some social service agency, but let the former

JVs live there for $200 per person, each month. However, the landlord, Rev. Dennis Muehe, who ran Catholic Charities in western Washington, told all the renters that on a moment's notice, he needed to be able to show the house to prospective buyers. This situation gave rise to a story I'll let Joe Rastatter write, since he had the better eye-witness view:

> *"Jack Morris was vulnerable on a couple levels. Jack was determined to live in community, but he hadn't informed the Seattle Archdiocese that he was living in Seattle, and he hadn't told them that he was living in a coed house with a bunch of 20-year-olds. The idea was to keep Jack's presence quiet. Usually, we'd get the word that Father Muehe was coming by to show the house. Jack would sneak out the back stairs and walk the neighborhood for an hour or so. One day, Jack decided not to leave the house, but rather to hide in his bedroom closet. I led the delegation consisting of Father Muehe and two or three prospective buyers through the house. I remember Fr. Muehe explaining how big and great the closets were. Father Muehe entered the room that Denny and Jack shared and tried to open the closet door. He got frustrated when he wasn't able to open it. Truth is, Jack was holding mightily onto his section of the doorknob from the inside so it wouldn't open. Finally, Fr. Muehe pulled so hard the doorknob came off and the door swung open. There, staring out, was a middle-aged, unshaven Jack, probably without his dentures. Of course, everyone in the delegation was stunned to see him. Jack hastily replied to their stares, 'Thank God you found me. I didn't know how long I'd be stuck in there!' I don't remember anyone saying anything next. With Fr. Muehe, the delegation backed out of the room and quickly left the house. A few months later, Catholic Charities sold the property, and we moved to a place on Capitol Hill close to St. Joseph Parish which we named Roundtable."*

My own live-in participation in this dream of starting a new type of religious life, namely *Roundtable Community* in Seattle, lasted about a year. There were many rewards and many challenges. The community continued successfully for ten years.

I was assigned to St. Joseph's Parish in 1974 to serve as assistant to the new pastor and my friend, Pat Hurley, SJ. Four priests, a big parish, and rectory life added up to too much elitism for my temperament, but I stayed there and performed my co-pastoring duties for three years.

In 1975, I met a very capable and inspired nun named Sister Elaine. I felt a deep enthusiasm and creative urge working closely with her to set up a half-way house for her sister and other people with mental illnesses. We called it TRY–Transitional Resources for Young Adults. It was, at its roots, another attempt at community building.

From what I was reading, I surmised that traditional Catholic life in Europe was collapsing. New transformations were happening in Europe earlier than what was taking place in the United States. I asked the provincial for a sabbatical to visit new spiritual communities in Europe. In June 1977, I landed at Shannon Airport in Ireland to visit an ecumenical community at Glencree, an old English fortress from the penal days. From there, I traveled up to visit Iona, off the Scottish Coast. Iona was Presbyterian in origin, but now ecumenical. Later I visited Lapiano in Italy where the Foculari movement was lighting up the sky, and which, in time, became a worldwide movement. Its foundress, Maria Lubich, was later beatified. I finished up with a twenty-day-retreat at Manresa in Spain, seeking the spirit of Ignatius of Loyola, to guide me. I left Spain on my fiftieth birthday, flying home via the Dominican Republic where my brother Pat worked with the U.S. Embassy.

I returned to St. Joseph's as a guest, still dreaming of starting new community life. In December, 1977, I talked with Provincial Loyens, SJ, and Peter Davis, SJ, about working fulltime with former JVs and starting communities that kept building the Kingdom of Christ, with the sacramental life of the Church at their core. They couldn't have been more supportive. I was planning to move to Portland and live with Larry Gooley in the JVC Northwest community we called "MAC house."

Inheriting my Ma changed all that.

CHAPTER 20

Taking Care of Ma

"A true community is formed from the realization of mutual weakness."

TAKING CARE OF MA WAS a singular and powerful journey. It was the most humiliating yet instructive episode in my life, dragging me back in time—her time and that of my father. It beat me up and tripped me up. It led me to ecstasies. I learned so much about God and the human condition because I was forced to replace my own ego-driven concerns with Ma's needs and desires. Taking care of Ma had three parts—at St. Joseph's, with Bill and Judy Kelly in Tacoma, and Ma's time in the nursing homes. It also led to major changes in Catholic Community Services in Seattle.

My brothers and I came of age during World War II. After high school graduation, each of us went immediately into the military and all at once Ma and Dad were alone. When I look back, I feel ashamed. I was totally insensitive to what the sudden absence of their three sons meant for them. It was especially difficult for my mother when the beds were empty and the house was silent.

My Dad died in 1957, close to 70 years old. Ma had been living near my brother Pat in Washington, DC, and then under the eyes of my brother Rob and his wife Norma in southern California, first on her own, then when dotage came on, with them. The marriage of Rob and Norma was on the rocks. Ma was growing inflexible; she was impatient with the grand-children. It was clear Ma needed to get out of there, but Pat was in the Dominican Republic. Rob and I considered my caring for her.

Morris brothers reunite years later at childhood home in Anaconda.

In desperation, Rob simply attached a note to Ma, put her on the plane for Seattle where I lived, and phoned to let me know she was on her way in the spring of 1978. It was my time to care for her. The responsibility was layered with sober joy and gratitude, but worry about how I would juggle this new duty with my Jesuit assignments.

Let me put "my caring" in proper focus. As a priest, totally taken up with my life as a Jesuit, I viewed my duty with a typical clerical mindset–taking care of Ma was the responsibility of either Pat or Rob, and both of them had valiantly taken turns caring for her for twenty years. Ever since my Copper Valley experience, coupled with my years developing the Jesuit Volunteer Corps movement, I was convinced the Church needed to invent new forms of community living. It needed a form that was a hybrid of the extended family and the community life of religious men and women. To my mind, this was the prescription for the new Church handed out at Vatican Council II. I wondered if God was speaking to me now through Ma's urgent needs.

I lived at St. Joseph's parish with three other Jesuits. Handily, there was a small, adequate guest room off the kitchen that became Ma's room for the next five weeks. I was determined to receive her, blocking out all uncertainties of the future. The three Jesuits couldn't have been more accepting. Ma was always joshing with them, soft spoken and easily smiling.

On July 1, 1978, Ma and I, with former JVs Bill and Judy Kelly, moved to a three-bedroom house in Tacoma, Washington. After their Jesuit Volunteer stint, unable to ignore the plight of the native children, Bill and Judy started their own home for distressed children. I was still searching for ways to carry on my dream of new community life within the Church. They, having been thoroughly "ruined for life" by their JVC experience and subsequent endeavors, were also interested in long-term community. We talked about the JVC insight that Christian community gave witness to the power of the Holy Spirit. David Rothrock, SJ, who had worked several years with Jean Vanier's worldwide L'Arche Communities, urged me to view my dependent mother as a blessing in disguise. Rothrock pointed out that my mom, in her vulnerable last years, was a perfect foundation for starting a new community. The handicapped and needy teach us the meaning of Jesus' words that weakness is strength, and that God chooses the weak and foolish to confound the wise. True community is about climbing down the ladder, not up; it tempers the human propensity to glide along on ego strength. Our little community, a few blocks from St. Leo's Jesuit parish, began with the hope that true community would arise out of acceptance of shared weakness.

It didn't take long before I started to enjoy serving my Ma. I felt totally needed in a deeply human way, more so than ever before. Ma couldn't hide her weakness. She was fragile, and I was strong. I had the necessary means to care for and comfort her.

The old frame house had an inviting back yard garden. One bedroom off the living room was for Ma, and we able adults occupied the second floor. From the front bay windows, we looked out over downtown Tacoma. To the east, we could see the massive, snowy Mt. Rainier.

Having served in Vietnam, Judy easily secured a nursing job. Bill did construction work, and the Jesuits funded me, although I also did fill-in ministry at the Catholic hospital two blocks away. All began well. We prayed, we shared our stories, discussed the future and got to know one another. Ma was the center of our caring, and she loved it. Overall, Bill and Judy were sensitive, warm and affirming. I thanked God for this new beginning. In our care for Ma, and in prayer and discussion, we laid the foundation for development of lay Christian community. We wrote letters and began planning for retreats and workshops to promote the possibility of a network of such intergenerational communities.

However, as time passed, Judy and I developed some interpersonal difficulties. We discussed it and prayed, trying to hand it over to God. But in mid-November, utterly frustrated with me, Judy walked out the front door, smashing a chair as she went (and later returned through the back door to resume our conversation). I didn't blame her. My headstrong stubbornness infuriated her.

By early December, we talked of splitting up. They wanted Ma and me to leave. Because of Ma's frailty, I wanted them to go. Early in January, Judy and Bill moved out. We never did properly reconcile. As a professional and a pastor, I let Judy down. It had been my duty to initiate this process, and I failed.

Ma's health was deteriorating. The unhealthy vibrations within the house didn't help her condition. Father Rothrock, on the pastoral staff at St. Leo's parish, was as restless a soul as I. He also sought new pastures. Together, we found time to visit the eastern most out-post of the Oregon Province Jesuits–Hays, Montana, on the Fort Belknap Indian Reservation. Dominican sisters and Jesuit Volunteers taught at the school. We thought perhaps we might begin building a Christian community there. Our provincial, needing someone at Hays, encouraged us.

Before I decided on the next move, my deck of cards scattered. I unexpectedly inherited new housemates, two very restless teenagers. Kata, the daughter of my brother Rob, came up from California to join me in

February, 1979. I suggested to Rob that she could help me care for Ma. Then two months later, my nephew Kevin, Pat's teenage son, joined us. Pat was second in charge of the U.S. embassy in Dominican Republic, and feared Kevin might be kidnapped. So now I had Ma and two uprooted teens. But it worked out well. Kata's presence meant I could get away for ministry and recreation. She was wonderful with Ma. Kevin found a gas station job. He decided, with my encouragement, to take a course in photography and that became his profession for decades.

In an April, 1979 journal, I wrote: "Lent has begun. I've been feeling badly because I haven't decided on any penance. Caring for Ma has upset every semblance of order. I didn't even get out for ashes. Last night, early in the morning, I felt Ma's presence next to my couch where I sleep in the living room. I'd moved down from my bedroom upstairs because Ma gets up, wanders and gets lost, sometimes stuck in a cold corner. I know she's looking for the bathroom. I threw back the covers and got up to escort her. She had fouled her pajamas, and I stepped right in it. I flicked on the light in the bathroom, pulled down her pajama pants, and applied a wet, warm towel to her bottom. The warmth made her urinate all over the floor. At 2:30 a.m., I sat back on the edge of the tub and laughed out loud—to think I was wondering what I should be doing sacrificially for Lent? Her pain and lack of control became mine. I got Ma cleaned up and back to bed. Then I cleaned up our tracks, and joined her on the other side of night."

Ma's condition worsened. I began talking to others, feeling guilty and admitting I couldn't care for her. On September 12, Ma ate her last dish of ice cream in the Tacoma house where we'd lived for fourteen months. She was turning 85. Choked up and depressed, I closed our house on Yakima Avenue. It was the end of another experiment trying to develop a new model of community life within the Church.

I drove Ma to Parkside Nursing home, just two blocks from the Jesuit residence in Seattle near St. Joseph's parish, where I'd take up residence. I figured that my frequent visits and attention would outweigh her new life in an institutional setting. How wrong I was.

Placing Ma in a nursing home was the hardest thing I had ever done in my life. God's word pricked me like a cactus thorn: "Honor your mother, and do not abandon her as long as she lives. Do whatever pleases her, and do not grieve her spirit in any way."[32] Deep underneath my hurt, I was keenly aware that Ma stood by me all my days of dependence, but here I was bucking God's word and guidance. I'd failed the one who had given her life to me.

I wrote in my journal, "I'm devastated, totally humiliated." I thought about calling this person or that, but I especially needed Sister Elaine, my dear friend who worked with Transitional Resources in Seattle. I wanted to share my confusion with her; I needed her comfort and companionship. I wanted her to help me make sense of my deserting Ma and handing her over to others. Yet I knew it was my journey, my personal desert. I felt I should suffer it alone to avoid losing any of the humanizing power of this sad, terrible moment. To disguise my misery, I put on a bright apricot shirt to visit Ma. She wore her yellow blouse and blue shawl. I fasted all day, an act of solidarity to be more intimately tied to Ma, trying to see this misery from God's point of view.

My September 13 journal entry: "I went down to visit Ma, greeting other residents I met in the hallway. Ma was propped up on two pillows with a bib. I gave her a bright greeting. No response. She looked sad and dejected as if to say, 'What did I do to deserve this?' Dried up hot cereal was plastered on her chest and arm. I cleaned her, kissed her hands and face, and embraced her. In a determined voice, she said, 'I want to get out of here!' Next, I lifted her from the bed–she was all wet. Anger and tears rose up in me, but I cleaned Ma up and situated her in the wheelchair. We spun down the hall and escaped out the front doors. The air was fresh. We walked two blocks to a neighborhood restaurant. Over tea, Ma said with a smile, 'This is nice, I don't want to go back to that place.'"

Over the months, Ma gradually gave me eyes to see, and so on February 16, 1980, I moved her from Parkside to Mount St. Vincent's with the Sisters of Providence, reputed to be one of the finest nursing homes in Seattle.

Jack and Ma commune together.

I remember writing in my journal in early spring: "Just the two of us are sitting having a snack and coffee. We chat. Then Ma goes silent. She lifts her chin with eyes fixed over my shoulder. She's tuned me out. I ask, 'What is it, Ma?' She doesn't respond. I reach across the table, touching her hand and again ask, 'What is it?' Without shifting her sight, she lifts her right hand and points toward her gaze. She says in a soft, deliberate, affective voice, 'Oh, son, it's so beautiful, and it's coming closer. It's so beautiful.' I ask, 'What are you talking about?' 'Well, son, it's out in front of me, there's this point and it has *everything* in it.' Then she shifts her gaze to me and says, 'It has nothing to do with you. It's just for me because I'm special.' I laughed and asked, 'What do you mean by that?' In her delightful

English way, she says, 'How the devil do I know what it means?' Then, in a healing way, 'Don't feel bad, son, you're special too.' And after a pause, 'Everyone is so very special.' She puts both hands over her bosom and gently says, 'But now I know *I'm* special.' This isn't an ordinary conversation. I try to engage her and talk about Moses and the mysterious bush that's on fire, but not consumed. Ma informs me that what she *sees* isn't simply in her imagination. 'When I lay in bed at night it's there, and I say over and over again, I'll follow you wherever you go. It's so beautiful and it's coming closer for me.' Her description was calm, serious and unapologetic."

April 2, I wrote: "Last night Ma called softly, 'Come here son, sit by me. Do you love me?' I bend to put my cheek next to hers; she's lying wide-awake. It's just beginning to get light outdoors. 'Of course I love you. I'll never leave you.' I kiss her. 'Something is going on!' she says. I ask what she means. She answers, 'I don't know, it's something different.' I move back enough to get a clear look at her face. I can't tell whether I'm viewing reality or creating illusions, but her face seems to have lost its wrinkles. I recall how Father Leo Eckstein told us that some few people, when they die, lose their wrinkles and become very beautiful. I ask Ma, 'Are you going to die on me?' She replies in a clear, untroubled manner, 'No, son. I'm not afraid.' We pray the *Our Father*, and then the Act of Contrition. Then she adds, and this was the first time I'd heard it, 'If I should die before I wake, I pray the Lord my soul do take.' Then she abruptly rolls away from me to face the wall. I reach over to touch her. She says, 'Blast it all, leave me alone.'"

April 3: "I'm happy thinking that perhaps the end is near. It will be a release. I'll be glad for Ma's sake and for mine. I have many beautiful moments, and feel blessed to be caring for her, but it is humiliating and difficult. My ego is being pinched. This brings to mind an incident in Anaconda, where I'd prayed my first Mass after ordination. I had been away for some years. We were invited to a tea with five or six of Ma's old friends. I sat and listened as they talked on and on, and finally discussed their husbands and lifetime gifts. Ma said in her precise English way, 'You know, my husband, John, was never much when it came to gifts, but he made it up in a big way–he died on my birthday!' She and I laughed. Her women friends were confused, but she was sincere. Dad had been wandering, now he was released, and so was she from worry about him."

October 11: "I'm sitting at the foot of Ma's bed. A bright yellow quilt covers her frail body. I often come just to sit, like tonight. She's been in some distress all day. She told me not to worry. Then, 'You know son, we don't have to worry. He sees all, knows all and forgives all. He takes care of all.' I'm amazed, just as I was yesterday, when she was feeling spry and being witty. I went along with her. I said, stroking my make-believe beard and without a smile, 'Yes, Ma, I see it now. You've got another fifteen years to go.' She simply chides, 'Who gives you permission to play with time?' At moments like this, when she's feeling pain and distress, I also see an active determination, a conflict in progress. She's battling something. Both in words and silence, she's communicating to me, 'Son, I'm all right. Don't be so dumb, so small. It's all right to feel pain, to be in distress. It's simply another kind of experience. It's not easy, but I've got it in hand. Don't worry.'"

I needed to do something with the shame I felt for not adequately caring for my own mother. In the spring of 1980, I went down to the Seattle Archdiocesan Catholic Charities office. Witnessing Ma's humiliations of decrepitude stripped away all ego defenses that hid from me the naked truth of old age. I asked the director what Catholic Community Services was doing for the aged. They had been talking about ministry to the aged but hadn't started a program. I offered my services as a volunteer for six months to put together a mission statement for developing a Christian response to the growing issue of the aged. We drew up a statement which their board accepted. Next, I searched several City of Seattle and King County offices trying to learn as much as I could about the demographics, needs, and services for the elderly.

The contract for the multimillion-dollar, citywide, federally funded volunteer Chore Services program, designed for in-home assistance to keep the elderly out of rest-homes, was coming up for renewal. The director informed me that a national pharmaceutical firm with no local base of interest held the contract but was failing to deliver. I asked whether the city office on aging would take a bid from Catholic Charities. They informed me that it would, with anyone who could get the job done right. I had an idea.

I rushed out and phoned the Jesuit Volunteer Corps office in Portland. I explained my inspiration for the placement of JVs caring for the aged. JVC Director, Larry Gooley, arranged to provide six full time volunteers, capable young men and women. The key was that they were genuine volunteers paid a subsistence stipend, which meant that Catholic Charities could come in with a low bid. Miles Otupal, director of Catholic Community Services, an arm of Catholic Charities, immediately caught the ball. He was ambitious, saw the vast unmet social needs of the city, and wanted to expand. The proposal made sense to him. I was certain we could offer the lowest bid for the Volunteer Chore Services program.

Coincidently, Brother Fred Mercy, SJ, a faithful, dear buddy of mine, was finishing up his degree in counseling at Eastern Washington University. Ten years earlier, he had opened up the highly praised Matt Talbot Center, a cheap, well run hotel in Portland for people who got trapped in the dark cellars of an affluent society. Fred was buoyant and happily alive. I phoned him and explained the situation. He signed on and moved into our Seattle Jesuit community.

The Chore program was a winner from the start. The Human Services agency of City Hall couldn't have been more pleased. Catholic Charities alerted Catholic parishes throughout the city, asking for in-house caregivers. Qualified, compassionate and honest women and men responded. The Jesuit Volunteers became the central staff, coordinating workers with clients, visiting homes and keeping records for City Hall. An unexpected result was the bright life the program brought to Catholic Community Services. The dedication of the concerned volunteers introduced a new flavor in the agency, which up until that time had concentrated on adoptions, foster homes, and child welfare issues.

I smiled and chalked this up to dear old Ma. Suffering the difficulties of caring for her had ignited this fire in me and brought the aged ministry to life in the Catholic Charities network. I became the Director of Programs for the Aged, Catholic Charities in Seattle and worked with a million-dollar grant. So successful was the work, that in a few years

Catholic Charities across the state of Washington were deeply engaged in the Chore ministry. I happily told Ma about my work. She smiled and said, "Son, I'm happy you're helping the old people. So many are neglected. I'm one of the blessed."

But something deeper and more mysterious was happening underground. The Chore program had become the seedbed for the next unexpected adventure in my life, a peace pilgrimage to the Holy Land.

CHAPTER 21

Bethlehem Peace Pilgrimage I: Origins and Inspiration

✦

"After the dropping of the atomic bombs and Japan's surrender, I signed on to join the occupation forces. When we arrived at Nagasaki I wasn't in a good place. The whole Tinian Island experience a few weeks previously had scalded my soul. I was confused and troubled with a growing feeling of dark guilt that wouldn't go away. We hadn't been in Nagasaki more than a week when I found myself making my way to the ruined hulk, a silent pile of rubble, the remnants of the Urakami Cathedral in Japan's most Catholic city. As I made my way into the ruins, into what had been the sanctuary, I saw something. I nudged it with my foot. I picked it up. It was a piece of the brass censor, designed to burn perfumed incense at worship services. As I examined it, it became a prism to my mind and heart. I saw the beauty and splendor of the cathedral that had been, the unfolding of Sunday Mass, a place of worship, a symbol of peace and harmony, a place of life dedicated to the God of peace. As I stood gazing, a foreboding silence seemed to loom over the vast ruins. No sounds of traffic, no bird song, no vegetation, no human voice." [33]

— *Fr. George Zabelka*

Father George Zabelka told this story in an interview with *Sojourners Magazine* on the thirty-fifth anniversary of the awful bombs in World War II that melted and annihilated soldiers and innocent Japanese civilians in

Hiroshima and Nagasaki. Roughly half the deaths in each city occurred on the first day from flash or flame burns, falling glass and debris. During the following days and months, large numbers died from the effects of gamma radiation sickness, burns and injuries. The death toll consisted of estimates only (confusion of the records, the many victims who died months or years later, and the political pressures to either inflate or underestimate the figures). I read an estimate that by December, 1945, as many as 140,000 had died in Hiroshima and 74,000 had perished in Nagasaki. Bomb survivors continued to suffer and die for years.

Zabelka served as the Catholic military chaplain in the U.S. Army Air Force to the 1,800 men of the 509th bombing squadron on Tinian Island, a speck on the map of the north Pacific. The unit, led by 29-year-old Lieutenant Colonel Paul Tibbetts, was on a secret mission known to only a few leaders. As pilot of the B-29 nicknamed the "Enola Gay," Tibbetts would drop a single bomb on Hiroshima. The peak temperature of the exploding bomb would be more than a half-million degrees Fahrenheit.

Zabelka gave communion to and blessed the Enola Gay's twelve-man crew before they took off from Tinian to fly to Japan through the predawn night of August 6, 1945. Don Young, the flight surgeon, gave the crew twelve cyanide pills, just in case. Lift off from Tinian Island started the clock ticking for 1,500 miles, and six hours of eerie anticipation. No one on the mission knew whether the bomb would work or what its effect might be.

At 8:15 a.m., over the massive city of Hiroshima, the whole crew was alert. They performed as practiced in their routine, and released the bomb. The crew had only forty-three seconds to make a steep dive away from the explosion and mushroom cloud. Shock waves rocked the plane. The devastation defied imagination. The atomic age was violently born.

Thirty-six years later, in 1981, the United States Navy commissioned the "Ohio" class of nuclear-powered submarines, the largest ever built for the Navy. Stationed in Bangor, Washington, the vessels were each armed with multiple Trident II nuclear missiles. At the time, fourteen of the Trident IIs together carried a significant percentage of America's total active inventory of strategic thermonuclear warheads. They had the potential to end life on this planet.

Responding to the presence of these fearsome weapons, local peace activists known as the Pacific Life Community, initiated an anti-Trident submarine campaign in 1975 in the Puget Sound area. I'd gotten involved in a small way. We shared a concern over the escalating nuclear arms race, and hope for a peaceful change. Sixteen campaigners contributed $100 each to purchase four acres that abutted the Trident nuclear submarine base on the Kitsap Peninsula near Bainbridge Island. We named the house located at our center for nonviolence, *Ground Zero.* A whole cast of characters assembled. Canadian, Jim Douglass and his wife, Shelly, spearheaded an impressive network of peace activists to protest in civil disobedience. Jim, a former professor of theology at the University of Hawaii, once told me, "We just can't give up. We're all complicit unless we stand forth and become part of a great *NO* to this nuclear madness." In a short time, our idea morphed into a national campaign of protest and civil disobedience against the Trident madness. Many of us clergy were arrested.

Robert Aldridge, a former missile designer, joined our effort. Robert, a Catholic like Jim, had resigned from Lockheed in 1974 when he discovered that U.S. policy had shifted from defense to a "preemptive strike posture."

Peaceful protests involving several hundred men, women and children, were organized at the Trident base. On special occasions, like the anniversaries of the Hiroshima and Nagasaki bombings, several thousand participated. We were encouraged that a groundswell for peace was possible, as newspapers, radio, and television reported on the escalating peace movement.

The protests accelerated when a community of eight Japanese Buddhist monks, with their drums and chants, moved into *Ground Zero.* They joined the collective *NO* with nonviolent daily leafleting, marches, workshops and prayer. The Nipponzan monks traditionally walked in many parts of the world promoting peace through their drumming and chanting prayer. They added strength, insight and drama. With meager funds, they began constructing a wooden peace pagoda.

I developed a friendship with one monk, Suzuki, a former electrical engineer who had worked on a nuclear power plant years before in Korea. "I became a new man through a conversation with one of the chanting monks," he confided. "I quit my job at the power plant and joined the peacemaking of the monks." He said, "Some talk about peace, some write about it. My job is to walk and pray for peace. It's a happy job. The body loves it. It brings peace to my heart, and I believe helps toward a peaceful world."

About a year later, activists led by Jack Chalmers arrived at *Ground Zero* after a 1,400 mile peace walk between San Francisco and Bangor. They testified to the powerful effect their walk had. They announced that Chalmers and others were planning a walk from the Trident base to Moscow, Russia. Without my knowing it, *walking for peace* entered my subconscious. It made sense to me—but something was still missing.

On the Christian front, ministers, priests, and sisters, often nudged by lay voices for peace, emerged within the movement. Archbishop Raymond Hunthausen of the Catholic Archdiocese of Seattle, shocked the world and became internationally known and saluted by the peace community when, at a Lutheran conference, he dared name the beast publicly. He called the Trident submarine base, "the Auschwitz of Puget Sound." He urged tax resistance. His bold words shook many in the American Christian hierarchy, and reached Rome. On June 12, 1981 in Tacoma, before the Northwest Synod of the Lutheran Church in America, he proclaimed: "Our willingness to destroy life everywhere on this earth for the sake of our security in America, is at the root of many other terrible events of our country." Affirming the need to explore peaceful avenues toward disarmament, he said: "I have recommended that our people (of this archdiocese) turn more intently to the Lord this year in response to the escalation of nuclear arms."[34]

Hunthausen's voice and presence at the *Ground Zero* center escalated the awareness of every religious community, Christian and non-Christian, in the Northwest and beyond. Scores of laity and clergy were now protesting and getting arrested. I recall Hunthausen coming up to St. Joseph's parish rectory where I was in residence, asking Fr. Pat Hurley, the well-known activist pastor, to accompany him on a visit to Jim Douglass in jail. The Archbishop and Hurley celebrated Mass with Jim. He wasn't, as he often said, preaching to anyone in particular, but simply doing what he personally felt called to do. The seeds he cast out were carried by the winds of the media across America, to Europe, Japan, and to Rome. Hunthausen's conduct jarred the typically moderate Catholic hierarchy.

In July, 1962, Hunthausen was appointed bishop of Helena by Pope John XXIII. Hunthausen returned from the Second Vatican Council a different man. He wrote: "It [Vatican Council] called us back to the primacy of love in our lives. I try to live out my ministry as a bishop in the spirit of the Second Vatican Council. I was liberated by that spirit."[35]

The Council's genius was not so much that of creating brand new ideas as one of taking ideas from, what John Courtney Murray once called, "the creative edge of the tradition," and placing them at the center. Continuity and change! The Council affirmed Hunthausen's native heritage, called back to the primacy of love and cooperation. It was in his gut from his boyhood, but the Council allowed what he felt to rise up and liberate him. Central were the notions of dialogue, shared responsibility, and trusting the gifts of others. It was from that inner true north that he often strolled in the cool evenings with other bishops hashing over the issues of war and peace. He felt that Pope John lived the question he wanted to live, ever faithful to the Gospel. The whole demeanor of Pope John was just simplicity: humility, a sense of wonder, uncommon common sense. He was fully human and believed that every day is a good day to be born, and every day is a good day to die. It was Pope John's persona that inspirited the unfolding of the Council. Dull, institutional uniformity often stifles the spirit. Hunthausen brought home something entirely different.

During the growing interest and activity of Puget Sound peace activism, I read the interview between Fr. George Zabelka and Fr. Charles McCarthy in *Sojourners Magazine* (August 9, 1980).[36] *Sojourners* was founded by Jim Wallis,[37] peace activist and proponent of Christian community, out of the evangelical Christian tradition. McCarthy was a lawyer and founder of Notre Dame University's Center for the Study of Nonviolence. He later resigned from there when Notre Dame invited the Reserve Officers' Training Corps (ROTC) program onto campus. The McCarthy interview arose out of a visit by Fr. George to McCarthy's parish in Flint, Michigan, to put on a workshop on nonviolence and the problem of apathy. Zabelka had been working with the Martin Luther King Jr. civil rights movement when he'd heard about McCarthy's work in nonviolence. The City of Flint had become an arena of overt racism due to the massive influx of southern Blacks to the expanding job market of the automobile and military industry. Zabelka and McCarthy became fast friends.

I'll never forget reading the interview:

*"**McCarthy**: Fr. Zabelka, what is your relationship to the atomic bombing of Hiroshima and Nagasaki in August, 1945?*

Zabelka: I was Catholic chaplain to the 509th Composite Group on Tinian Island, the atomic bomb unit. At the time, Tinian had the largest airport in the world.

McCarthy: Did you know that the 509th was preparing to drop an atomic bomb?

Zabelka: No one knew but a select few at the top. We called it the "gimmick" bomb, a top secret weapon. I never did speak out against it. On Judgment Day, I think I am going to need to seek mercy more than justice in this matter. As a Catholic priest, my task was to see that the boys conducted themselves according to the Catholic Church on war practices. I, with most chaplains, was quite clear and outspoken on such matters as not killing prisoners nor torturing them. But we said nothing or little about the destruction of civilians, always forbidden by the Church. If a soldier came to me and asked if he could put a bullet through a child's head, I would have told him absolutely not. That would be mortally sinful. Tinian, as I said, was the largest airfield in the world. Three planes a minute around the clock could take off and land. Many of these planes went to Japan with the express purpose of killing not one child, but the slaughtering of hundreds and thousands of children and civilians—and I said nothing. I knew more than many what devastation we were commanding. I was counseling young men who were hospitalized, losing their minds over what they were experiencing. One man told me he had been on a low-level bombing mission, flying right down one of the main streets of the city. In the middle of the street, gazing up, was a lone, dear child looking upward in wonder.

He knew that in a few seconds this child would be burned to death by napalm which he had already released. Yes, I knew, but I never once gave a single sermon against killing civilians. Only later could I sum it up: I had allowed myself to become 'brainwashed!' I was told by the military, and implicitly by the church leaders, that it was sad but necessary. The question of its morality never seriously entered my mind.

McCarthy: So you feel that because you did not protest the morality of this bombing that somehow you are morally responsible for the dropping of the atomic bomb?

Zabelka: I say all of this as one who was part of the so-called Christian leadership of the time. So you see, this is why I am not going to the Day of Judgment looking for justice in this matter. Mercy is my only salvation."

Fr. Zabelka, in his direct, honest and revealing interview, had been carrying this guilt for 35 years. His was the story of a tortured soul. His way of repentance was manifested in his dedication to racial justice and nonviolence. He was desperately seeking contrition.

I asked myself, why was I so caught up in this nuclear arms peril? There's something about my hyper-responsible personality that leaves me vulnerable. I felt pulled away from the ordinary tasks of priesthood. I felt driven to stand and point to the greater enemy–the force of evil–behind the fear justifying these weapons. Was I the one who lived in unreality because I saw the madness that could bring us to the brink? How should I cry out? How should I become, with others, prophets of sanity and light?

Everything in my own inner stirrings about hammering swords into plowshares was ready to ignite. Zabelka's disarming story and the interview by McCarthy sparked to life the shreds of inert tinder in my psyche, particularly when Zabelka joined all this military madness with the Christian Church. It was the missing piece that set in motion the crazy, foolish, preposterous Bethlehem Peace Pilgrimage, a seven-thousand mile walk through eleven countries to the birthplace of the Prince of Peace.

The interview continued:

"Zabelka: Things, since these terrible deeds 35 years ago, haven't changed. Mainline Christian churches still teach something that Christ never taught, or even hinted at, namely the <u>just war theory</u>. It has been completely discredited theologically, historically and psychologically. So as I see it, until the various churches within Christianity repent (re-look and reshuffle their priorities) and begin to proclaim by word and deed what Jesus proclaimed in relation to violence and enemies, there is no hope for anything other than everlasting violence and destruction...Communion with Christ cannot be established on disobedience to his clearest teachings.

McCarthy: What kinds of immediate steps do you think the church should take in order to become 'the divine leaven in the human dough?'

Zabelka: Step one is we've got to insert <u>prayer for our enemies</u> as absolutely fundamental. This is the mustard seed. I offer step two at the risk of being considered hopelessly out of touch with reality. I would like to suggest that there is an immediate need to call an ecumenical council for the specific purpose of clearly declaring that war is totally incompatible with Jesus' teaching and that Christians cannot and will not engage in or pay for war from this point on in history.

McCarthy: Do you think there's the slightest chance that the various branches of Christianity would come together in an ecumenical council?

Zabelka: Who knows what could happen?...One thing I'm sure of is that our Lord would be very happy if his church would again unequivocally teach what he unequivocally taught on the subject of violence."

These words stirred me up. They broke me open. Alive and hopeful, I knew something must be done. Pacing my room excitedly, I said out loud, "I'm going to walk to Bethlehem for peace!" Upon uttering this pronouncement, I felt dismayed and foolish. Yet, I knew a fire had been lit.

I don't know how Bethlehem arose as a destination. In a typical Ignatian retreat, one meditates on the truth surrounding Jesus' birth, but I had never once thought of personally going to Bethlehem. Jesus came as the Prince of Peace, and he was a great walker. The only word that describes my personal, inner event is "enthusiasm" *(en theos)*, meaning filled with the excitement of the Spirit, inspired of God. Temperamentally, I'm something of an enthusiast. Life easily excites me and awakens feelings, but this was a major quake.

I had to align this pilgrimage with my life's quest for authenticity, integrity, and, if you will, holiness. It had been my conviction that when I died, when I came to the moment of judgment before my God, I would be asked not if I helped stop the arms race, nor how successful I was in my priestly career, but how I responded to the times in which I lived. Did I recognize evil? Was I willing to shift my priorities, and pay the price to move from conjecture to thought, from thought to plan, from plan to action?

Within the hour, I sat down and pounded out a letter to this Fr. Zabelka, suggesting that we organize a walk–a pilgrimage for peace–to the birthplace of the Prince of Peace, and yes, to call for an ecumenical council for peace. Next morning the fire was still burning. Devoid of doubt, I wrote a second letter telling George that I wasn't crazy. I told him who I was and what I'd done, and that we had met before at a house meeting in Tacoma after his talk on the enemy of peacemaking–apathy. Three days later, Zabelka phoned me, "I got your letter, Jack. It sounds like a good idea. Let's keep working on it."

I worked up a flyer on the walk, and sent it to him for his input. The next thing I knew, he'd doctored it, printed it, and handed it out. I had no idea that he was 67 years old and retired from active ministry due to two serious heart attacks. The McCarthy-Zabelka interview rang as true as a great bell announcing peace. What it revealed was the spirit of an unusually altered man, a compelling individual who didn't shy away from truth and responsibility.

Just two weeks later, in my job as program director for Elderly Concerns at Catholic Charities, I headed for a meeting. With me was Bill Ingalls-Cox, part of the Jesuit Volunteer Corps team at the agency. On our drive,

Bill asked what was new. I told him I was going to walk to Bethlehem for peace, and I told him all I knew about Zabelka. He said, "Wow, you mean in Pennsylvania?" I told him, "No, where Jesus was born."

Ten days later, Bill phoned to say his house of seven Jesuit Volunteers wanted to join the walk–Bill and Pam Ingalls-Cox (Spokane, Washington), Marcus Groffman (Albuquerque, New Mexico), Laurie Hasbrook (Milwaukee, Wisconsin), Mimi Ward (Cape Cod, Massachusetts), Alice McGarey, (New Canaan, Connecticut) and Bob Patten (Portland, Oregon). They became the core group along with Mary Jude Postal. Eight months later, Steve McKindley (Mennonite Volunteer from Everett, Washington) joined the group after hearing Fr. Zabelka speak at Notre Dame.

Original group plans the Bethlehem Peace Pilgrimage.

Our first group meeting was at South House, one of three Jesuit Volunteer community houses in Seattle. It didn't work out too well. Mimi had brought home a street person who named himself Eugene Debs, after the famous union organizer. My brother, Pat, was in town from

Washington, DC, visiting Ma and me. Pat thought this talk about a peace walk to Bethlehem was folly. Pam, Bill and Marcus Groffman, and perhaps Mimi were excited, but Alice and Laurie were a little skeptical. While I was confident the walk to Bethlehem would unfold, I didn't have a clue as to how. When Bill initially asked for a meeting, I responded free of expectations, but now they asked for a second meeting. Perhaps something really was happening. Soon our meetings at different locations turned into a growing upbeat relationship between all of us. After the third or fourth session, Alice said, "If this is real, and it's supposed to happen, then we've got to do some praying around it." That led to a weekend get-together once a month for retreat and prayer.

Three months slipped by while I continued to work for Catholic Charities and looked in on Ma. We were into 1981. The pilgrimage group firmed up, speaking more and more about "our" walk. Other JVs and friends became interested, but our commitment needed to become concrete. I proposed that we meet on the Feast of the Annunciation. At Mass, each of us would say: I am going for sure, or I'm not going. Zabelka came out from Michigan to join us. At the offertory, we each announced our position. George and I were in. Mimi, Bill, Pam, and Alice all said yes. Three others backed out. Pam put it well, "It's like when Bill and I got engaged. Unless something terribly unusual happens, I'm walking." Laurie thought she would just walk for the summer, but later decided she *couldn't* leave.

As the peace pilgrimage unfolded, two quandaries assaulted me–what about my religious superiors, and what about Ma? I feared that the pilgrim road might wend me right out of the Society of Jesus. Throughout my journals, in entry upon entry, I pondered Ma's ever deteriorating condition. I wanted God to take her home, for her sake and for mine. Because the Jesuit Volunteers wouldn't finish their commitment term until August, we knew we couldn't leave before the following spring, some fifteen months hence. For sure, I figured, Ma would have taken flight.

The heart and mind of the Bethlehem pilgrim group arose from seven members of the Jesuit Volunteer Corps communities in Seattle who worked with the poor. Their year-long Jesuit Volunteer adventure was risk-taking and countercultural. It proved to be a formation challenge, a practicum, an ongoing honest sharing in learning how to be real, to sacrifice, to admit faults, and to forgive. Neither they nor I fully grasped that their year of volunteer service was really just boot camp, preparing them for a two-year, nonviolent assault on the utter folly of nuclear arms.

For the Jesuit Volunteers' parents, their children's earnest spirituality and idealism were sometimes upsetting and confusing. A typical phone conversation between a prospective pilgrim and parent:

"You're what? Walking to Bethlehem with some far-out Jesuit priest? This is absolutely crazy. You've just given a year to the Jesuit enterprise. This isn't why we slaved to send you to college. You've got a career to think of."

"Well, yes, mother! But we've got to face it. Russia and the U.S. are on the edge of a nuclear holocaust. It's about saving the world."

"Oh my God, I'm sure this nutty priest has brainwashed you. I told your father I didn't like sending you to a Jesuit university—all this foolish idealism around Jesus and St. Ignatius."

"I'm sorry, Mom, but I've got to take a stand."

"Well, take a stand, but a walk of seven-thousand miles to Bethlehem is madness. Have you lost your mind? I suppose you'll all pray the rosary as you walk across the ocean! Excuse me, dear, as you can tell (a long pause), I'm terribly upset. Be careful in your think-ing. Don't make any definite decision yet. I'm going to send you some scary articles on religious cults and brainwashing. I'm just warning you because I love you. Oh, and tell that Jesuit he's crazy."

Brother Fred Mercy joined our group. He was not a former Jesuit Volunteer, nor a "peace-nik." He never intended to walk, but he was drawn to the pilgrimage because of his interest in Christian community, and he saw this as a way to learn more about it. He confided in me later that the walk changed his ideas about the nuclear problem. It changed his whole life: "When we love one another, work together, and are all headed in the same direction, there is an unbelievable power."

One cannot understand our walk to Bethlehem without appreciating that the late 1970s and early 1980s held a deeper current that compelled us. The Cuban Missile Crisis of 1962 brought home to the world the voracious menace of nuclear weapons. Just off Florida, the world watched helplessly as two nuclear Goliaths stood toe to toe, defying one another. All nations held their collective breath, wondering if this would end life on Earth. In the U.S. and Russian standoff, we understood the warning of the French leader, George Clemenceau, that war is too dangerous to be entrusted to the military. The advice of President Eisenhower in 1961 was also compelling. Our nation must be on guard against the temptations and propensities of the military-industrial complex. In the Pacific Northwest, these concerns spawned the local nonviolent peace movement which peaked with the announcement that the Bangor submarine base on Hood Canal was readying to receive its first Trident nuclear submarine. It seemed militarism was driving our nation and the world. By the late 1970s, it became clear that living on planet Earth was getting downright precarious.

The secretive and disgraceful dropping of atomic bombs on innocent Japanese civilians, August 6 and 9, 1945, did indeed end World War II, but at what price? With ideological divisions and the continuation of the arms race, the Soviets soon had their own nuclear stockpiles. The United States lived in fear of being attacked by nuclear weapons, and several presidents threatened use as a deterrent. The fact of nuclear weapons brought home to thinking minds in every nation the dread expressed by Robert Oppenheimer as he witnessed the explosion of the first atomic bombs during their testing: "We knew the world would not be the same."[38]

Oppenheimer testified[39] in late 1953 security hearings: "When you see something that is technically sweet, you go ahead and do it, and argue about what to do about it only after you've had your technical success. That is the way it was with the atomic bomb." But I believe Oppenheimer knew that he and other physicists had partaken in something destructive and sinful.

CHAPTER 22

Bethlehem Peace Pilgrimage II:
Walk Across America

"If the nuclear peril is the moral issue of our times,
then my entrance into God is through that challenge."

IN OCTOBER 1981, WE SENT out the first *Pilgrims' Progress* newsletter leading with: "Although our first steps toward the Star City are still six months
off, in reality we began moving out a full year ago." In Latin, *to pilgrim* is
to go on a journey. The end of our journey would be to arrive home, at the
birthplace of the Prince of Peace. The logo of *Pilgrims' Progress* was a dove
bearing an olive branch. Seattle Jesuit Volunteer, Mary Driscoll, gave us
our motto, adapted from a medieval pilgrim verse from days when believers
all over Europe made holy pilgrimages to Bethlehem on foot:

> *"All roads lead to Bethlehem, and one day all must follow them, and*
> *be ye great or be ye small, may the sweet Lord Jesus bless you all upon*
> *those roads to Bethlehem."*

To our surprise, I received a letter from Jerusalem, Israel that made us feel
at one with the Christian community of the holy city.

> *"Dear Father Morris,*
> *Your walk has become known over here. I'm enclosing this list of Christian*
> *and Jewish communities who have pledged prayer support for your walk.*

Let me explain: a fellow countryman of mine from Holland had left his faith as a young soldier, and then roamed the world. As old age and some illness began to take over, he returned to his faith and took up residence as close as he could to the basilica of the Nativity. It became his custom to go each week to the Jesuit Bible Institute in Jerusalem to read in their library. He came to me one day announcing that he had read of your pilgrimage in an American publication. It sparked something in his heart. He wanted to be part of what you were doing. Though he found difficulties in getting around, he personally went from one religious community to another, promoting prayers for success of your wonderful endeavor. John Spath died just after Christmas. Among his belongings was a list of communities that will be praying for you.

My religious congregation runs a hostel near St. Peter Galicantro, on the edge of Jerusalem. I am the chaplain and guest master. Please honor us by staying with us when you arrive. We have plenty of beds, and with all the troubles, I'm sure the number of tourist-pilgrims will be sparse."

On April 8, 1982, Holy Thursday, we closed down and cleaned up our rented staging center, a house in central Seattle dubbed *Lothlorien* by Steve McKindley, the Mennonite Volunteer who had joined our group early on. Steve said, "It is the central place of safety, a place of dreams and strategizing against the forces of evil by the forest elves of Middle Earth in J.R.R. Tolkien's *Lord of the Rings*. It was also called Golden Wood, and a "space out of time." For seven months, our group at *Lothlorien* existed in a space out of time, up to our elbows in planning, soliciting help, developing contacts across America and Europe, raising funds, and gathering necessities for the journey: two vehicles, a small enclosed trailer, tents, banners, a cooking stove, traveling kitchen, and literature. We also participated in the ongoing protests at the Trident base. We edited and sent out the newsletter of the Chalmers' group, *March to Moscow*. Their experience proved a fortuitous gift to us. Month after month, the marchers shared openly the stresses of the road and the struggles of community.

Jesuit Volunteer, Mimi Ward, said, "I can't believe it's actually happening. It seemed like all we did week after week was plan and write letters, placate parents, answer inquiries, hold meetings, develop mailing lists, and solicit others to join us. Now the clock strikes. We're doing it. I've always loved walking. Now I can do it every day, all day, month after month, out there in God's glorious world."

That same evening, twelve pilgrims (three others of the group would join us before the week was up) gathered at *Ground Zero.* Full of anxiety and gladness, we were aware that our adventure to walk from this place of darkness almost seven-thousand miles through eleven nations to the birth-place of the Prince of Peace, was finally a reality. As a group, we had no money to get across the ocean. Some details would just have to unfold. We celebrated the Eucharist that Holy Thursday evening. In John's Gospel, the Last Supper was enacted at the very time in the Temple of Jerusalem when the lambs were being slain for Passover, the Jewish symbol of journeying out of bondage in Egypt. They were saved by the blood of the lamb. We felt we would be too, as we recited Jesus' prayer, "We pray so that they may all be one, as you, Father, are in me and I in you, that they also may be in us, that the world may believe that you sent me."[40] Our prayers were for each of us, our small group, and the whole human race. Then we cooked a simple dinner, toasted our pilgrimage, and talked late into the night.

We set out on Good Friday, April 9. We chose that day, recalling the death of Jesus, to draw attention to the capacity of nuclear weapons to crucify the whole world. Christians of every brand celebrated Jesus' way of making peace on this day. We woke early to a clear sky in anticipation of a large crowd of supporters for our 11 a.m. departure ceremony. News stories in daily papers of Tacoma and Seattle, the Catholic Archdiocesan press and numerous bulletins and newsletters had spread the word. Some of the pilgrims had been interviewed on radio and television. In our yearlong lead-up, we had participated in *Ground Zero* resistance programs, and were known among many in the vibrant, geographically broad peace network.

Steve McKindley called Bethlehem "Star City." It beckoned as a holy place of destiny, grace, and human struggle. To act as pilgrims lifted our journey out of the more aggressive and mundane military term of marching, lending it spiritual power. Our chosen name and destination added drama, direction, and definition to our protest of the militarism expressed in the Trident submarine base. Our motives encompassed dimensions beyond politics. We were declaring our faith as fundamental to halting the madness of the nuclear arms race.

Foremost a spiritual pilgrimage, the walk was a call to religious leaders and all peoples of faith to take responsibility for the potential destruction of the human race, and to begin the laborious task of building a more just world order. In the United States, we intended to charge up grass-roots, middle-of-the-road folks to join in a peace movement. We would focus on outreach and education through brochures, worship and prayer, media contacts, and peace education presentations to family, community, school and church groups along the way. We planned to raise support for a great council of world religious leaders–Christian, Jew, Muslim, Hindu, Buddhist, and Native American–to demand an end to the voraciousness of the arms race that steals bread from the world's poor.

Bethlehem Peace Pilgrimage poster.

Peace statements with twenty-five million signatures had been gathered by activists. We wanted people to walk from all over the world and make the longing for peace visible. We were the Bethlehem Peace Pilgrimage (BPP), but we also encouraged simultaneous walks from San Francisco, Portland, and Vancouver, British Columbia, even New York. Our aim was to link with existing disarmament programs and peace projects. We were dreaming a foolish dream, but we hoped for the blessings that make dreams come true.

We sketched a tentative timetable across America. Covering 120 miles a week, our walk would take us from April to November, 1982, to travel the 3,700 miles from the Trident base into Seattle, down to Portland, on through the magnificent Columbia Gorge, over the Rockies, across the plains and Appalachians and on to Washington, DC by mid-November. As the walk unfolded, our *Pilgrims' Progress* mailing list grew to 3,500 and generated financial help and much correspondence. In it, we quoted what is attributable to Martin Luther, "If you preach the Gospel in all aspects with the exception of the issues which deal specifically with your time, you are not preaching *all* of the Gospel."[41]

We staged our departure celebration right in front of the Ammunitions Gate on the east side of the Bangor Trident submarine base. Many military guards were on duty with clubs and holstered guns. Most of us had witnessed such gatherings before and were not intimidated. I looked out over the crowd and prayed, *"O God of Bangor, God of Bethlehem, giver of all who ask, bless us on our way. We deliberately choose to begin our journey on this day when the universal Church remembers how you sent your Son, Jesus, to bring peace and healing to our broken world. We thank you for this wonderful turnout of fellow peacemakers, and ask that you guide and protect us as we make our way across America and Europe to Bethlehem in Palestine, birthplace of the Prince of Peace. Let us all labor together to turn swords into plowshares. Amen."*

Father Zabelka, our oldest pilgrim, was introduced and gave the first talk. "Thank you, all of you, for coming out. The importance of standing up against the darkness of these weapons cannot be over-emphasized. Thirty-seven years ago, a few weeks after the atomic bombs were dropped, I was in Hiroshima with the occupation forces. I have seen with my two eyes how such weapons decimate whole cities, leaving behind a legacy of immediate and painful dying of innocent civilians that goes on year after year. I mean even until today, some are dying from the radiation of those bombs. The bombs absolutely annihilated all plant, animal and human life."

Zabelka went on, "I'm an old man now but I am driven by my silence then to shout now as loud as I can to bring a halt to the use and manufacturing of all nuclear weapons. I see our pilgrimage as a sign of hope, a belief that together, we, the ordinary, little people, can change the course of history...There are no winners in a nuclear war. We've been marching toward this time ever since Cain slew his brother Abel. Faith that works deeds of peace is the only solution."

Archbishop Hunthausen delivered the main talk. His presence was like a rising sun. He had become a star in the peacemaking world by participating in demonstrations at Bangor and speaking up boldly: "Stand up here and now and be counted!" After our celebration at the base, we began walking, entering into the Stations of the Cross along the way to St. Olaf Catholic Church in Poulsbo.

St. Olaf parishioners greeted and welcomed us with a special potluck dinner. I wrote in my journal at St. Olaf's: "I'm resting in the social hall, quietly sitting on my stretched out sleeping bag. I'm tired, overwhelmed and awed by the whole day. All around are pilgrims and others, happily conversing, laughing and sharing impressions. The local press couldn't have given better coverage. We pilgrims felt our efforts at outreach paid off like a royal flush in spades."

On day two, we stopped at the grave of Chief Seattle at the Suquamish Tribal Cemetery on the Port Madison Indian Reservation in Suquamish, Washington. A current Native American prayer leader with some of his people, met us and led us to the grave. Our large white-on-green PRAY FOR PEACE banner was held high. We circled the grave as he set afire a cedar smudge. With an eagle feather, he wafted the pungent smoke over the grave. He circled the crowd and did the same over us. He reminded us that all of nature whispered of peace, and gave us sacred herbs and soil to take to Bethlehem. Pam Ingalls-Cox carried them to Bethlehem, depositing them twenty months later. After the pilgrimage, reciprocally, she returned to Chief Seattle's grave and laid soil she had gathered from the Holy Land.

Rain pelted down as sixty walkers made our way to the Winslow-Seattle ferry. With several peace banners afloat, we trudged two miles to the Jesuit, St. Joseph's Parish on Capitol Hill, greeted with a community dinner. Three-hundred fifty people joined us to celebrate a special sunrise Easter Sunday Mass.

At the end of Easter Mass, the pilgrims were called before the congregation to be identified and blessed. We each received a circular, blue and yellow threaded badge fitted with a neck band reading, Bethlehem Peace Pilgrim. We filed out of church into a major downpour. One woman was overheard, "Holy thunder, and they intend to walk all the way to Bethlehem! May God bless 'em." Due to the rain, nervousness, and the crowd, the driver of our red pick-up truck, donated by Zabelka, had an accident. The trailer was damaged and needed repairs. Bob Patten smiled and said to me, "God's reality therapy." Bob held out his hands to be pelted with the heavy rains. Two dozen hearty souls walked the day with us to St. Philomena parish fifteen miles south, where we were warmly received. Laughter greeted us as they led us to chairs in front of which were placed buckets of hot water with towels. I doubt if any of us had anticipated such attention, nor the delight of dunking our cold, soggy feet in soothing, warm water. Another wonderful potluck dinner followed singing, prayer and our first formal peace program.

The next day, we made a lunch stop at the Visitation Sisters' Convent on the way to Tacoma. They wanted to be part of what we were doing. After a fine meal, we bid them farewell. "Not so fast," one of them said. "When one of our visiting Sisters departs, we send her off with a blessing song. Now gather together, and we seven Sisters will gather around you." With arms and hands outstretched over us, they sang, *"May the blessings of the Lord be upon you, we bless you in the name of the Lord! May the blessings of the Lord be upon you, we bless you in the naaame of the Looorrrd."* Ever after, all across America and Europe to Bethlehem, we imitated this ritual whenever guest walkers left the walk. The ritual verse often brought tears to those who walked with us.

Our next destination was St. Leo's inner city parish in Tacoma. It was an alive, service oriented parish in the Archdiocese of Seattle, hosting a soup kitchen, a Catholic Worker House, two L'Arche homes for the developmentally disabled, and a drop-in center. Many St. Leo's parishioners were involved in nonviolent protests dating back to the Vietnam War. Charismatic Jesuit, Bill Bichsel, was for years the joyful figurehead of St. Leo's nonviolent collective stance against the darkness of military might. Father Bichsel had been arrested numerous times, and was saluted by several civic organizations. Co-pastor, David Rothrock, was largely responsible for bringing the L'Arche communities to St. Leo's. He had lived with the L'Arche Movement founder, Jean Vanier, at Troile, France. As he said to me once, "I found in L'Arche a meaning and vitality that until then was missing in my life." By sheer chance, visiting Rothrock in Tacoma that night was John Drury, a L'Arche companion from England. John played a mean guitar and composed and sang songs well. During the program at St Leo's, he gave us our pilgrim song:

> *"O let there be reconciliation,*
> *May it spring throughout creation,*
> *From every one to every nation,*
> *Oh let there be reconciliation…."*

Pam had brought her guitar and now she had our signature song. And sing it we did at every program and place, hundreds of times across America and Europe.

It was the middle of April. We walked straight south along the verdant corridor from Seattle to Portland for 190 miles. Easter joy filled us as spring beauty exploded around us. Each day we relished the spring rains, sunbursts, the greening fields and forests. Rushing streams gurgled, birds warbled, the backroads beckoned. George said quietly to me, "If we had tails, they'd be wagging."

Every day was brand new. Brother Fred said, "I'm as happy as I've ever been." And it seemed we all were. It's because we were using our physical bodies for a purpose. Walking was therapy, and put us in touch with mother earth. We felt alive and free, on the road day after day finding new joy and delight in the wind, rain, sun breaks and fresh air. Our leg muscles were firming up and everything we ate tasted better. We believed our walking and our presentations were making a difference.

Months before the walk started, and continuing each day, I struggled with my deepest self. Becoming a pilgrim meant that dear old Ma at 90 years old would have no family member to visit her. It was with hidden shame that I told her I planned to walk to Bethlehem for peace, and that I wouldn't see her for months. My rationale was, yes, we are called to leave even mother and father to do the will of the Lord. She was at Mount St. Vincent's, well cared for, and she did have weekly visitors, including Charlene Collora and Madeline Douglass, Jim Douglass' mother. However, I was concerned. As the pilgrims faced east on the Washington side, hugging that great river for more than 120 miles through the Columbia Gorge and then over to Pendleton, Oregon, I took a quick exit on the bus back to Seattle to visit Ma. My absence from her of almost a month was the longest time I'd left her since my care for her began seven years earlier. After my brief visit, and a difficult goodbye, I rejoined the group four days later.

The Columbia Gorge was spacious and dramatic, and the small communities welcomed us. Each day of the pilgrimage, we basked in the ever changing wonder of our fair and bountiful land. To love and reverence mother earth is fundamental to making peace. Some nights, after our presentation, we pitched our tents to sleep under the stars. The darker the nights, the brighter were the constellations. We laughed and chatted as we ate and shared stories around an open fire.

Our group passed through windswept Eastern Oregon. A peace group at the small town of Union hosted us. We stayed at Kimbro Farm with hosts Bill and Lucy who were ardent in their peace commitments, and warm with hospitality. As they walked with us for several days, we talked about a post-walk peace community. "Why not set it up at our place? We've got a couple of old buildings that would be fine with some fixing."

On May 11, 1982, we crossed a milestone. Washington and Oregon were behind us. At Twin Falls, Idaho we were 650 miles out. We went crazy with excitement when someone happily pointed out that we were one-tenth of the way to our destination in Bethlehem. So far our journey had been brilliant and enlivening. Not only still intact, we were becoming a genuine community.

A meditative moment for Jack and George Zabelka in Oregon © Bill Cox.

Mimi Ward reflected all our thoughts: "I'm in love with the experience we call the USA. I'm in love with the farmers and the small townspeople who in profound and simple ways express their concern over thermonuclear war. I'm in love with the eyes of both the very young and the very old, eyes that are full of life, questions and answers. I'm in love with all those normal people we meet who don't think we're crazy to be walking to Bethlehem as a prayer for peace. I'm in love with the windblown wheat fields and the arid expanses spotted with sagebrush, mustard, wild asparagus, with the shapes of the mountains and the iridescent colors of common ground cover. I'm in love with the singing meadow larks, the soaring hawks and the laboring blue herons. I'm in love with being in the rain or the heat, with the cows and sheep. I'm in love with God who created it all and saw that it was good."

Several factors, including the organizing of our social structure, knit us together: the walking itself, which got us out of matters of the head; the continual positive response of every community in which we stopped; the variation in revolving leadership and jobs we were assigned; and our daily gathering together. We came to know one another's ways quite well. We knew those who snored and those who didn't, those who liked oatmeal, and those who didn't. Being the second oldest at 55 years, I was always glad for the consistent generosity and attentiveness of the young folks to the minutiae.

We elected a new leader every six weeks; she or he chose two co-leaders. During that time, they made all the decisions. But we also faithfully held a business meeting every week, and a personal sharing session. The Sharing Meeting, as it came to be called, was a continuation of Holy Communion at Mass. It was the glue that held us together. We would all sit in Quaker worship silence, with no one person officially directing, in a circle in a room or outdoors under a tree, often at our evening rest stop. We'd each retire to the inner self. After a while, someone would say, "I'll begin," and proceed to say whatever she or he felt; it might be joyous, it might be sad, or reflect upset or hurt. Sometimes common themes would emerge like weariness or fatigue, or a common joy at the responses, but it had to be personal, and about what was going on inside of "me." The aim was to allow each person to share in a safe and trusting way, in which we all aimed to be attentive, respectful, sensitive, and caring. I remember Fred saying something like this: "I'm beginning to see that the people at our stops are more touched by who we've become as a group, than by what we say. They see clearly our sense of commitment, our gratitude, our easy joy, our determination."

There were many logistical parts to the pilgrimage machine: care of large quantities of printed hand-outs; vehicle maintenance for our pick-up, trailer, and the Volvo advance vehicle; a treasurer; care of large banners; buying and cooking food and clean-up; contact with the home office in Seattle; the monthly newsletter and press contact; a guest master to attend to the ever changing guest walkers; and a thank you person who gave to each host a signed photo-card of the pilgrims.

We had decided our weeks would consist of six days of walking, with one full day of rest. Our goal was to walk about twenty miles per day–averaging 120 miles per week. Early on, we established a routine: rise at 6:30 or 7 a.m., eat a breakfast of oatmeal, French toast and coffee, circle up for prayer and instructions, and hit the road in twos and threes. We'd take turns carrying banners, and handing out literature in villages and towns, stores and restaurants, and to passers-by. The breakfast cleanup team with George's red pickup and small yellow trailer, caught up and passed us, going in advance to establish a welcome lunch and refreshment stop. Finding a proper place for lunch was the most formidable task of the cleanup crew. If it was hot, they sought a shady tree; if windy, get 'em out of the wind, and if it was raining, get 'em out of the rain. It was interesting, as the jobs rotated, that the complaining about inadequate lunch stops diminished. Once you had the job, you knew it was catch as catch can.

After lunch, walking resumed. Often the old timers–George, Fred and I–lagged behind to take a snooze, or as we put it, "to do spiritual reflection." We got so we could catch a snooze almost anywhere. It was good to be so attuned to the elements and Mother Nature. After a while, the body adjusted to the wind, the cold, and the long days on the road.

The advance team members typically drove into towns further along our route, looking for a church spire where they knocked at the door and asked for the pastor. The goal was to see if the pastor was accommodating, and explain that we were a group of Christian peace pilgrims, walking in witness to the birth place of the Prince of Peace. We said we were endorsed by Catholic and Protestant bishops and we offered a program–pray with the people, sing, give testimony to why we were walking, and show a film, *The Last Epidemic,* produced by Physicians for Social Responsibility, soberly depicting what one nuclear bomb would do to San Francisco, London or Paris. As we handed the surprised, sometimes skeptical pastor our flyer, we silently waited in prayer. As for sleeping, all we asked for was a single room big enough to roll out our sleeping bags and cook for ourselves. It was when we said there were twenty of us that we really caught their attention. And sometimes we had more. Each of us had our own stories of nervousness, doubt, and strange encounters in our own assignments of doing advance work, but to our constant amazement, the sentiment of the citizenry was hospitable. In our eight-month trek with more than 150 overnights, we suffered only three refusals.

We slept outdoors, in church sanctuaries, a fire station, in a couple of restaurants. At times we were farmed out to host families. Full of gratitude and solicitude, they wanted to be helpful, but we were often so tired, we preferred the neutrality of a hard floor in some hall. After resting, some of us wrote letters or went into town until the time for our program and potluck supper.

We initiated fabulous potluck presentations across the country. The turnout was consistently high. After eating, we'd put on our program and sing "Let There Be Reconciliation." We took turns presenting and testifying. The most common questions asked were: *How are you going to cross the ocean? What about the Russians? Wouldn't it be bad to unilaterally disarm? How can religious people influence politics? And what can I do, as a nobody, against a problem so massive?* Zabelka often teased at the end of a presentation, "Isn't it wonderful the idealism and commitment of these young people for peace? Do you really want to know why *I'm* walking?" He'd pause and look out with some deliberation, "It's you women! I mean day after day, I've never eaten so well. In fact, excuse me, but I'm always waiting for the meeting to get over so I can have three or four delicious desserts." They'd all laugh. Then he'd offer them an invitation to come walk with us the next day.

Peace felt like it was only a potluck supper away. We drooled and prayed thankfully at dinners cooked by others across the land. We felt our salivary glands dance at the variety of potluck dishes served. We cooked about one meal out of every seven. But food is for the soul, too. It is God's device for making friends; companion means 'one with whom you break bread.' There was no better way to break down barriers than meals between strangers in our own land, meals between Russians and Americans, and recreating the Eucharist, the meal to which God invites friends, enemies, and all, because we are one family.

Some problems did surface along the way. One involved our married couple. It took three months for Pam and Bill to have the courage to say that they were different. As a married couple, they felt they lacked privacy. The group heard their words. From then on, the first task of the afternoon crew when arriving at a destination, was to save the most private room, corner, or isolated spot for Pam and Bill. Another problem that came up was the constant attention of the press, radio and television. Zabelka was our celebrity and I got some attention. But the women, quite rightly, wanted to be included. We all examined our presentations to make sure women and men shared the spotlight, and that everyone felt involved and appreciated.

We hadn't been on the walk for more than a few months when an incident occurred that I won't forget. Several of us were milling around. I've forgotten the conflict, but Pam, with her red hair, came up deliberately face-to-face with my stubbornness. She stood directly in front of me, her arms straight at her side, and fists clenched. Like firm hammer strikes, she said, "Jack Morris, I hate you, I hate you, I hate you." Then she walked away. The fact that she could do that, she dared to be true to herself, impressed me enormously. We've been great friends ever since.

The United Nations held a Special Session on Disarmament. We had a BPP discussion and determined that with the help of our benefactors, we would send Alice McGarey and Steve McKindley to the events. Their mission was three-fold: to gain a sense of the international spirit for disarmament at this historic meeting; to keep our own message on track; and to make contact with European peacemakers. Alice and Steve would fly from Salt Lake City to New York City, and also lay the groundwork for our arrival on the East Coast.

On June 12, we joined sixty people from Logan, Utah in an ecumenical prayer service. It was held in solidarity with thousands gathered across the country, especially in New York, calling out for a bilateral nuclear weapons freeze. It was here that we also picked up our first Muslim peace pilgrim, Bookda Gheisar, from Iran.

Two days of hiking through the beautiful Wasatch National Forest where we communed with wildflowers and shimmering aspen, brought us to the Trappist Abbey of Our Lady of the Holy Trinity in Huntsville. We were invited by the monks to join in a votive Mass for Peace. Richard Rohr, OFM, the Franciscan celebrant, was visiting from his New Jerusalem

Community in Cincinnati. He spoke to us of our responsibility as peace-makers not to bring further division, but a reconciliation of differences. He read from Thomas Merton: *"If we want to bring together what is divided, we cannot do so by imposing one division upon the other or absorbing one division into the other. But if we do this, the union is not Christian. It is political, and doomed to further conflict. We must contain all divided worlds in ourselves and transcend them in Christ."*[42]

By June 17, we'd arrived in Salt Lake City, having hoofed it for more than two months. Our feet were beyond the blister stage. We'd sung and testified for peace before two score groups, in the sanctuaries of the Mormon, Buddhist, Protestant and Catholic Churches. The fact that each of these diverse places opened their doors to us was a living witness that differences could be transcended in the search for peace.

We received an important and affirming letter of endorsement of our pilgrimage from Mtoshi Motoshima, Mayor of Nagasaki, Japan. We also learned from the Internal Revenue Service that our BPP organization was granted its tax exempt status.

Joe Allen of Nampa, Idaho, walked with us for a while. He was a B-17 gunner in World War II where he took part in the bombing of Dresden, Germany. He recalled the firestorms that the napalm bombs caused in that city—tens of thousands of civilians incinerated. We shared our war experiences and vowed to keep working for peace. Then a pilgrim named Jim walked with us. His plane had gone down in enemy waters. He was a prisoner-of-war on Kyushi Island, Japan, for over three years. He recollected how, after August 15, 1945, some B-29s flew over his prison camp and dropped aid packages. Fr. Zabelka had flown over that place, and actually saw men scurrying to retrieve the parachuted aid.

Zabelka told the story of meeting Dick Sherwood of Salt Lake City at the Cathedral of Peter and Paul where George preached at each of the four Sunday Masses. Dick was a B-29 pilot from the 505th group on Tinian Island. His plane was assigned to take pictures of Hiroshima two hours after the bombing on August 6th. He remembered flying just one-hundred feet above the devastation. Dick had whispered to Fr. George that his assignment was to fly low, and to make several passes over the breathtaking ruins, snapping pictures. It looked like a moonscape, the river below covered with floating bodies. Thirty-five years later, this scene still haunted him. He had never talked about it with anyone until his tears flowed with Zabelka.

We arrived at the loading dock of the Hercules Corporation plant in Magna, Utah, a thousand miles along the railroad tracks that carried missile components for the Trident submarine. Mary Jude Postel, who did the advance work from Boise, Idaho to Salt Lake City, walked and wrote about the state of our democracy: "Here, with the missile components, the U.S. government manufactured all manner of explosives for our defenses. A faceless plant belching tons of acrid smoke into the blue sky stood behind a gigantic perimeter fence. Several thousand people were employed in this bleak landscape. At lunch hour, the employees strolled in and out of the main gate. Thirty of us, pilgrims plus locals, spread out with leaflets in hand and our peace banners raised high. Most employees took the flyer, but didn't talk. One woman slowed down in her car. She slipped a piece of paper into Steve's hand as he gave her a leaflet and drove off. Steve called to those near him and read the woman's words, 'Greetings to all of you. I'm sorry I cannot physically protest with you today, but in my heart I am. I fully agree with your cause and am working with local groups in Salt Lake City to further it. I feel like a hypocrite working here but I have children to support. I so want to meet and talk with you, but we're being watched. Thanks for stopping at Hercules along your way. Peace and love.'"

Some people we encountered wondered if the Bethlehem pilgrimage would accomplish anything. It was a legitimate question. In Nampa, Idaho, a group called the Canyon County Chapter of the Snake River Alliance was formed as a direct result of the Bethlehem-bound pilgrims' visit. They worried that Idaho was becoming the nuclear garbage dump for the rest of the country.

On July 18, we pilgrims fanned out to eight different suburban Denver churches to give sermons, announcements, and teach Sunday school lessons. Later, we met with U.S. Congresswoman Pat Schroeder at our picnic-in-the-park. In the evening, longtime peace activist, Liz McAlister, spoke passionately on the seriousness of the nuclear threat. Half the walkers attended a week-long "Peace Revival" sponsored largely by the Denver area Mennonites, while the rest continued to follow the star eastward across Colorado.

Jack and George, roadside in Colorado © Bill Cox.

On July 29, our group crossed into Kansas, two-thousand miles and over half way across the country. The small town pastors of eastern Colorado were friendly, but the generosity and openness of the Kansas towns on highway 36–St. Rancis, Atwood, Oberlin, Norcatur, Norton–were over-whelming. Food was brought to us, potlucks appeared out of nowhere, café waitresses picked up the tabs, civic swimming pools opened late at night for our use, and we were invited to join Rodeo Days in Philipsburg with our peace banners and leaflets. One pilgrim thought he'd entered a subculture specializing in loving kindness.

By the end of August, we arrived in Kansas City. I didn't think we'd ever get across the plains. Coming in, we held vigil at the Bendix Corporation plant–one of those awful war manufacturers. It felt good to pray. The Catholic Social Justice office of the diocese worked hard to set up television, radio interviews, and speaking engagements at five or six places.

Rabbi Mark Levin, who grew up in Romania where tens of thousands of Jews were carried off to Hitler's ovens, invited me over to the Temple for Shabbat services. Bookda, our Muslim pilgrim, spoke at a local mosque. Like everywhere, the Catholic Sisters were present and very active in the peace movement. Tired, we thanked God for all who took us in.

Imagine the hot asphalt highways of Kansas in late August. Each one of us was exposed to the penetrating sun that was so necessary for growing acres of corn. One particular day, I was with Bob looking for a lunch stop. On a rise, we saw a single house three blocks off the highway. We hoofed up, sighting an empty carport. Our skin was brown as hazelnuts; we wore short pants and long hair. We knocked. An old woman came to the door and opened it a crack, "Yes?" We smiled as Bob told her about our walk. He slipped one of our flyers through the door. She closed it, returning a few minutes later, "Yes, you can use the porch for lunch." We thanked her, guaranteeing that we'd leave things tidy and neat. The gang found their way to us in twos. Pilgrims could smell lunch four cornfields away. We were just about finished when this elderly woman came out and quietly asked if two of the "boys" would come with her. She went down into her basement and filled two boxes with peach, plum, and pear preserves in mason jars. She looked over the group and said, "I want to be part of what you are doing. This is all I have to give."

One of our preparations for the walk was to address the possibility that walking for peace might upset some people. It could be interpreted as anti-American, even unpatriotic. For some, talk of disarmament might threaten their livelihoods or push their fear buttons. We needed to know how to relate to people who disagreed with us and judged us, so we invited a professional from Fellowship of Reconciliation to address a nonviolent response to confrontational situations. We imagined the mindset of people who oppose discussion of peacemaking. We talked about our need to use nuanced language, to be lighthearted as well as serious, to be good listeners, and always courteous. We role-played possible responses to verbal and physical disruptions or violence at meetings and on the road. Ironically, our own mindset needed fine-tuning. We had to wring out our own biases and sense of moral superiority. One result of those meetings was addressing our dress code. The women decided to wear skirts to be most respectful of strangers. We anticipated trouble coming from small, isolated communities such as in eastern Colorado or Kansas. How wrong we were. Only a few people drove by and gave us the finger. A few more would shout, 'Go do it in Russia!' Only two or three towns found us unacceptable. Most likely our non-threatening title and destination, as well as our literature, had something to do with our overall acceptance.

At the beginning of September, we scanned the wide open plains of Missouri. Autumn beckoned. A young man, Ron Rankowski, joined our walk for a few days. He showed us a map of the more than one-hundred missile silos in Kansas, a kind of minefield of missiles, all aimed at people in Russia—each one over one-hundred times more powerful than the bomb we dropped on Hiroshima. We stopped at one silo right next to the highway. Unless you knew, it looked like a regular farm gate. We found it unlocked. Steve, Bob and Mary Jude went in to view the silo and walk around it. Before we knew it, an army jeep roared through the gate. Two soldiers who looked like teenagers, raised bulky, ugly rifles, pointed toward the three. One got on his walkie-talkie to report, 'They are unarmed…a whole group of peace-niks.' The rest of us outside sat down on the grass. Laurie lit a vigil lamp. We began praying. Almost immediately, a highway patrol car pulled up, 'What are you guys doing?' We said we were promoting peace. We were just praying. The officer calmly, authoritatively, said, 'Well, hurry up with your prayer; you're making the whole United States Air Force nervous.'

Feeling autumn in the air, I wrote:

Precious sun-drenched days, tamed warmth
Perfect true blue sky, playful birds skimming high
The rains stayed, each tree shimmering like fire,
Clap your hands, join in the cosmic dance!
Twirling, swirling gold red slippers
Nudged by autumn's scented breath,
Gliding, spinning from branches high,
Clap your hands, join in the cosmic dance!

We didn't believe our spirits could soar higher, so marvelous had been the reception across the plains. Just as we had often watched the clouds pile up across a vast sky, then dump rain with thunder and lightning, we experienced the spiritual waters for which we'd prayed as we neared St. Louis.

St. Louis was unforgettable–for the event at The Shrine Of Our Lady Of The Snows, for the peace movement, and for our pilgrimage. The Oblate Fathers of Mary Immaculate (OMI) coordinated our arrival. They understood the dynamic connection between overt, nonviolent peacemaking and Catholic spirituality, contemplation and action. They printed and distributed flyers by the ten-thousands and solicited countless significant endorsements for our walk. They flew in nationally known comedian, activist Dick Gregory. We heard him speak boldly like a prophet of old: "In the Bible, God called the Israelites harlots, and their leaders he called pimps because they kept betraying their marriage covenant with God. Pimping is pimping whether you are betraying young women with money or making weapons to destroy God's most dignified creatures."

The OMI brought in professional music, lined up television, newspaper and radio interviews, and convinced the City Council of St. Louis to proclaim that Sunday, September 12, 1982 was *Bethlehem Peace Pilgrimage Day.*

With banners held high, we walked to and under the magnificent Arch marking St. Louis as the Gateway to the West. After our rally at the Arch, Dick Gregory took our big yellow peace banner and led a crowd of more than 350 across the Mississippi River into Illinois. The group included two city aldermen, the hard working folks from the National Nuclear Freeze Office, and an unprecedented number of African Americans side by side with Dick Gregory, who passed through East St. Louis and on to the national Marian Shrine Of Our Lady Of The Snows.

The Shrine Of Our Lady Of The Snows, comprised of two-hundred glorious acres of rolling lawns, verdant trees and bright flowers, was dotted with various scenes from Mary's life. For us, the stay meant three unprecedented nights in the same place, in beds with clean sheets, and deliciously prepared meals. It also allowed us a two-day retreat to pray and reflect. Father Larry Rosebaugh, OMI, a long-time peace activist, offered two conferences. The last time I'd seen Larry was after several years with the

Milwaukee Catholic Worker when he came to Seattle. His calling was to be with the poor. He could sleep anywhere. Rumor had it that Larry once embarked on an old rusty, one-speed bike for southern Mexico from the Midwest. That's more than 2,500 miles. When I saw him, my first question was—did you make it to Mexico? He said in his understated way, "Yes, after all, not much can go wrong with a one-speed."

Jack, Fred and pilgrims cross the great Mississippi.

The time with the Marians refreshed us. I was gifted with a spacious new feeling about Mary and peace. For the vast majority of Christians, except for Catholics and the Orthodox, Mary is marginal, and for most of them, they are taught a disengaged personal piety. In truth, Mary epitomizes those forces which are contrary to war—paying attention to what one is given to do, and to do it with a full surrender of will. Mary was alive, alert and quite aware of the reality in which she had to raise her son.

Less than five miles from Nazareth was Rome's largest fortress-garrison in Palestine. Like every mother in Nazareth, Mary cautioned her child to beware of these men of war. We speak of Mary as mother, and also of Church as mother. Why? Because our very baptism means to imitate Mary, to surrender to the Holy Spirit and give birth to Christ in our time and our place.

Fred and I were Jesuits, Kevin Lafey was a Carmelite priest, Janet Horman was a Methodist minister, and George Zabelka, a diocesan priest. We partook in frequent celebrations of the Holy Eucharist, usually led by either Zabelka or me. We had Mass in chapels and outdoors. We faithfully conducted our weekly sharing meeting, and in retrospect, this was our primary prayer. After a while on the road, this time together became a bonding. We saw how much alike we were, we felt the pain of one another, and above all appreciated and heard one another's interior longings. Yes, I am not alone. I have brothers and sisters who care. I am held and respected. I don't have to hide my weaknesses.

Sometimes, three or four pilgrims could be seen fingering their beads as they walked together praying aloud, "Our Father who art in heaven…. Hail Mary, full of grace…" But walking itself was a form of prayer. As Lafey said when we finished the U.S. leg, "The biggest surprise was how well we got along, and how well we handled tensions and disagreements. The walking itself has a lot to do with it. It's almost as though tensions, doubts, and anxieties work their way down through the body into one's legs and feet and into good Mother Nature, who exchanges it with harmony and gladness."

Prayer happened on the walk mainly because the core group rose out of their year of service in the Jesuit Volunteer Corps where volunteers learned in practice much of what we were trying to implement. Discerning God's will for us and the world was foremost in our hearts. That deliberate effort to align our wills with that of God–what I call prayer–was a foundational practice in generosity of spirit and a willingness to dare. The volunteers had joined the JVC movement to give something back, to make a difference. The pilgrimage was just one more step in the living art of prayerful action and contemplation.

Walking the miles while praying.

For me, the core members of the group were "five loaves two fish" individuals, acting like Jesus when he encountered the crowd exceeding five-thousand men, women and children. Jesus looked to his disciples to do something to sustain the people after they'd trekked so far, even though the food supply was limited. Jesus said, "There is no need for them to go away; give them some food yourselves." Then he said, "Bring them here to me," and he ordered the crowds to sit down on the grass. "Taking the five loaves and two fish, and looking up to heaven, he said the blessing, broke the loaves, and gave them to the disciples, who in turn gave them to the crowds. They all ate and were satisfied, and they picked up the fragments left over—twelve wicker baskets full."[43]

They were satisfied with what they had been given. Significantly, it does not say that Jesus multiplied the loaves. In sermons on this text, I've given the example of the Sisters of Providence and the Jesuits, both groups made up of ordinary women and men, certainly neither wealthy nor excessively brilliant. How could those little Sisters throw up magnificent hospitals wherever they went, and the little Jesuits raise up universities and high schools? And our pilgrimage? All of these are examples of groups made up of "five loaves two fish" people. Miracles happen simply because generous, bold hearts together conspire and dare to act.

When we set out, we didn't have money to cross the ocean for the European leg of our journey. But we encountered many "five loaves two fish" people along the way, making everything possible. One man in eastern Pennsylvania stood out. As our walkers strolled through a neighborhood in a small town, we observed a man raking up the autumn leaves. Each twosome that passed greeted him and chatted. At the end of the day, the man handed $20 to Mary Jude and Laurie. Jim, Fred and Mimi all reported the same gift-giving from him! He said he wanted to participate in making peace. A week later, we held a vigil in front of the White House in Washington, DC. Who showed up but this elderly gentleman from the small village? He must have asked for "the Father" because one of the pilgrims led him to me. He said, "That day you passed our church, I'd been home and got the feeling I should do something for the Lord. So I went over to the church grounds and was raking the leaves when your group passed. Your bright ways, your dedication, your taking time to chat with me, made me want to be part of your pilgrimage. He reached into his wallet, extending $300. I said thank you but reminded him that he'd already given. "No," he said, "I want to give more. I'm promising to send something each month until you reach Bethlehem."

A Mennonite minister in Pennsylvania understood the cost and impact of discipleship. He asked me, "Do you know why I came out for your presentation tonight? I've been in peace work all my life. You won't tell me anything new, but it isn't every day I meet people who believe in something so much that they're willing to walk half-way across the world for it. I came out to be touched by you. Commitment," he said with a warm firmness, "rubs off."

Our 3,700 mile trek up and down and across America was almost over. We had experienced wonders: Missouri's alluring swimming holes; Illinois' flat fields full of tall ripe corn; Kentucky's dense hardwood forests and tobacco barns; Ohio's great river that leads to the West; West Virginia's tiny communities and hollows; and Pennsylvania's Pittsburg, our place of vigil at the corporate headquarters of Rockwell International, a premier nuclear weapons manufacturer. We sojourned back into West Virginia, Maryland, then into Virginia, heavy with political history and juicy firm apples.

On November 13, we arrived close to the end of our transcontinental walk. We ate our last breakfast on the road in Langley, Virginia, at the Quaker Friends Meeting House. It was a short six miles across the Potomac River into Washington, DC. More than one-hundred supporters met us at Chain Bridge over the Potomac and walked with us up to Georgetown University where we were welcomed by veteran peacemaker, Dick McSorley, SJ. Next, it was on to the White House.

Pilgrim, Laurie Hasbrook wrote, "As I stand and vigil here in front of the White House in our nation's capital, I am awestruck. Not by the grandeur, but by the fact that little Laurie Hasbrook, with her fellow pilgrims, and in the name of tens of thousands of little people, can come here and declare that our small, individual voices do count! Hear us, we cry out, stop this damn crazy arms race. It is not the way to peace."

In Washington, DC, the Benedictines for Peace sponsored an all-night vigil on the eve of the annual meeting of the American Roman Catholic Bishops Conference–about 275 bishops. They came to hammer out a document on peace and the arms race. The meeting attracted international attention. More than one-hundred people prayed through the night to bring the light and courage of the Holy Spirit to the bishops. We gave to each of the bishops our letter to religious leaders of the world. At noon, we hoisted our banners and, joined by a few supporters, walked four miles to the massive Pentagon where we prayed. Having begun at a place of darkness–the Trident submarine base–we couldn't end in another shadowland, so we walked east a hundred yards, symbolically headed for Bethlehem. Overlooking the Potomac River, we sang, *O Come, O Come, Emmanuel.*

We had all matured in our Christianity. That maturity was like a cantata with many notes. The notes told us when to work, when to play, when to pray, when to enter into silence, when to pay attention to the city of man and woman. Our bodies had fasted and been fed. Our minds had been tested. We had expanded our creative powers, our community bonds. Feelings of gladness and gratitude became favorite chords in our song.

Of course, we felt ecstatic as we neared our final American destination. We'd walked across America crying out for peace. Each one of us planned to continue with a nine-month trek across Europe. The wonderful Christian Brothers De La Salle promised us a big, ten-bedroom house on Broad Street in Philadelphia to live rent-free from November, 1982, until March 10, 1983, the date we planned to embark for Europe. During that time, some pilgrims planned to stay in Philadelphia, others would make return visits home; some needed to find jobs to refurbish their finances. All needed a good rest. We gathered for three days of meetings to talk about the route and timetable through Europe. Not wanting to walk through the European winter, we decided to begin in Ireland on St. Patrick's Day. We chose to go via Ireland, Scotland and the whole length of England because our aim was to bring the voice of peace. Going where English was the native language likely furthered our effectiveness.

I knew I would return to Seattle for Thanksgiving. I worried that I had deserted my 91-year-old Ma. I took comfort realizing I had fifty days of visiting with her before starting the second leg of the journey. Several times during this period, I fumbled, trying to explain to Ma that I was continuing on this long walk across Europe to Bethlehem. I was a pilgrim because I had to be. She heard my words and knew the meaning. I felt her sadness, and her steel resolve. I imagined she would say: "So what's new? I've survived this long without you and I'll keep going. Go on your blasted trip." But there was not one word from her inducing guilt. That too was Ma, part of her beauty, and why I admired her. She always taught us that we each had to do that to which we were called.

CHAPTER 23

Bethlehem Peace Pilgrimage III:
Walk Across Europe

"May the road rise up to meet you.
May the wind be at your back." – traditional Irish blessing
(and we added…May the pouring rain cease,
and the hiding sun one day shine.)

Ireland

AFTER A THREE-MONTH HIATUS, THE pilgrims rendezvoused in early March, 1983, at the Jesuit Seminary at Rathfarnum, outside of Dublin, Ireland. The Jesuits gave us eight days free board and room for our now nineteen pilgrims. This was no small gift. We incorporated four new members into the core group. The pilgrims hitchhiked two-by-two down to Cork, Ireland, while Fred and I went to Holland to purchase a Volkswagen van.

Upon arrival in Europe, we immersed ourselves in peace work already lined up for us. We participated in "Peace Week" activities in Dublin, speaking in churches and schools, joining with Pax Christi in a Walk of Remembrance, and talking to the press.

Continuously aware of our need for heaven's help, we began the nine-month, three-thousand mile, eleven country trek across Europe on March 17. It was St. Patrick's Day in Cork, and we asked St. Patrick for protection and guidance. Two of the pilgrims had gone over earlier to lay the ground-work across Ireland, Scotland and England. Others worked on contacts in each of the countries we faced. Our purpose and presence was announced publicly several times, "They've walked across America and are now here to join us to pray for peace in Ireland and around the world. You are most welcome."

We marched in Cork, Ireland's famous St. Patrick's Day parade with our peace banners held high, and packs loaded with flyers to hand out. Imagine! We were walking for peace in Ireland and the world. We part-nered that day with fellow peace activists from The Irish Campaign for Nuclear Disarmament, and PAX Christi.

St. Patrick's Day was only the first of many parades in Ireland. We were led into towns with brass bands, and the next day out of towns to the drumming and trumpeting of bands and bagpipes. Each Sunday we had more than one-hundred walkers who joined in. As we got near Dublin, Jesuit seminarians from several European and African nations joined us. In Kilkenny and other towns, bright, laughing, uniformed children were let out of school to walk with us for a few hours. The children met us with posters and songs. Mothers with small children cheered us with, "We've come to walk a few steps with you."

For the next three weeks, we headed north through Dublin, to Belfast, and Larne. The days were lengthening, but winter's rain and chill still held sway. The weather was wild–snow, hail and rain every day–and yet bursts of sunshine radiated across the land and into our chilled bones. How wonderful to be warmed by cups of tea and offers of biscuits, beds, love and attention. We walked alongside ancient ruins into Fethard, the oldest chartered town in Ireland, beneath the sweeping arch of a rainbow over lowing cattle.

About five days out, we spied a bent old woman standing under the eve of a decrepit thatched hut. A shawl covered her shoulders and head. A thin voice sang out, "Come in off the road. Have a cup of tea. I've been waitin' fer ya. I saw ya on the telie." One of us said, "We just had a cup of tea." She shot back with, "Mind ya now, it's not every day the Yanks come down my lane. Come in and meet an old biddie." Five or six of us peeled off to accommodate her. The drab place hadn't been white-washed for twenty years. In the corner, there was a broom, shovel, and a rake partly hidden by spider webs. On the wall were pictures of Mary, Joseph and President Kennedy. The tea kettle sang. She had a circle of chairs ready and we sat. She then bowed to each with, "Yur welcome, yur very welcome." Then she looked at me, the oldest of the group, "You're the Father? Well, it's a grand day, and it's not just going to be tea, Father. She moved quickly to hand out cups. I was handed a glass, someone else received a cup, another got a jar. She announced with a smile, "We're all going to have a wee bit of *the Craetur!*" She came to each one with this quart mason jar full of white lightning. Laurie was first. I was fifth. By the time she poured mine, my eye caught Laurie's face as she clandestinely emptied her lightning through a hole in the floor.

When the woman poured a wee bit, I asked why the Irish called it "*the Craetur?*" She drew her head back, looked at me and said, "Don't ya know? It's God's special gift to the Irish. The Romans came to these parts. They didn't stay because they didn't have the gift that gives us hope." She went on, "I'm all alone here; my man's been in the ground for many a year, and my boys have gone to make their way in life. Sometimes my heart feels heavy and hard as stone. But, I have *the Craetur*. I pour a bit and quietly sip it, and, glory be to God, before I know it, the sun's come out, and I'm feeling warm all over." She keeps her gaze on me, "It's the same at night, every night–just me and the tickin' of the clock. Before I get down to pray, I pour a bit, and sip it. Again, glory be, all at once, the curtains part and all the stars are out. I don't feel so alone." She goes on, "Ishkabaha–the water of life. God's gift to the Irish." Then abruptly, with heightened voice and a serious frown, "Now it's a gift. We don't abuse it, cus if ya do, it'll cast ya into hell to squirm with the very snakes themselves." Before we departed, she pressed a pound note into my palm, "I wish it could be more, Father." We departed, chastened, enriched and delighted.

Often individual families took us in. We marveled at the heavy burr or brogue. At times we laughed after exchanging a few misunderstood words in their homes or on the road. The hospitality was gentle and warm, but they wanted to talk and talk and we were often dead tired. Some tension existed because several members of the group preferred to stay together in community rather than split up in separate homes each night.

In addition to language, one of the main problems on our European leg of the pilgrimage was the different culture. Ireland's main meal was lunch and ours was dinner. When we came in hungry at the end of the day, ready for dinner, we received tea and biscuits. So, we reduced our walking schedule from our normal twenty miles a day to fifteen miles.

Our group was received by church and civic officials in towns and villages as celebrities, but most of all by the ordinary folks as part of family. It helped to be a Christian group on our way to Bethlehem. They listened to our story, asked questions and celebrated with us in and out of churches. Children along the way often carried our banners and handed out flyers. We talked in halls, churches and schools, and were treated to theatrical presentations. We frequently showed the Maryknoll movie *Gods of Metal*,[44] highlighting the issue and the response of the American churches to the destructive potential and astronomical costs of the arms race.

Local councils gave us money as did nuns and priests. On the streets, old women pressed Irish pound-notes into our hands, "God bless you, this is my small way of going with you." Young and old seemed informed not only about the nuclear war issue, but about the harsh activities of the United States in El Salvador and Guatemala. Of course, Irish tradition had been sending out missionaries, priests, brothers and nuns for generations; the people have a wonderful global consciousness. We marveled to have bishops, and yes, two cardinals, Protestant Church officials, as well as members of the Irish parliament who met with us and actively listened. Our walk was a touchstone.

Our group accepted opportunities to meet political leaders. Governments were where decisions were made to resist or to stockpile nuclear weapons. In Dublin, we sat down with three members of the Irish Parliament to discuss Ireland's role in the growing European resistance to nuclear weapons. Some of us also went to the American Embassy. We met with the Lord Mayors of Dublin, Cork, Port Arlington and Dundalk, as well as several town councils. In churches, we spoke and prayed for peace with sisters, priests and ministers, and with Roman Catholic Bishops in Dublin and Callan.

On Holy Thursday, as we walked the streets of Dundalk, a Roman collar stepped in front of us. It was none other than the Catholic Primate of Ireland, Cardinal O'Fiaich. He introduced himself and said, "I want to walk with you, and pray too." He walked a couple of blocks and led us into a church, "We know here in Ireland the price of peace, and you, walking across America, also know. We need the Lord's help. I couldn't allow you to escape without walking with you a symbolic step or two, and praying. It makes all the difference." Outside he said, "You're doing a grand job and I thank you for coming to Ireland. You're a blessing to our troubled land." He continued, "Today, as you know, is a holy day about that most holy of all meals. Jesus gifted us with the Eucharist." Handing over to one of the leaders of the day a generous gift of money, the Cardinal said, "Here, go have a good meal *on the Church* in Ireland." And we did, choosing where we'd get the most for his money, a Chinese restaurant.

On Good Friday, exactly one year since we took our first steps toward Bethlehem, we crossed the tense and dangerous border into Northern Ireland, such a suffering boundary between southern and Northern Ireland. Our arrival had been advertised. We embarked upon the Stations of the Cross, seven on each side, each station a killing-place in the ongoing "troubles." The night before, three of us were billeted with a family. We told them of the 'morrow's doings,' and our need for a sizable cross to lead us. Brendan, the father, said, "I've got just what you need. After we eat, we'll go over to my shop. I'm a woodworker. I've got two lengths of oak, six by six. Can't think of a better use for it." Like the day itself, the cross was heavy.

We anticipated the Stations as a meaningful reinforcement of how and why our journey had begun, but we had no idea it would mean so much to the several hundred Irish people, Catholics and Protestants, who walked with us praying. Each Station was a significant place of suffering: a massacre, a school bus bombing, or children killed in crossfire. This living symbol of their suffering touched us all. Many wept, and in the end thanked us for the gift of this very real prayer.

In Belfast, four days later, we talked and prayed with the Executive of the Presbyterian Church of Ireland. He too thanked us, commenting how helpful it was for outsiders like us to come prayerfully to them. "It helps us to keep on." In Belfast, we saw some of the most devastated ghetto areas along the *peace line* separating Catholics and Protestants. Belfast's own story was dreadful, painful and tense as it held the ghosts of bombings, Catholics vs. Protestants, IRA, Shankhill Road, death, mob violence and fear. Even in the face of rolls of barbed wire, soldiers with machine guns, army trucks, metal fences, and stone fences with broken glass, the people wanted to relate, to talk to us, to tell their stories.

The Irish viewed the paranoia of the U.S. and Soviet governments toward each other with a clarity and concern that many U.S. citizens lacked. Several towns and cities along the walking route were deemed Nuclear Free Zones. The Irish commitment to neutrality and peace was strong. They knew it required church involvement.

Our walk through Ireland concluded faster than we wished, yet we got a feeling for the suffering history, the graciousness of its people, and the beauty of the land and sea. I learned three amusing things: Boston, Massachusetts is a suburb of Ireland; every Irishman has relatives somewhere in America; and each spring day has within it the other three seasons. The people were generous, humorous and inclined to overstatement and indirection. Malarkey, blather, blarney, hooey, gift of gab—all because of exaggeration that comes from the fertile Irish imagination. As one Irishman said, "We are devious." One said, "We are lazy." Another said, "We are not lazy—we are all poets and philosophers."

Scotland

On April 8, we boarded the ferry at Larne to cross the North Channel to Stranrane. We waved goodbye to our poignant month in Ireland. Scotland would also be brief. Peace groups met us in Glasgow, at one time, the second city of glory in the Commonwealth. They took us to the anti-Polaris Peace Camp at Faslane. Here, NATO wanted to place a Trident submarine

base. We visited the permanent, bleak, tent peace camp of a score of protest-
ers. Our presence seemed to affirm their work. Such camps were sprouting
up at military bases across Great Britain. From Glasgow, we hoofed three
days eastward to Edinburgh, delighted by our meetings with rural folks.
Afterwards we'd laugh. The conversations were in English, but the brogue
was thick and led to crazy misunderstandings.

Arriving in Edinburgh was a happy event. Pilgrim walker Dean exclaimed,
"Thank God we're no longer moving toward the North Pole. My bones are
tired of the cold winds and rain. From here on, we're equator bound."

Fr. George, Brother Fred, Fr. Kevin and I were put up by the rector of
the Cathedral. Rightly so, we got flak from some of the female pilgrims on
our privileged clerical status. After we'd cleaned up, a tall figure in a black
overcoat sauntered in. With a warm smile he said, "Welcome to Edinburgh
and Scotland." It was Cardinal Gray, the Catholic Primate of Scotland,
known for his concerns for peace. "I want to toast and bless you on your
mission of peace." He shook our hands, then reached into the wide pocket
of his coat and held up a quart bottle of Scotch whiskey, "The wine of the
country." We all laughed. His pleasantries were down-to-earth. We talked
for half an hour about the peace movement and the Catholic Church's
need to be more active. He ended by getting up, looking to the priest who
had followed him in, and said with an expansive smile, "Father Mac, show
them the pope's toilet." Our spontaneous laugh was punctuated with question marks. With that the Cardinal excused himself.

The rector, Fr. MacDonald said, "Come with me and you'll understand." He had a twinkle in his eye. He led the four of us through narrow halls, down steep, groaning steps into the rear of the church. There
he opened a door with a grand gesture and said, "There it is! The pope's
toilet." He told us the story behind it. "The Holy Father, Pope John Paul,
was coming to Scotland. We were all quite excited. One day an advance
man came—a stuffy, unsmiling fellow wanting to see where the Pope would
stay, where he would vest up for Mass, and, yes, how far away from the
sanctuary was the closest toilet. I gave him the tour. All was well except the
toilet was deemed too far from the sanctuary. The pope needed something
closer. We had to put in that special accommodation, costing more money,

time and worry than we'd have liked–you know a rush order with pipes, new walls, and all." Fr. Mac broke us all up with, "And he didn't even use it!" Back upstairs, we toasted wonderful Pope John Paul II, the new facility, but not the pope's stuffy emissary.

Leaving Edinburgh, we entered into immaculate rolling hills with wooly sheep and lambs, and wide open spaces of Northumberland, looking south into England. Just near the border, we detected the sound of bagpipes. There on the crest of a knoll, in the gently falling rain, were two pipers all decked out in colors and kilts, piping us on our way. It was a gesture of farewell. Their costumes, splendid demeanor, and plaintive notes gave life to our feelings of gratitude and joy. Fred said, "Just think of all the military glory connected to the piping of Scott soldiers in far off wars." May they more and more be pipers of peace.

England

England! That meant only another forty-five days to mainland Europe. Day by day, through the rolling plains and hills, gray skies and hours of slanting rain, we trekked on. All around us, spring flowers emerged in tidy yards of the many villages. Everywhere were sheep, hedges and stone fences. The ruins of old monasteries and churches, as well as Hadrian's Wall, woke us up to ancient history. At the Wall, we paused and chatted with a local constable who told us the Romans came to stay in 43 A.D. with three legions, some 20,000 soldiers. The Wall runs east and west for seventy-three miles where Britain is the narrowest. It was erected to protect the southern regions, their empire, from the menacing Picts, a tribal people who lived in what is now eastern and northern Scotland during the end of the Iron Age and early Medieval times. Every mile had its castle, and there were seventeen great forts built for 800 troops. Settlements in time had grown up along the barrier. The Roman presence ended in 410 A.D., called back to ward off barbarians closer to Rome.

One of the most sinister and chilling modern stops was at Menwith Hill, a gigantic installation secluded in the serene Yorkshire countryside. It operated in total secrecy. Through Menwith Hill, we were told, the U.S. National Security Agency monitored every international phone call and telegram to and from the United States, seeking out enemies of the United States. Its headquarters in Fort Meade, Maryland, was a place that rivaled the Pentagon. It was created by President Truman in 1952 in the grip of fear from the Cold War with Russia. The NSA was built on the same fears that constructed Hadrian's Wall centuries ago.

The days lengthened as we walked on roads that dated to Roman times. We conducted many evening programs, testifying, telling stories of our walk across America and singing our peace songs. The people who came out to be with us didn't need convincing that nuclear disarmament was a life-and-death issue. They were involved in local peace groups, or in the nationwide Campaign for Nuclear Disarmament.

BPP pilgrims hold peace gatherings across Europe © Bill Cox.

Each pilgrim delighted at telling how faithful we were to the pub scene for forty-seven days from Cateleugh, at the top of England, to Canterbury at the bottom. Locals told us, "Sure, that's the way the pubs are—they'll receive you well. Just go in, tell 'em you are Yanks going to peace. Then to be sure, lift one for me." And that we did. Each day, twenty dripping pilgrims, sometimes augmented with guest walkers, unpeeled their rain gear to enjoy an hour of warmth in the comforting ambiance of the English Pub. Each day, the advance twosome figured our distances, chose a pub, and went in to converse with the proprietor. Never refused, we were even welcome to bring in our own food. Some purchased coffee, tea, or a Guinness. I think we'd have died on the way, saturated with rain, if it weren't for the heavenly warmth and openness of that grand institution—the pub.

At Milton-Keynes, we prayed at the Buddhist Peace Pagoda with members of the Japanese Nipponzan Myohoji Order. These monks and nuns walked and chanted for peace in places around the world. We visited the Molesworth and Greenham Common Peace Camps, near RAF bases scheduled to host U.S. first-strike cruise missiles.

Upper Heyford, a small town north of London, was the site of one of the biggest military airfields in England. It stood as part of NATO's aim for a first-strike on Russia should it prove necessary. George told a story of our England experience: "On May 21, the Christian Campaign for Nuclear Disarmament (CND) staged a march and demonstration. Several thousand Christians from all over Britain came together. Our BPP contingent joined the massive crowd at Bicester. It was a beautiful spring morning with hundreds of banners unfurled over happy faces of young and old, and mothers with baby carriages. High and low clergy joined the solid, clear voice of the Christian laity. Everyone communicated the message: stop the nuclear arms race that leads only to suffering and death. The crowd stretched out over a mile on the eight mile walk to Upper Heyford. Singing could be heard; even a trumpet sounded, celebrating Peace Pentecost, the name given this event. The chairman of CND presented a blooming cherry tree and cross to the base commander. Then, it seemed all at once, loud thunder and lightning, and the heavens opened up. Before we knew it, we were slogging along in deep mud. Paths became streams. The crowd began merrily singing, *Our God Reigns (rains)!* When we arrived at the peace camp to greet those holding a constant vigil, we were wet and cold. The planned service went on for the hundreds who persevered in the eight-mile trek. The Bishop of Kensington began the service in his rain-drenched, mud-splattered purple cassock. Powerful prayers and readings followed." Zabelka added with a smile, "I gave the shortest homily of my career and said that this walk was faith in action. We can't have peace without paying the price. We the people must be as willing to go to peace as we've been going to war. Only then will we bring the peace of Bethlehem to the world."

Coventry was an important stop on the European leg of our pilgrimage, where the historic St. Michael's Cathedral had been largely destroyed during the Nazi Luftwaffe carpet bombing of England in World War II. Now the site stood as a place actively making peace with Germans and others worldwide, in their "Covenant of the Nails" program. Zabelka and I pensively explored the ruined, yet renewed Coventry Cathedral together.

On we walked to Canterbury Cathedral, a site that took us back 900 years to Archbishop Thomas Becket who was murdered in Canterbury Cathedral in 1170 by the faction of King Henry II. When Becket was canonized a little over two years later by the reigning Pope Alexander III, Canterbury became a holy site, a place of pilgrimage. The animosities engendered here between church and state simmered for 400 years, erupting again with Henry VIII and Thomas More.

We let the dense history of England sink in as we gazed at towering Canterbury Cathedral. Off in the distance we could see the white cliffs of Dover. France and mainland Europe were just across the choppy Channel.

France

When the firm, round-coming sun
reminds us it's May
All of life turns to life,
Seed to shoot, boy to girl,

Flowers from stems and roots,
Every end has a middle which has a start.
May's flowers fill the mystery of fresh starts,
May's birdsong and green life
Build a cradle to budding flesh.

Only the flower, bright with harmony's light
Brings the secret of starts and middles,
The meaning of roots and stems.
Patience and peace become one
who lives in stemming,
May tells us in blossoms in bunches,
In flowers galore – all of nature's uproar,
Tripping over one another splendor
At the root of all May children.

– Jack Morris

We waved goodbye to England in late May as we crossed the Channel to Dieppe in Normandy, where the Allies in World War II suffered 1,400 casualties.

My first sensory impression was the delicious warmth and promise of the French sun. Secondly, it was our first experience where we didn't know the language. We were hampered because only Laurie Hasbrook was fluent in French. Perhaps it was no accident we arrived in France the day after Pentecost Sunday, and sang, "where you shall speak your words in foreign lands and they will understand." Our power would consist of our call to walk faithfully, to live together in harmony, and to remain hopeful.

In contrast to the meticulously neat and sedate England, France was vibrant, boisterous, and informal. Our walk through the patterned fields and small villages along the Seine River to Paris seemed like art to me. The back roads were lovely but confusing, so we left little paper arrows at questionable intersections to mark the way.

Far too often, we stayed up too late at too many meetings as the French set out to solve all world problems. And the long, cold, damp walk through

Britain had taken its toll. We began to bicker and quarrel. It became harder to pray together. Several pilgrims came down with colds and flu, forcing one, then another, to lay behind to rest, mend and catch up. We failed to address the signs of failing morale, and kept trudging on.

Then, beyond Paris in Burgundy, we came to the amazing ecumenical monastic order of Taize, with more than one-hundred brothers of Protestant and Catholic traditions from thirty countries around the world. Thousands of young people made pilgrimages to Taize every year for prayer, Bible study, community work, and sharing. The Protestant founder and leader of the community, Brother Roger Schutz, met us outside the village. He personally welcomed us and led us to their center. Bill gathered up everyone's Birkenstocks for repair in Cluny. For three luxurious days of rest and reflection, we began the task of going inward and healing as a group. We rested, prayed, and spoke truths to one another that sometimes felt uncomfortable. It became clear that at different points along the way, due to sickness, exhaustion, petty upsets and emotional ups and downs, our walk had been on the edge of disintegration. Thankfully, it always came back together. Going inward always aided that process.

In 1960, Thomas Merton, OCSO, wrestled with the uneasy state of his search for a position on public issues of war and violence. Father Merton had a growing conviction that the military power of the United States, having been weighed in the balance and found wanting, faced a dreadful judgment. He began to write on these matters. When he was partially silenced by authorities in his order, he began sending out mimeographed essays. These became his *Cold War Letters*.[45] He felt that the advance toward nuclear war was evil, even criminal. He urged all people to act and to give moral voice to the crisis, no matter what it took to get it out there, even if you had to scribble it on the backs of envelopes. Our pilgrimage was one way of writing *peace* on the backs of envelopes.

By June 26, we were at the eastern edge of France. The hills to the Alps were beckoning and our walking consisted of much up and down in the rain. We all threw in our thoughts about what we would most remember in France: the healing Taize retreat; ecumenism; inquisitive, animated and hospitable French people; wine, cheese, bread, cherries, big rose windows, coffee in large bowls, nettles, red poppies, snails, and robust French farmers.

Switzerland

We arrived in Geneva, Switzerland, on June 30 before we were ready or rested. In the afternoon, we met with religious leaders from the Middle East at the World Council of Churches. We also met with church leaders from the Lutheran World Federation, the Alliance of Reformed Churches, the Conference of European Churches, and the Metropolitan Emilianos of the Greek Orthodox Church. The police escorted us through Geneva. Because so many words had been spoken in Geneva at all the disarmament negotiations, we decided to walk in symbolic silence. A man on the sidewalk stopped and clapped; a worker silenced his jackhammer as we went by; some walked a few steps with us; a woman gave us a bag full of juice and glasses. A small group of pilgrims met with the team of START negotiators for the Soviet Union who promised 'no first use,' an agreement to *freeze,* and troop reductions in Eastern Europe. They said their position was for peace–if the United States cooperated with their bold initiatives. We appeared on National Soviet Television.

After leaving Geneva and walking along the lake all day, we stayed in our first, large, atom bomb shelter with one-foot thick walls and doors. Inside was a hospital with no windows. The Swiss government required all buildings to have such shelters, and people to have a small A-bomb shelter in their home! It was haunting to realize people were actually preparing for nuclear war.

High in the spectacular grandeur of the Alps, we stopped the walk for a marvelous retreat, as many in our group were worn out and tired, or recovering from sickness.

We eventually ascended the Gran St. Bernard Pass on a beautiful clear day, with twenty-four vibrant kids from Grenoble walking with us. Just as we passed the border of Switzerland and Italy, the French students left the road to frolic, skiing down through the snow on their feet. In Aosta, Italy, we circled up with the French youth group, sang songs, and bid them adieu. It was sad to see them return home.

Italy

Italy brought giant mosquitoes, hot weather, marvelous hospitality, many peace programs and wine. Somewhere along the way, I picked up the name "Giovanni (John) Montana," after football great Joe Montana. We stayed in churches in small villages and cities along our route from Vercelli to Ponte Nuovo, Milano, Modena, Bologna, Florence to Rome. Every day of walking brought encounters with gracious strangers and the pain of letting go of the people who had lodged in our hearts.

Four more Japanese sisters joined as guest walkers in Bologna–joining their Sister Genevieve Masuo, who walked with us from Geneva to Bethlehem. On August 6, we began fasting on and off until August 9 in remembrance of Hiroshima and Nagasaki. Thirty-eight years ago, Japan and the United States were at war. Now–Americans and Japanese–we were walking together for peace.

Months of community discernment, prayer and discussion, led to our decision on which route we would take to reach the holy land. We considered three alternate routes. Should we walk as we originally planned through Turkey, Syria and Jordan? Should we walk through Yugoslavia and Greece, sail from Athens to Haifa, and walk from Nazareth to Bethlehem? Or should we walk through Yugoslavia and Greece and take a boat to Egypt and then up through the desert to Bethlehem? Would Turkey allow the pilgrimage in? Would war erupt between Syria and Israel? Everyone we consulted told us it would be an extremely dangerous route and that we wouldn't be able to walk much of the way, but six people thought we should go that route anyway. On the days we stopped to pray specifically for an answer, we found our group evenly divided over these possible routes: the tally was six-six-six. What mattered more than the route itself, however, was our process as a community to peacefully work out our conflicts and disagreements. As the time grew closer to a decision, everyone realized they might have to give up their preferred choice. Fr. Zabelka suggested we surrender to chance and "draw straws" to determine our route. A moment of astonishment followed as we realized we were all prepared to accept whatever outcome the drawing of lots produced. I think we had faith that any third of the group couldn't be totally wrong. We prayed as we drew lots. The plastic spoon marking the group's final choice was drawn by guest walker Sister Genevieve. Yugoslavia, Greece and Haifa would be our route.

We reached Rome on August 23, 1983, where we stayed with the Sacred Heart Sisters. The next day we had an audience with the Pope—joined by fifty-thousand other people! The Peace Pilgrimage was mentioned. Afterwards, a television station rented six taxis to transport us to a meeting with several pastors, where there was television coverage. The Sisters bustled about to make sure our needs were attended to perfectly. The morning we left, alongside our coffee, milk and rolls, were plastic bags with our individual packed lunches, and holy cards to take on our journey. Thank you, dear Sisters.

The first day of September marked a joyful celebration from dawn to dusk in Cassino, Italy as our own Mimi Ward and Steve McKindley exchanged marriage vows. The ancient Roman amphitheater behind the school on the hill was a spectacular venue for a ceremony. However, we got kicked out when the local caretakers thought we'd broken in, so a whole line of people carried chairs up above to a clearing that would serve as an outdoor wedding site. The mountains facing us and the Benedictine Monastery high above made for a picturesque setting. The Monastery dining hall was transformed into a banquet room. The carrot cake and potatoes were baked in the kitchen, but the rest of the food was prepared on our little camp stove. I prepared the sacramental ceremony, while others set up candles, covered tables, and arranged fruit and nuts. The pilgrims cut hair, resoled Mimi's shoes, designed a wedding card, decorated a hotel room, and finished the bride's hair-band of hand-sewn flowers. A few bought wine and champagne and arranged for music and circle dancing later in the evening. The joyful event brought all of us into a holy communion.

Yugoslavia

On September 17, we embarked on the ferry from Bari, Italy to Dubrovnik, Yugoslavia. When looking for sunglasses, two walkers had the first impression that shops were less about choice than necessity. After leaving Dubrovnik, we headed for Molunat, a beautiful village on a little inlet of the ocean. I told everyone they couldn't get lost as long as they just kept hugging the ocean. But as I was leading us out of town, I took the wrong turn, and had to wind my way back. On September 22, we had a business meeting, and all agreed to take up a collection to send Fred to see a Greek island, recognizing his deep desire for that.

We left the coast, what we called the "Yugoslav Riviera," and began our walk into the hills. Up and down. Beyond the tourist area, we saw horse carts, peasant women dressed in black, tiled roofs on ancient houses, pigs and chickens freely roaming, beautiful rivers and marshes. Across a lake was Albania, that country which was shut tight from the outside world.

On St. Francis Day, October 4, we wound our way up the switchback trails with people chopping wood, walking cows, tending farms and fields. The vegetation changed from chaparral to deciduous forest. Colors of fall brightened with the elevation. On a grassy hill, as we waited for our van with lunch to arrive, we were suddenly greeted by a car. Was it curious locals? Instead, it was members of the Peace League of Beograd (Belgrade), a group that had been finding us everywhere on our route. Were they tracking us for our protection, or were they threatened by our presence? The questions were both comforting and disconcerting. In a nearby village, we were invited to stay in a boys' camp being refurbished by laborers. We ate "Zvonko soup" (hearty lima bean) for dinner as the workers watched us eat. Their dress? Hats, utilitarian clothes, rugged faces. This was our first pilgrimage through a Communist country. The workers, fixed on their tasks, had no families with them and no place else to go. Their days consisted of work, eating, drinking, sleeping, and work again. We caught a glimpse of color television and watched President Reagan speak, his words dubbed in Serbo-Croatian. What might he have been saying, and what might it mean to these people?

A friendly militzia had offered us a stay in the Murino Police Headquarters building, but he had to confirm the invitation with a higher up. Hours later, suspicions aroused because we were religious. They demanded our passports. And Janet Horman had chosen a spot in front of their local war memorial to build a campfire and boil potatoes, which also set off alarms.

Later that night, we camped at the summit of the mountains beneath a canopy of constellations. We spotted a welcome café with checkered tablecloths and devoured thick goulash, corn bread, and sweet tea. Our tents dotted the hillside behind the café. We could hardly sleep because our camp was overrun by shaggy sheep. The tied up donkey brayed, pigs grunted, and passenger buses stopped to look at us.

The landscape of Yugoslavia unveiled itself in its varied glory. Trees displayed their uproarious fall colors, blanketing the rocky hills with splashes of orange and purple. Sunset and dawn provided daily spectacles. Everywhere we walked, carts and horses passed us. We witnessed olive-skinned women with white scarves, multicolored flowing dresses, and billowing pants. Local markets were filled with live chickens, prepared cheeses, chestnuts, hooked rugs, and used clothes. Our band of pilgrims attracted their attention. Maybe they saw us as "American" gypsies since we joined them at the river to wash our clothes. We didn't fit any mold. We were a Japanese nun and a tall red-haired American, a blend of the USA, Canada, Great Britain, France, Iran, West Germany and Japan. The deeper we got into the country, the more we observed turbans and Mosque towers. When camped, we would sometimes hear women singing Eastern tunes in a minor key. Or we'd hear Albanian men drinking beer, singing their songs, and enthusiastically smashing their glasses as the music intensified.

We celebrated Bob Patten's birthday on October 18 at a camp where neighbors brought apples and firewood. Pilgrims broke out guitars and sang late into the evening. Bob danced around the campfire, beating a pan. The boisterous occasion alarmed local authorities. Suspicious, curious policemen demanded to see our passports, while Janet tried to explain that is was just a birthday celebration. On October 21, Mary Jude turned 24 years old. She was treated to breakfast in bed, with Fred and Jim serving as singing waiters. On October 22, I was the birthday person, turning 56 years old. It seemed a good time to share some stories about life in the novitiate, and my thoughts on the adventure of aging.

The next day we woke up to cold rain. George celebrated Mass in a crowded, but dry, tent. Several pilgrims were sick and needed to rest in a nearby monastery. No monks were living there, but some congenial old folks led us inside to a room with a warm stove to thaw out. Some of our crew left for an advance trip to the Greek border; many pilgrims stayed all day in local cafes. One priest at the monastery showered us with icon postcards, a Macedonian New Testament, candy and brandy. As we continued our walk the next day, the Red Cross dropped off coats, soap, dishtowels, shirts and handkerchiefs. When we got to the town of Demir Kapija, we all lined up for haircuts and shampoos for a hundred dinar each. The barber preferred women to men, proposing marriage to every woman in our group.

For forty days beneath the Yugoslavian autumn sun, our feet fell on communist ground—a nation under the red star. Pilgrim knowledge is existential, rooted in the senses, harvested on the move. To those senses, we perceived Yugoslavia to have a familiar communist "smell"—human lives that were low on wages and freedom, long on ideology, indoctrination and control, high on collective promises. One religious leader said, "surveillance is a primary occupation," while another apologized for not allowing us to use his office for a mailing address. "It's too delicate; I'm sorry." Religion, we learned, was tolerated as a private affair of the unenlightened, although generally free of overt persecution.

Yugoslavia also revealed familiar, homey scenes: families at the beach, parents proud of their children, groups of hardy workmen, boisterous and jovial as any, urging us on. Young lovers could be seen transcending party affiliation and government interference. We watched boys of ages 11 or 12, astride a jackass ascending a mountain path, or driving a loaded mule to market, or herding goats. Girls, high on the slopes, knit while following two or three cows. Indeed, Yugoslavia, with five national groups, four languages, three religions and a communist form of government, was not America, but how it captivated us. It didn't deserve the dreadful and poisonous fear of the Cold War American hyperbole, "better dead than red."

For myself, I felt sure I could have found union with God, joy in my priesthood, and laughter anywhere – even if I lived in Yugoslavia. I knew this because along the way, day after day, pilgrim-knowledge brought convincing evidence that life here was human and not so different from rural life in America. People were happy or not, felt free inside or not. How our spirit responds to our circumstances, whatever they are, is what matters.

October 29 was the last full day of walking in Yugoslavia. We felt a bit wistful. However, all the pilgrims had been promised hot baths at the end of the day in the rehabilitation center called Banja. It was a glorious way to say goodbye to Yugoslavia.

CHAPTER 24

Bethlehem Peace Pilgrimage: IV
The Final Stretch

"But now they desire a better homeland, a heavenly one.
Therefore, God is not ashamed to be called their God,
for he has prepared a city for them."[46]

Greece

AFTER AN EIGHT KILOMETER WALK to the border, we had no trouble crossing into Greece. We camped in the woods above a village and were greeted with shouts of welcome by young Greeks who joined us at the campfire. They wanted to know all about our walk and about American music. The next day was Halloween. Clouds and rain blew our way. That night we stayed in the Kastanas schoolroom where we took turns acting out and guessing the lives of the saints.

After a few days, we arrived in Thessaloniki with its ancient Christian Churches, modern buildings, and noisy streets. The quantity of goods in the marketplace and on grocery store shelves, was overwhelming. We asked ourselves the question raised by our experience of communist and capitalist cultures: which was more disturbing—too little or too much? We knew we would always measure the excess of capitalism against the sparseness experienced in Yugoslavia.

Sister Nicodeme and Sister Nina joined us in Pirgos, bringing with them $1300 from their order, Le Montena Convent in Japan. We couldn't believe our windfall. That amount seemed overwhelming and would pay for our ferry from Piraeus to Haifa.

On November 6, Sunday, we participated in a Peace Rally in Thessaloniki. Seeing thousands of people marching into Aristotelous Square, holding banners and chanting for peace and disarmament, was boisterous. It presented a touch of disorderliness unlike Yugoslavia, where the public seemed obliged to be politically silent. A street corner drew speakers: Germans, Americans, Japanese, and Greeks who spoke English. Some of the crowd shouted anti-American slogans aimed at the American arms race. We were relieved to bring the news that we were Americans for peace. For most of our journey through Greece, we were met with gracious hospitality. As word spread about what we were doing, one mayor put us up in a hotel and called the next mayor in the next town to expect our arrival.

Thanksgiving Day was spent in Halkida, Greece. By then, there were thirty-one of us, from Canada, Great Britain, Japan, France, Iran, West Germany and the USA. We held Mass at noon followed by a spread of chicken, fruit salad, rice, baked tomatoes, potatoes, salad, wine and beer around a table set with candles, peace cranes, and a cornucopia of almonds, oranges, apples, and flowers. Afterwards, we read letters from the families of pilgrims, and sang early Christmas carols in several languages.

It was during this time that George Zabelka fainted. We knew he had a bad heart. We got him into his sleeping bag. I sat with him while he talked and dozed. I kiddingly said, "Now that we're almost finished, you're going to ruin it all by dying right here on me!" He laughed. I asked seriously, "You're not going to die are you?" George answered, with an edge of annoyance, "How the hell do I know?" Then I pried, "Are you ready?" He calmly said with the confidence of one who has faced that reality many times, "I'm ready and more than ready. I've thought about it all along our journey…and it wouldn't be a bad way to go. I don't want to end up in a damn nursing home." But George survived.

We held a meeting and talked about our future as a big group. No one had specific plans, but several pilgrims reflected on the many ways the walk would change their lifestyle choices upon returning to their country of origin. Since the anti-war effort in the United States was more politically driven than spiritual, we talked about committing our energy to building a more spiritual peace movement.

Four days later, we arrived in Athens. Our arrival there jolted us, because we had thought for so long that Athens signaled the near-end to our journey. We had to leave Bookda Gheisar in Greece because she was an Iranian citizen. If she came with us to Israel, her passport would contain an Israeli stamp, preventing her from ever returning to Iran. We felt anguish that, after walking with the core group all the way from Logan, Utah, she couldn't finish the journey to Bethlehem.

On December 3, we were on the beach, contemplating Haifa and our next country, Israel. As we thought about the Occupied West Bank, we wondered what we had to contribute in this destination land of ours. Gratitude, hope and peacemaking were the gold, frankincense and myrrh we hoped to carry to the birthplace of Jesus.

The ferry boat took us to the lovely island of Rhodes, and then on to Haifa, Israel. We docked at 7:30 a.m. Before everyone was processed through Customs, George intoned in a provocatively loud voice, "We denounce all war!" to warning looks from some of the pilgrims.

Israel

Each pilgrim remembers stepping foot on the ground in the land of Abraham, Sarah, Isaac, Jacob and Moses. It is the land of Hassidic and Sephardic Jews, Orthodox and Russian Jews, of Muslims, Palestinians and Christians. Here we were in the crucible of wars and fears, and the home of the Prince of Peace.

On day six of Hanukah, we met with the mayor of Haifa and leaders from the Catholic, Greek Orthodox, and Druze communities. Amid the clicks of cameras, the mayor shook our hands and welcomed us, announcing he looked forward to the day when Jews would no longer be compelled to fight to preserve their people who had been so battered by history. I spoke about the call to all Jews, Christians, and Muslims that we must resist the temptation to worship the gods of militarism.

We met with leaders in the Partnership Office for Jewish-Arab Dialogue, down the street from the school where we lodged with the kindly Sisters of Nazareth. Josef Abilea spoke to us of his confederation idea rooted in the social ethic preached two-thousand years ago in the Sermon on the Mount. He described his own spirituality as based on the Jewish ethics lived by the early Christian communities. We wanted to know from him what he thought our walk would mean in this land. He said the nuclear arms race was remote from people's attention here, but witnessing committed people who personally sacrificed for peace would mean a great deal. A Jewish man asked us how we maintained hope in the face of the Russian threat of nuclear weapons. The Arab Christian pastor, who chaired the Partnership, said to this Jewish man, "Shmuel, your brother was killed by an Arab bullet, but you haven't stopped believing that we can make peace. My cousin was killed by a Jewish bullet, but I haven't stopped believing either."

We passed out pamphlets in English, Arabic and Hebrew that said, "Though we walk in the name of Jesus, we believe the deepest wisdom concerning the making of World Peace lives in the reservoirs of all faiths."

The coming road to Nazareth was arduous. Twenty-five kilometers from the home where Jesus, Mary and Joseph lived, we grew pensive. We were walking the same hills they had walked. In the fertile Jezreel Valley, some pilgrims encountered an Israeli soldier who spoke fluent English. He told them he had witnessed a man shoot his best friend in Lebanon. That same killer then shot his own wife. The soldier had Arab friends whose brothers hated them for talking to Jews. He said all this happened out of pain, ricocheting back and forth between cultures, families and generations. This Israeli soldier seemed satisfied to be a soldier, but he also wished us well. He kissed our peace pamphlet and ran off, gun in hand.

My dear friend, Maureen Casey, had rejoined us after months of nursing her daughter back to health following an accident. We were all so happy she had returned.

Our communal journal described the baptism of walker, Yvette Naal, in the Jordan River near a woodsy, calm spot downriver from the official "Pilgrim Baptismal Site." Father Benoit Charlemagne entered the water with her. Benoit cried out, "Yvette, what do you ask?" and down Yvette went three times, in "nom du Pére, du Fils, et du Saint Esprit." Still in the water, the group laid hands on and prayed over her. She received many hugs, and then disappeared behind a grove of trees, emerging in a white dress with a rose garland on her head. For a finale, they broke out into song. Yvette ended the celebration with the Prayer of the Ark:

"We are all strangers and pilgrims…let us make of where we chance to be a temple…blow on us, Lord, blow our prayer into flames, so that our hearts of sticks and stones and their fickle spark of life may somehow serve Thy glory."

Our group was intent on spending time with both Israelis and Palestinians. We headed west toward Hadera after Nazareth to walk in the state of Israel before crossing over into the Occupied West Bank, where we witnessed ruined homes and destroyed fields. Only by walking through the villages and refugee camps did we learn first-hand of the suffering of the Palestinians: expropriated lands, imprisoned people, children shot for throwing stones, and new homes bulldozed by the Israeli government because a family member was suspected of belonging to a forbidden group. Walking for peace amid such oppression was painful. Our prayers for peace were welcomed by interfaith groups, schools, churches, families and community centers.

We arrived in Jerusalem on December 20, spoke to students, journalists and prayer groups, and spent the next few days exploring the roots of our faith. Friday evening, December 23, we participated in the Shabbat meal of gracious, local Jewish families. Then came Christmas Eve, and our last night's walk into Bethlehem.

Fr. Benoit Charlemagne described it:

"It was a black night when we came to the small back road that would lead us to the Shepherd's Field. Garbage lined the roadside the last few kilometers. Enveloped in darkness, we saw nothing but the occasional light from a pile of burning debris which brought with it acrid smoke and odors of decomposition. Now and then we heard the haunting sound of dogs barking in the hills around us. The long procession of nearly two- hundred people from many countries walked on in silence along this desolate road, so full of symbolic images."

At midnight, the silence was punctuated by the bells of the Star City. It brought us hope and relief. We were so tired of walking. Twenty months had passed on foot, up mountains and across plains, through cities and villages of three continents and eleven nations. Gratitude washed over us. In the midst of so much human hopelessness, we were here at last to celebrate Christmas in the very place where Jesus was born on the darkest night of the year.

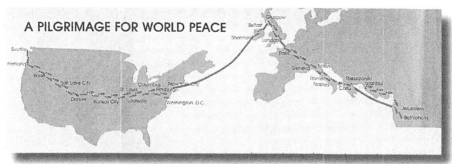

Journey from Bangor to Bethlehem.

The single most astonishing aspect of the pilgrimage was that no one chose to quit. Throughout almost seven-thousand miles, we held together as a community, as a communion body. Bookda had to drop out for reasons beyond her control, but twenty of us completed the journey, including all twelve people who took the first steps on Good Friday, April 9, 1982, from the gates of the Trident Submarine base outside of Seattle. We all walked the last twelve kilometers, our final steps from Jerusalem to Shepherd's Field on the outskirts of Bethlehem, on Christmas Eve, 1983. The night sky was radiant, and peace seemed possible. Zabelka said, "We are all children of God, and we are all threatened by the sword of Damocles." Then he bent over and whispered to me, "Jack, I'm getting old, and these last months were tough, but damn it, we made it. I think I'm in ecstasy!"

Every day on the road, out of a silent yearning, we had said the World Peace Prayer. We said it at the final point of our pilgrimage in Bethlehem:

"Lead me from death to life, from falsehood to truth;
Lead me from despair to hope, from fear to trust;
Lead me from hate to love, from war to peace;
Let peace fill our heart, our world, our universe."[47]

Bethlehem was surely not an end; it felt like the beginning of our work. Our journey promised to be a proverbial acorn, a compact seed that would grow and become a mighty oak within each of us.

CHAPTER 25

Bethlehem Peace Pilgrimage V: What It Meant To Me

"God is faithful to those who lean upon His mercy
and search the way for peace."

NOTHING SO FAR IN MY Jesuit life held a burning candle to our long, arduous, and passionate trek from Bangor to Bethlehem. I knew I would return home with pockets full of spiritual treasure–joy, contentment, community, reverence for the awesome worth of the human body and mind, and the spirit of God in His people throughout the magnificent earth. I believed that God wanted to put peace in the center of the Church's thinking.

To journey as a pilgrim is to find inwardness as you go outward and onward. The call to silent prayer and a simple lifestyle was the call from God to go to the desert–a place where all contrivances, artificiality, and noise disappeared. As a pilgrim community, we were stripped and humbled when others in our traveling tribe reflected back to us the poverty of our own fallen natures. It was in the silent love of God that our hearts were nourished and fed, our weary bodies were healed and justified, and our restless natures found peace.

Praying together and in silence had proven important along the seven-thousand mile journey. It had stitched our band together as a community and fueled our inner hearts. Living close to nature for months told us of the preciousness of silence. Dew never falls on a loud and blustery night, nor can God's healing power come to a restless, word-cluttered person.

Without silence there can be no birth of words that nourish and connect, and without such words, there is no meaning, and without meaning there is no communion. Part of my discovery of Bethlehem was that those who live without silence make noise without meaning.

Bethlehem for me was a symbol of hope, the place where Jesus was born. It was a complicated place: tender and tough, signs of weakness and power, hopeful, yet oppressive, highly personal and cosmic. It was about gift-bearing magi and their long, foolish journey of risks and trust. It was about walking the earth and watching the stars. Bethlehem was about Mary, whose whole life proclaimed a blazing "yes" to God. It was about Joseph, the just one. It was about the birth of a child called the Prince of Peace, who continues to be born wherever men, women and children are willing to choose life over death.

Martin Buber, the Jewish philosopher and mystic, regarded tragedy to be an essential element in human existence, that tragic loss seems married to life itself. Just so, Bethlehem was also the beginning of the road to Jerusalem and the mysteries of sacrificial, paschal suffering.

As our walk ended, I thought about the nature of power. A nuclear weapon's explosion is the twin of the sun. Both are massive, incomprehensible fire, yet the power of each is so different. Like twins separated, one is homeless, lost and angry, the other remains true to its Originator, and to itself. One brings darkness, the other true light. A nuclear explosion blinds every eye, scalds all flesh, and transforms all buildings into debris. It sucks up oxygen, sterilizes the earth, pierces the genetic code as a killing germ for ages to come. It can bring on a never-ending night. Undisciplined power is violence itself. The sun, on the other hand, trumpets forth spring's glory—brilliant flowers, soft grasses, gamboling lambs, and lovers swooning. The sun is power, and nuclear energy is power. The problem isn't power; the problem is the misuse of power. Is it used as a blessing or a curse?

Power can be good and necessary. Jesus knew it took power to banish evil, to bring healing to every soul, every family, and to lead the world to the Reign of God. It takes power to give away my possessions to another, to risk being kind. Jesus' call for discipleship (to grow in disciplined power) is what Gandhi and Martin Luther King Jr. heralded. It's about soul-force, about the power of listening and controlling anger. To condemn all power is to take on a false innocence. Yes, we must condemn the misuse of power, the misuse of authority, the misuse of flat logic. Jesus came to show us a new strategy and shouted this out from the cross. The scriptures relate that he could have called upon twelve legions of angels to destroy those who were attacking him, but Jesus' fulfillment came from his lips, "Father, forgive them; they know not what they do."[48]

We witnessed, all across the globe, adults and children crying out that the military and governments, and all the monuments glorifying war, have got power all wrong. Nuclear weapons will save no one. They mock Christ's nonviolent sacrifice of returning, not evil for evil, but good for evil. How strange, that to preserve our American way of life, we are willing to spend billions of dollars for wars that everyone loses.

I also saw God repeatedly in the desire for Americans to walk with us, in the grit of Irish, Yugoslavians and Palestinians, in the haunting visage of so many Europeans who knew war all too intimately, and looked upon us with hope for a better world.

God was present in our little band of pilgrims–determined, imperfect, complicated, forgiving, prayerful and honest. We sang, laughed, hugged, complained and cried. We welcomed strangers all along the route. We walked through the phases of the moon. Our band stepped to the sound of gentle rain on our capped heads and through the harsh roar of traffic. We had prayed for our enemies until they become like ourselves. We fell in love with each other, with God's people, and the great round world. Above all, I learned the deeper meaning of dependence on others for purpose and meaning, for food, lodging, interpreting foreign tongues, and pointing the way forward. I rediscovered that God is more present to us than we are to ourselves. God is faithful to those who lean upon His mercy and search the way to peace.

And truthfully, there is no way *to* peace. Peace is the way.

The Concept of Pilgrimaging – by Jack Morris

"The concept of pilgrimaging is as old as the human race, imbedded in practically every religious tradition. It is a spirituality that invests the individual with power; it steps outside of technology, it steps outside of all those buffers we build around ourselves to protect ourselves from reality. Once you set a destination that gives meaning to you, there's something that bursts open in you. There is grittiness to the journey that gives off joy. It has filled me with excitement. I feel real hope. It has convinced me of the power of the individual—just being a person.

We can rediscover ourselves, redefine what it is to be human. It isn't something that belongs to the past, it is something that has power today…you put your feet step after step, you plant it on good mother earth, you hear the rain, you smell the rain, you taste it, the dust, the wind, you hear it. We are in contact with the elements of the earth, God's creation, in a new way day after day, we feel something different…and I think what it means to be in contact with God.

It is simpler, plainer. I believe pilgrimaging is a form of prayer that involves one's intellect, one's will, imagination, and memory. For us to have an authentic spirituality of pilgrimaging, we must go back to the reality of being a pilgrim physically. To say that we are developing a spirituality of pilgrimaging is to reassert what is already there, what is real, and to make sense out of the fact that we are moving in the stream of life…The pilgrimaging reality has brought together for me the concept of community; it has grabbed hold of the issues of the day, our quest for peace and justice; it deals distinctly, critically, and really kind of severely, with life-style, and it bonds one in solidarity with others, where we share our anxieties, our doubts and fears. We feel we are in solidarity with everyone who is on the quest to make the world a better place.

Something has happened to us because of the journey. And along the way, people salute us, they cry, they give us money, they invite us into their homes, churches open up to us. People are identifying with our pilgrimage as a sign of hope. And they see there is a way, perhaps, to break through darkness and to bring new light."

(From the YouTube video by Bill Cox https://www.youtube.com/ watch?v=xbC5G-kqzMM)

CHAPTER 26

Examining My Affections

"I knew it was essential to live out the words of my vows."

AN EMOTIONAL UNDERCURRENT HAD FLOWED with me all during the walk across America and Europe. I felt my friend, Sister Elaine, with me in my heart. She and I had developed a special relationship in 1975 as we created the Transitional Resources for Young Adults program in Seattle. At the beginning of the pilgrimage, Elaine walked a few days with us in solidarity. She knew the pilgrims and they knew of my care for her.

After several months on the road, I felt her distant support for me wane. But I carried her spirit. My emotional side wanted to be with her. Yet, I knew on a deeper level that the fundamental orientation of my being was to my chosen life as a priest. Jesus was *real* to me. I had promised to stand with him at the cross, whatever the personal sacrifice. I was not a mere leaf in the wind or a cork bobbing on a brook's surface; I was choosing to make an act of will. I was doing it out of love for the Lord, the one true servant whom I considered God. Across the plains and mountains of both continents, I tucked this text in my wallet:

> *"...For His sake I have accepted the loss of all things and I consider them so much rubbish, that I may gain Christ, and be found in him... It is not that I have already taken hold of it or have already attained perfect maturity, but I continue my pursuit in hope that I may possess it, since I have indeed been taken possession of by Christ [Jesus]."*[49]

I knew it was essential to live out the words of my vows, deeply aware that I was called to be a priest. That meant living with the celibate reality restricting clergy against marriage, even though at times, it was a very personal struggle. Over the years, my flesh and spirit had pulled me toward the beauty of both Maureen and Elaine. I remember Dostoevsky's idea that the only way the world will be saved is through beauty. I was so glad God created women–how they moved, their wrists and fingers, their necks and curling hair when they turned their heads. So sacred was their place, that when I observed a pregnant woman, a gentle prayer rose up in me, "God bless you." I was nurtured listening to women's voices, and was set alive by their singing. I felt moved toward reverence, a feeling of God's sweet presence. The paradox was this: that a woman's beauty didn't end there–it pointed to the divine.

I imagine most priests live in the tension that celibacy imposes. It is an active sacrifice that requires on-going self-examination and prayer. It's worth noting that during the first several centuries of church history, celibacy was a matter of choice for bishops, priests and deacons. St. Peter was married, given that he had a mother-in-law who Jesus healed. In the twelfth century, a rule was approved at the Second Lateran Council forbidding priests to marry. In the Latin Catholic Rite, only celibate men are ordained as priests. This is not necessarily the case in the Eastern Rite Catholic churches. Celibacy is meant to reflect life in heaven, a detachment from the ways of the sinful world; men consecrate themselves with a pure and undivided heart to the Lord. In marriage vows, a couple promises faithful commitment to each other, where God is the subject of love flowing through the relationship. It is unfortunate that we have not, as a Church, honestly explored the question of whether to allow the option of married clergy.

Jesus said so much about poverty and so little about celibacy. Priests should choose celibate freedom by choice and by love for Jesus. Outside of Christ, it seems to me, it has no meaning, except the outward sterility which is perceived. It remains genuinely unproductive unless it is freely chosen in love, as an act of faith for the good of the Church–a living body of the faithful seeking mercy and redemption.

It's not the end of the world if we are sometimes tempted or if we sometimes fail. We are all human. Some are more domesticated than others, some less passionate, less sensuous, some with deeper insights of faith, centeredness, clearer direction. Who knows the reasons? We are all born into time, and the only self that is real is the one that is. I do myself an injustice wishing it otherwise, or comparing myself with others. I must always say, "For all that has been, thank you, and for all that will be, yes."

What matters is that we work to become more authentically true to the power that God infuses in us. We can ask of life only one moment at a time, and labor to be true to that moment. What is essential is to sow our very life with courage, honesty and integrity.

CHAPTER 27

Goodbye to Ma

"May each one born of woman know that he is because of her."

BEFORE FRED AND I COULD return from our Bethlehem Pilgrimage to the United States, we needed to dispose of our Volkswagen van. After several weeks, we finally found a buyer—an English fellow we met on a boat. But first we had to drive it to Yugoslavia to get my passport stamped "no vehicle." Otherwise, I was stuck in Europe. It cost us $900 to sell it for $750.

The delay in returning to Ma's side filled me with anxiety. I needed to get home. Before the walk started, I wished she'd be set free from her frail body of only sixty-three pounds. Now I hoped she could hang on until I returned.

Would she be alert? Would she know me? Could we communicate? Charlene Collora had written me, reporting that after my departure for Europe, Ma turned inward, communicating with no one. Now that I was coming home, Charlene buoyed my spirits by describing Ma's reaction when she heard the pilgrims reached Bethlehem. The news was broadcast on *Good Morning America*. "Violet," Charlene whispered to Ma, "Your son, Jack, reached Bethlehem. He finished the long journey." Apparently, the windows to Ma's inner self opened. To the surprise of the staff on her floor, she talked up a storm for two straight days. The head nurse later reported, "It was so unusual, I made sure it was recorded. I think she was silently in vigil with you. News of your arrival made it a grand time to celebrate. It was her journey as well as yours, and now her waiting could end."

Driving over the high arching bridge into West Seattle on that first day back, I felt tense and preoccupied. All that mattered was seeing Ma. As I steered into the parking lot of the Mount, I realized how much I needed this visit. I was also aware that I hadn't felt absent from her during the intense months of the pilgrimage. I took the elevator to the fourth floor, turned down the hall, and entered the dining room.

The moment I spotted her, my heart stopped. She sat in a wheelchair amidst a crowd of frail residents, some feeding themselves, some getting help. I felt terrible sadness for the weeks and months she'd been waiting alone. Her shriveled, bony body and a thinning, gray head of hair stuck out at me. How could she become any wispier? A gentle breeze would blow her into eternity.

My thoughts raced. I reckoned with the fact that I'd freely chosen to go off and leave her behind. I'd wrestled with that decision before departing across America and Europe. It never got easier. I believed then, and I still believe, that this painful sacrifice would, along with the sacrifices of so many other pilgrims, contribute to an opening for God to give the gift of peace to our suffering world. I felt that my dear Ma, from her incapacity and place of waiting, was also doing her part for peace. Everything we do has cosmic significance. Our choices tilt the universe toward the light or toward the dark. As individuals, we are never unimportant. I knew, as every son and daughter instinctively knows, a parent, no matter how vulnerable and confined, is of inestimable value. They constitute the emotional core of our own security system.

I walked to Ma's side and bent low. Our faces almost touched. I placed my hand tenderly on the tiny contours of her shoulder and gently kissed her cheek. Tears of gratitude welled up in me as I thought of her waiting for my return. Then, I shuddered at the dark side of the thought. Was it too late for recognition? She turned slowly. She was living half way between this world and the next. The light of recognition came into her eyes, and I could see her fumble for words. Then her eyes rolled back and slipped away.

I wheeled her into the hall and down to her room. I bent near again. She labored to bring her eyes back into focus, to climb up out of that dark, mute well. I moved in and put my arms around her. She instinctively rested her head on my shoulder as she'd done so often before. Ten minutes later, while I looked at her, Ma's eyes stopped rolling for a few seconds. With a soft, half smile, her reed-thin voice said, "I like you."

She recognized me as familiar, but I wanted more. I wanted a bright smile and words of greeting. I wanted her love. I wanted to tell her that I was home and I loved her and thanked her for her patience. Guilt, regret and apprehension rose up in me. My troubled feelings weren't just about her. She and I were connected, body and soul. Something of me felt pulled into the pit. Her plight would one day become mine.

The sadness I felt as I walked out of her room that day was as much for me as for her. Looking back, I realized that we harbor shame and dread for our human condition. Decrepitude, total dependence, and the threat of death, undo and rattle us all. We shrink from reality. Jesus' words that those who mourn with those who mourn are blessed, is a corrective to our fear. As I left the building and drove away, I wiped away tears of confusion.

Another day came. It was the beginning of February. Ma and I sat with the plants and paintings in the lobby of the Mount. Large windows opened onto the hilltop view of Elliot Bay and central Seattle. So often in the past, Ma and I had sat here, or outdoors on summer days, like two lovers, holding hands, silently looking and glad to be together. But now her head wobbled back; her eyes wouldn't focus. I felt she knew I was at her side, but she struggled with her affliction.

I wanted her to say my name. I prayed for that. But just that she was here, alive, having waited for me, was reward enough. I pondered how mysterious is human existence. A very limited circle of light surrounds us; beyond that, we conjecture. And when it is our own mother who wanders beyond that circle of light, we feel the chill and apprehension of that other reality beckoning. How do we think about it? My brain leads me through a trapdoor with no exit. But my faith is what straddles the apparent separate realities, and helps dissipate the dread and fear. From that vantage point, I know all is well–God will wipe away every tear.

I'd been home a week. Visiting Ma was my compelling duty. Even with its edge of sadness, it was a gift. After almost two years on the road, I found it hard to believe I no longer had to pick up our gear, pack the van, and move out every day to a new location. I felt a melancholy for the pilgrimage. I missed our camaraderie and the joy of adventure. I missed our prayer and sharing circles, our sense of high purpose. But I also acknowledged the rewards of homecoming: visiting Ma, seeing old friends, the triumph of a journey completed, a comfortable bed every night, and staying in a room where I could lay things out in an orderly way, and come back to them at the end of the day.

I witnessed Ma as she slowly, laboriously emerged out of some inner, oppressive world. Perhaps God's healing power worked through my presence, my words of love and comfort. I watched Ma's lips formulate like a mantra the words, "I want to go home." It was so hard to endure her weakness. I couldn't help her to go home, to get beyond this world. I could only wait and pray. The timing of nature wasn't the timing of the heart.

For ninety years Ma's heart had beaten, never stopping, faithfully pumping blood, thousands of gallons through her veins. What a mystery? I, and my brothers and their families, and so many friends, had been supported and nourished by her great love. She was as devoted to us, as constant, tireless and dependable as her own beating heart was to her.

Another day, another visit. The day began sadly, but ended in triumph. I worked hard to get Ma's unused teeth in her mouth. I wanted her to try solid food for a change. She'd subsisted for months on a monotonous liquid diet. Ma looked at me after the first bite with steady, knowing eyes as though she'd climbed out of a cave. The solid food, in a way, symbolized that. After eating, all at once she puckered her lips and leaned my way. She planted a kiss right on my lips. I went into orbit. To celebrate we took a spin outside and then gobbled ice cream with chocolate syrup. I left her side feeling like the world was packed with rainbows. Outdoors I paused, inhaled the fresh air, and observed the spectacular panorama of the Seattle skyline. I noticed the soft air on my face and a dab of blue in the overcast sky.

A few days later, I drove to the Mount again. After a little wheelchair spin outside the building, Ma and I returned to her room and resumed our favorite pose. I sat far up front on a chair and put her wheelchair directly in front of me so we could face each other. I pulled the wheelchair forward between my legs. That way we got close enough for her to bend forward from her chair to lower her head onto my shoulder. I then easily wrapped my arms around her. Our cheeks touched. She breathed softly. Her blue eyes seemed more controlled, less chaotic. Some terrible storm had passed. Our togetherness relaxed me, freed me from my anxieties. Who, I wondered was comforting whom? Then, Ma unexpectedly flipped on the light switch near her. Lifting her head up and looking directly at me, she said, "My son Jack. You're *my son* Jack!" Tears of joy poured from my eyes. I couldn't believe it. She smiled knowingly. We belonged to each other once again.

After two weeks of visiting Ma, I felt the need to make a retreat in order to more fully process the enormity of the peace pilgrimage. I needed to ask and pray for an answer to—what is next in my life? I needed time alone. I began a retreat in Enumclaw, Washington on February 20, 1984. I thought I left Ma in good shape. A few days later, on February 23, I received a call that she was in a high fever and was surely dying. I immediately drove into Seattle in the early afternoon. I stayed by Ma's side. Her breathing was labored. I believe she vaguely sensed my presence. I got down next to her, softly talked, and gently recited her favorite prayer, the *Our Father*. I stayed all night, and slept fitfully on one side of the bed. It was good being with her. Weighing less than sixty-five pounds, she didn't take up much of the bed.

With the coming of light, aid workers began their busy routine. The nurse told me her condition had stabilized and her breathing had returned to normal. I decided to go home briefly for a shower and shave before returning to her side.

As I read the morning paper from home, the phone rang. Ma had just died, alone in her room.

CHAPTER 28

Bethlehem Peace Farm

*"A community is only being created when its members accept that
they are not going to achieve great things, that they are not going
to be heroes, but simply live each day with new hope, like children,
in wonderment as the sun rises and in thanksgiving as it sets."*[50]

— JEAN VANIER

AFTER MA PASSED OVER AND was buried, I evaluated my situation. How
could I go on as if things were normal? In times that are unhinged, where
would I place my hope? Should I retire to the edge of a nuclear installation
to pray, to create a hermitage for others to pray, to pit my God against the
nuclear deity? I needed to pay attention, listen, and find a place for my soul
to live.

In the afterglow of the Bethlehem Peace Pilgrimage, my restlessness
and commitment to build a permanent community of peace reared up. I
believed it impossible for me, for former Jesuit Volunteers and pilgrims,
and for others to fully live the Christian message outside of community.
Divorce, hoarding private property, obsession with technology and enter-
tainments–all because our culture had abandoned living together in love,
trust, and mutual support groups. We paid a high price for false concepts
of well-being.

I chose to follow an inner calling. It was a dream based on the theological
concept of Trinity, three persons in a passionate dynamic of love and sharing.

The mystery of God is the mystery of relationship, of community. To grow, we need to share our deepest selves–our hopes, our fears and our doubts–with companions (*cum panis*–the company with whom you break bread).

I had received an okay from Oregon Provincial Tom Royce, SJ, to investigate the possibility of continuing with the Peace Pilgrimage group by setting up a community in northeastern Oregon, namely, Kimbro Farm. With much disappointment the prospect fell through, so our investigation shifted to a location in the Seattle Archdiocese.

In August 1984, we moved onto a forty-four acre farm on Coal Creek Road, two miles from Chehalis and four miles from Centralia, Washington. The project to build a retreat center for former Jesuit Volunteers and pilgrims was an effort to continue the spiritual growth and ministry of JVC members who sought an extended commitment. It was conceived as an educational, back-to-the-land community. I crafted a curriculum for a Peace School and said Mass at three parishes between Chehalis and the coast. Larry Gooley (who had been JVC Director for nine years), Brother Fred, myself, and a few of the other peace pilgrims who were involved included Mary Jude Postel, Maureen Casey, Paddy Martin, Alice McGarey, and Bill and Pam Ingalls-Cox.

We would weave together a Bethlehem tapestry from several threads: to live simply and close to the earth; physical work; disciplined hours; spiritual direction; and to celebrate our joys and sorrows in personal and communal forms of prayer and worship. We would link our prayer with merciful works–feed the hungry, welcome the stranger, clothe the naked, and visit the sick and imprisoned. Hospitality would be central to our service and we'd live out the spirit of the early Christians, where the whole group held everything in common, united in heart and soul.

Like a newborn baby, we spent the first nine months struggling to stay alive, to establish basic coordination. We often had three or more meetings a week. Our identity was tested, personalities rubbed together, work assigned, prayer models and times were explored, tensions rose and fell, and relationships were bruised and reconciled.

Our 1910 farmhouse, five out-buildings, and unpainted barn were adequate in their austerity, but a thousand loose ends needed attention. We set in place basics like rooms for ourselves and for guests, but we needed an adequate facility to host workshops, and private and group retreats. We wanted to build hermitage huts in the woods where people could come to develop the art of listening, allowing God to speak to the soul in solitude. We turned the grain house into a small chapel.

Over the months, probably five-hundred guests visited, about two-hundred overnighters sleeping on floors and in the barn. In spring of 1985, several former Jesuit Volunteers celebrated Passover with us on the Farm. For Easter, we had another crew of former JVs and pilgrims. On a hillside overlooking our small valley, we kindled the new fire, sang songs, watched the dancing flames, and recognized Jesus Christ as the light and warmth of the world.

On Christmas Eve day, 1985, we were all expectant as we thought of our evening walk two years earlier to Bethlehem from Jerusalem. On that night, we realized the journey was coming to an end and we needed to set our sights on something beyond the next day's advance trip. One of the delights of the Farm was the continual recalling of stories of the peace walk as we hosted guests and visitors. It was hard to let go of the experience.

If Bethlehem Farm meant anything to me, it was the sharpening of focus that all people and all life are connected, dependent upon, and rooted in the earth. Half the acreage on the Farm was flat pasture, the other half rose gently into a forest. We acquired our first animals and planted an apple tree. Our bee hives, fish farm, our colonies of moles, our friends the geese, sheep, chickens, cows and rabbits instructed and intrigued us. In a former age, fidelity of humans to the land was clearly delineated; it was a commitment to choose stewardship. God made us of the earth, and as a species to find peace, we needed to reestablish that fundamental covenant with the sacred cycles of life.

The stated purpose of the Farm was to be a collective witness for peace. We would read and discuss biographies of Martin Luther King Jr., Dorothy Day, Caesar Chavez, Dietrich Bonhoeffer, Jaegerstatter, and Gandhi. It was a retreat center dedicated to forming lay ministers for peacemaking and ecological care. We needed to address the overwhelming problems of war and the arms race through action. We talked of taking vows of personal and political nonviolence. The Farm would be one location; other action sites might include pilgrimages to places housing missiles and along railroad tracks which carried missiles. Former JVs, the Bethlehem Peace Pilgrims, Jesuits, and others were all welcome, but we planned to recruit only those willing to devote a year and who had a desire to search with us to form community. The world repeatedly goes to war. Our dream was to help call the Church to go to peace.

We advertised on our brochure a training program of nine-months duration. It would be the start of a movement called "Going to Peace" and would be qualitatively different than just an absence of war. I knew conflict could never be eliminated from the human experience. But the purpose would be to understand the significance of conflict, and to guide human assertiveness as a movement against evil. As nations recruited the young for war, the Church would evangelize the young for peacemaking. With Jesus, we would learn even to love our enemies.

There were times when I thought our effort to focus on the huge distant reality of nuclear war was just a grandiose illusion. What could we really do to stop evil? Was our effort at the Bethlehem Farm just a mirage used by our psyches to avoid the daily, hum-drum routine of insignificant acts? Were we escapists or were we realists? Were we listening to God, or to our own fractured and bruised spirits? Was I caught in a web of righteousness, allowing myself to feel superior to others, more concerned with God's will than others? Lord, I prayed, let your Spirit guide me, and not my ego.

Together, we also grappled with the practical concern of how to bring in income and sustain our efforts in a depressed economic region. We worked the Farm and held jobs beyond the Farm, but the collective income was never enough. In January 1986, some of the threads began to fray. Tensions about income and lack of gainful employment eroded confidence and hope. Some members felt irrelevant, and others were absent for periods of time.

I was reminded of the prayer, correctly or incorrectly attributed to Archbishop Oscar Romero: "It helps, now and then, to step back and take the long view." The Kingdom of God, he reminds us, is not only beyond our efforts, but even more compelling, beyond our vision. "We accomplish in our lifetime only a tiny fraction of the magnificent enterprise that is God's work. Nothing we do is complete, which is a way of saying that the Kingdom always lies beyond us. No statement says all that could be said. No prayer fully expresses our faith. No confession brings perfection. No pastoral visit brings wholeness. No program accomplishes the Church's mission. We are prophets of a future not our own."[51] We are simply those who in our own turn plant seeds hoping they will grow. I wanted to be among those prophets of peace.

Community is our calling, but so difficult to fashion and sustain. Many such efforts were rising up in this country in both Protestant and Catholic traditions—Sojourners, Charismatics, Holy Savior. Our Farm experiment in community never gained the momentum to truly stabilize or to solve the question of our basic identity. In a complex way, our efforts eventually got a vote of no-confidence and the Oregon Provincial pulled the plug. Fred and I left. It was hard leaving the Farm after two years of hard work. We believed we were on to something solid; it was just taking more time than we anticipated.

Fred opted to go to Yakima, to St. Joseph's parish. I put in a request to do a Peace Studies program with John Howard Yoder at the Mennonite Seminary in Elkhart, Indiana from 1986 to1987. Larry stayed on at the Farm, trying to carve out something in conjunction with JVC. Over the years, the Bethlehem Farm evolved into a Catholic Worker farm.

From 1987 to1989, living at St. Joseph's parish in Seattle, I became Jesuit Father Terry Shea's co-founder of the Oregon Province Peace and Justice Center. Later called the Inter-Community Peace and Justice Center, it was based out of Seattle University. Everything told me the Peace Center with its position papers and intellectualizing wasn't where I belonged, and yet I tried to be obedient. If obedience was the center of abandoning the ego, then I felt like I was battling God in my rebellion against this assignment. I filled my personal journals with questions. How could I be true to my own being and self-emptying at the same time? I was afraid my ego would drive me right out of the Society of Jesus. And to what? Emptiness, a non-identity, a vacuum where demons rush in?

I began saying Mass at Mount Virgin in Seattle, working with Laotian-Hmong-Kmuhu refugees who I came to greatly admire. I envisioned this as a way for the Peace Center to go on. In 1990, I was named pastor of Mt. Virgin parish.

The summer of 1991 was designated the Year of Ignatius. With walking still in our bones, Fred and I made a pilgrimage to Spain with twelve others. To pilgrim was our Jesuit heritage. St. Ignatius of Loyola, the founder of the Society of Jesus, was a seasoned pilgrim; in fact, he referred to himself and signed his letters "The Pilgrim." St. Ignatius had made a pilgrimage to Montserrat after being injured in battle. Ignatius desired that all Jesuits experience the power of pilgrimage–the humbling dependence, troubling disconnectedness, freedom, exhilaration, and simple, cheer-giving attitude. And so Fred and I walked from Loyola to the eleventh century Montserrat Monastery. We prayed for peace and justice as we walked in the footsteps of St. Ignatius.

CHAPTER 29

Uganda, Africa I:
How Shall I Walk with the Refugees?

✤

*"I could see that the African spirit—with its commitment to
communal, relational identity—offered gifts to our atomized
western world."*

ON MY SIXTY-FIFTH BIRTHDAY, SOMETHING stirred in me to take one more
wide swing through the stars in the company of the Jesuit Refugee Service
(JRS). Led by a hundred Jesuits, 150 lay people, and sixty religious men
and women, the JRS worked in over thirty-five countries. JRS was born in
1980 when Superior General Pedro Arrupe, SJ, gave the call for Jesuits to
get involved in worldwide refugee relief efforts. Inspired by the JRS commitment, I thought about losing life to find it. Why not explore, break
my patterns of comfort, and surrender myself to this beckoning mission?
I applied to serve, and in November, 1992, our Oregon Jesuit Provincial,
Steve Sundborg, SJ, approved my request. My assignment was to serve at
Rhino Camp, Uganda, on the Nile River near the Sudan border for two
years.

Echoing beneath my resolve and excitement were inner voices of
doubt and recrimination. *"What's wrong with you, Jack? Can't you ever
stay in one place? You are ever foolish, fleeing your work. Why can't you live
in the ordinary? Why are you forever wandering, running from the core, and
playing on the margins? This will be dangerous—and frightening. You are
too old."*

But Martin Buber's phrase came back to me about a kingdom of danger and of risk, a kingdom of holy insecurity. I felt I was being called to detach from all of my securities, and to journey as a pilgrim once more.

How would I walk with the refugees in Uganda? Did I have the courage to enter into this mass of struggling people, often traumatized by poverty and horrors beyond my experience? Did it make sense for an old dog like me to venture there? A mere three degrees north of the Equator, I would encounter starving people, severe malarial conditions, vast Nile basin swamps, the dreaded tsetse fly, a Babel of tribal languages, polluted water and frontier living. But something bright, a genuine joy in my deepest self, awakened in me.

How would I know this work was the will of God for me? Lay theologian, Frank Sheed, in his book "Theology and Sanity," helped me sort it out. God's will would consist of work I'd never thought of before. It would cost me something. And, however little I trusted my capability, my life experience would have prepared me for it.

From the beginnings of my vocation, I'd been attracted to the margins–Alaska, the Jesuit Volunteers, the long road to Bethlehem, now Africa. This fresh start connected me to Jesus, who made himself vulnerable, living with and for the poorest of the poor. Perhaps beneath the surface, I dreaded living a default life, an accidental life of some other person's determining or assigning. Choosing Africa grew organically out of my baptism: I wanted to put myself in the way of grace. The affirmation of the Provincial released something in me that quieted the accusing and doubtful inner voices.

The more I read about Africa, the more fragile and volatile the continent seemed. I felt a need to divest myself of belongings, to bare myself in poverty to the Spirit, to live where suffering couldn't be avoided. Every article I read was a lamentation. Every story contained the seeds of unfolding tragedy, always stemming from a colonial era of brash Western imposition upon the continent. Holding the refugees in my prayer as I prepared to leave, I followed my heart, sensing that their needs and mine would somehow meet. I had faith that the refugees, in their vulnerability and unearned misery, would thrust me into the presence of the crucified Christ. Perhaps accompanying them would also, in some small way, bring light to them in ways unknown.

I knew there was an immense distance between refugees and their condition, and me and my situation. But I trusted that the Holy Spirit, who called me to this journey, would bridge that gulf. All life is divine—even life awash in misery, and life dimmed by the distance of not knowing another's misery. I trusted God would emerge to break through ignorance and distance, free of borders and boundaries. As a Jesuit, as Church, as mission, I knew God wanted me in Africa.

The plight of the refugee could be abstractly sensed in figures from the United Nation's High Commission on Refugees (UNHCR). The population of 2.5 million the UN had cared for in 1970 had grown to eleven million in 1983. Ten years later, I would arrive in 1993 to serve a small portion of nineteen million desperate people. However, the UN counts as "official" refugees only those who cross borders. While these are deemed entitled to official international financial assistance, another twenty-eight million people that year had been put to flight within their own countries. These internal refugees were buffeted mercilessly by wars, economic dislocation caused by multinational corporate power, persecution based on race, religion or nationality, and other human rights abuses.

As I looked forward, I also looked backwards. I knew, after serving as pastor for almost four years at Mount Virgin Parish, it would be hard to leave. That community included Italian immigrants as well as the Hmong, Lao, Kmuhu and Lamet refugees from Laos for whom I'd come to feel much affection. By 1993, we had become a parish family. As the mystery of my own experience would unfold, these four Asian tribal groups had given me a foretaste of the bitter shocks and confusion of the refugee experience.

These Asians had arrived in Seattle a dozen years earlier, forlorn and confused, burdened with cruel, soul-breaking memories of indescribable experiences. Mountain people living a simple, pre-technological existence, they'd been caught between communist insurgents and the Western power and influence of first the French, then the Americans. Now, they had to deal with an utterly alien culture in the United States. Like plants brutally torn from their native soil and carelessly transplanted into foreign soil, they struggled to retain what they could of their ways of work, family life, language and culture, while adjusting to the English language and American values and patterns of life. Survival on their parts required great will to accept radical change. It also required generous welcome and openness from us Americans, and patience by everyone. Leaving my community made me sad. But I had to go.

CHAPTER 30

Uganda, Africa II: Adjumani

✥

*"Weeping, laughing and praying, they waited for God
to one day lead them in an exodus from this bondage
to their home land."*

On September 12, 1993, I arrived in Nairobi, Kenya on the eastern ridge of Africa. The Nairobi climate, with its thin mile-high air and breezes, was fabulous. Nairobi was filled with crowded streets and the constant movement of vital, lean people on foot. There was a miniscule middle class. Unemployment was 30 percent, under-employment much higher. Nairobi was described to me as a city in which a third of the people hire a second third at minimum wage, to protect their property from the final third.

The streets were bustling, but beneath the seething human traffic was a stark reality that broke my heart. Cheap Western merchandise was available for purchase. But mostly the streets were lined with little stands of "merchants" waiting to derive a scrap of livelihood from passersby, selling an ear of corn or a banana, a bit of gum, candy, or a single cigarette.

Refugees consisted of many extended families, usually three generations. They had been driven from place to place for years, as the war, like an evil tide, flowed and ebbed from one location to the next. Crossing into Uganda didn't promise a land of milk and honey, but it was better than entering either Ethiopia or Zaire. Dictator Mobutu Sese Seko's unpaid mob of an army in Zaire roamed and pillaged both local citizens and refugees.

It was reported that these mobs would raid refugee camps and strip the inhabitants of all they had, including every stitch of clothing. Escaping refugees arrived loaded down with grim memories of witnessing rapes and unspeakable forms of physical and emotional brutality to family members.

A woman named Clemintine told me she had fled the Nuba Mountain region in Sudan two years earlier, where a systematic rape program was underway. Soldiers, she reported, were given incentives to "purify" the people. Every child born from a Muslim father became, in their eyes, a Muslim. Mothers watched their young daughters and sons ripped from their homes and handed over to brutal Arab slave traders. As the Khartoum, Sudan government troops moved south, Christians, many of them members of the Nilotic tribes, were given three options—flee, be killed, or submit to coerced, radical Islamic conversion. These were the people to whom I would minister.

Sudan had become a British colony a century earlier. The British initiated a policy that sharpened the enmity between the Arab and Moslem north, and the exploited Christian and Animist south. Anti-Arab sentiment in the south arose from centuries of the predatory Arab slave trade. British colonization brought missionaries into the south during that period. By the time of my arrival, over 50 percent of our refugees would be Christian, largely Catholic.

Beginning in 1955, Sudan's more developed, Islamic north sought to compel submission by all tribes to their creed and government. The south rebelled, and seventeen years of war broke out. That war was followed by a ten-year truce. As Islamic fundamentalism gained ground during that time, war erupted again. The declared aim of Khartoum in the north was an Islamic nation with strict Sharia Law (Islamic Law) imposed politically as the law of the land. The secular judiciary was effectively destroyed. There was widespread torture, enslavement of women and children, and amputation of limbs as punishment for thievery. Isolated cases of actual crucifixions were reported.

When I first visited the JRS Refugee Clearing Center in Nairobi in 1993, the office was managed by Eugene Birrer, a Bethlehem Father from Switzerland. His JRS work was under contract with and funded by the

UN High Commission for Refugees as well as private, church sources in Europe. Birrer worked with a dozen employees, handling all new refugees coming into Nairobi. I encountered my first refugees as we drove through the gate. The eyes of two score black people stared at me. We had a car, food, security, control of basic resources; they had nothing but a will for their own survival. A thousand discordant, deeply troubling thoughts and feelings ran through me as I peered into the gulf separating them from me. Their collapsed world collided with my own intact, first world circumstances enclosing and protecting me like a glove.

These refugees were most likely from Sudan, Ethiopia, Rwanda and Somalia, but they could also be from seven other distressed African nations, driven from their homes by war and hatred, forced to wander. As explained by Birrer, "There are always more than we can handle. It's a steady stream that at times turns into rough waves of human need." The JRS had to build a high fence and tall gate at the street entrance with guards in order to get their work done. Inside the compound were sun shelters. Twenty people at a time were admitted from the waiting crowd outside. Who knew how long they had awaited their turn, or how desperate they might become? One by one their needs were determined and they were processed. More than 150,000 refugees lived in wretched slums in Nairobi, and woke each morning to join the masses of local residents searching for sustenance.

JRS in Nairobi provided start-your-own business assistance to entrepreneurial refugees. There were seventy-five projects from shoe-makers, chicken growers, furniture makers, bakers, and clothing menders. With grants from Europe and the USA, the office supported refugees' transitions into a sustainable life. I first met Abdul, a refugee from Somalia, sitting in an alleyway with a clutter of old battered shoes and a few new ones around him. He had a small stool, a little bag of tools, and a box of thread and leather. His shop was a make-shift wall of cardboard to protect him from the equatorial sun. Abdul arrived in Nairobi three years earlier with his wife and six small children. Because of hunger and lack of medicine, two of his children died. When I greeted him, I learned he was earning his way and feeding his family because of this JRS business program. Abdul flashed me a big smile. When he learned I was a priest, he held his hands together and bowed. He was grateful to Allah for life.

On September 19, 1993, I flew to Kampala, Uganda on my way to the small settlement of Adjumani. In the airplane, I was thrilled to look down on the vast blue surface of Lake Victoria, three-hundred miles across. Winston Churchill called it "the pearl of Africa." I wondered what Uganda had in store for me, and I remembered T.S. Eliot's words that old men ought to be explorers.

Kampala was still recovering from the dreadful war years of Idi Amin and Milton Oboto. In another time, it must have been a gem of a city, resting among the rolling hills flowering with lavish banana and mangos leaves, plovers perched on high trees, the heart of the famous Buganda kingdom still intact when the British colonials arrived. I saw intense poverty everywhere amid a fever of human movement. People who yearned to be industrious were desperate to survive. I witnessed drinking beyond limits, violence, robberies and burglaries. I learned that a diocesan priest was ambushed the night before I arrived. The thieves stopped his car and took his entire Sunday collection—about $200, a fortune in Uganda.

Nine hours of continuous driving up to Adjumani, my destination, couldn't have been rougher. It felt like an agitating washing machine. The black-top road ran out half way, as did the lush tropical verdure. My car mates, Sisters Dorothy and Maureen, veterans of many trips, didn't seem to mind. Celso Romanin, SJ, an Australian director of the Adjumani JRS project, commanded the wheel. When asked later about wildlife I'd seen, I remembered only three monkeys. Wars, starvation and wanton destruction by soldiers left a harsh mark on the native fauna and flora, as had a hundred years of systemic deforestation.

Small and ugly, Adjumani was two-thousand residents amid a mean clutter of dilapidated frame structures ringed by helter-skelter huts. A major crossing point on the Nile, the town appeared on most Ugandan maps prior to World War II due to its proximity to Sudan. Cotton growing and ginning, along with local marketing of maize, sorghum, and millet crops, gave this East Moyo district town a sustainable economy despite twenty years of brutal war. Dead and deteriorating power lines arched toward the earth along the roads south. Both electric power and black-top ended abruptly at Gulu, about 110 miles southeast. After seven years of peace, however, modest stability was emerging as trust seemed to be slowly returning. Adjumani's L-shaped main street was wide, allowing streams of walkers and a few vehicles, as well as rainy seasonal floods. At one end of the L, stood the impressive mission operation, built fifty years ago by the Comboni Fathers of Verona. At the other end, was our Jesuit compound.

Twelve of us lived in the Jesuit Refugee Service compound. Four of us slept in the only house, where we all ate, relaxed, and entertained one another. Several grass huts accommodated the other staff as well as guests. A large hut served as an office. Within were seven working desks, two computers, a copy machine, and shelves of books and manuals. We had four, all-wheel-drive vehicles, two Land Cruisers, and two Toyota Hilux pickup trucks. Two young women cooked for us. Three Sisters were the backbone of JRSs educational outreach work, running more than twenty-eight "under-the-trees" refugee grade schools, and one secondary school serving a refugee population of about 130,000.

Jesuit Refugee Service outreach in Uganda.

One day we drove to see the Nile. I was excited to view that romantic river where baby Moses had been hidden, where silent pyramids stood, where Anthony and Cleopatra bathed. This was the Nile whose thousands of miles of mysterious courses once set all Europe on edge to claim the wealth it promised. En route to the great river, we passed through four refugee camps, Robidere, Alere I, Ogujebi II, and the enormous Ogujebi I. These camps made me forget all about the Nile's allure. What I saw fascinated, appalled, and confused me. All along the fifteen miles of road between our compound and the Nile, hundreds of black men, women and children, like streams of satin ribbons, moved in both directions. Women, with babies strapped to their backs, balanced sacks of grain or heavy loads of wood on their heads.

Our vehicle bumped and jerked up through Robidere. Suddenly before us, down a long slope about five miles away, across the tops of the sea of grass refugee huts, flowed the mighty Nile. It was already a watery giant, as far as 3,500 miles upriver from Cairo. The river's beauty and riches were seductive—hippos, crocodile, papyrus, irrigational waters, teaming with fish. Fishermen stood on the shores with large catches of fish, hoping for a sale. But I was warned of the shadow side of the river. With malarial mosquitoes, tsetse flies, and belharzi parasites, her waters could be as lethal as the venom of a cobra. Local citizens usually selected wisely to live a good distance from her banks. Refugees, however, had no choice. They were placed where citizens refused to live. I was appalled to observe mothers both bathe and slake the thirst of their infants with these waters.

We approached this beach landing, a bustling, vibrant market with several dozen energized, laughing people. It was a swimming spot for children. While a thousand eyes stared at me, I detected nothing but curiosity. As we prepared to leave, I gazed once more out across the slow, deep waters of the Nile, moving north to Sudan and on to the Mediterranean. I pondered how many thousands of years these beautiful black people, whose smooth ebony skin reflected the sun, had found their livelihood on these beneficent shores. And how many had also suffered early death from the river.

From the strands of many conversations, I surmised that the refugees were both wise and industrious. Women were the haulers and held the community together; they were like the steel girders of a building under construction. Either nursing a new infant, carrying one on the back, or bending over the fire cooking, women were hard working, lovely, and motherly.

When refugees arrived at a newly assigned location, hundreds poured into a camp. Women and men began to construct a domestic world. The UNHCR would drill bore-holes for wells in anticipation of fresh water. Some wells yielded plentiful water, while at other pumps, "the water was tired." Imagine five-hundred to twelve-hundred people dependent upon one well pump, one spigot. From early morning to late at night, children and women, young and old, gathered to wait and pump. Men never pumped nor carried water. At times, there were fights at the wells between tribal groups or with local citizen groups. Refugees constructed shelters of plastic tarp or round straw huts with a roof like a mandala, and dirt floors. They built latrines. Cooking apparatus and bathing screens appeared. Where land was allotted, they would clear, dig, and plant. They built schools, chapels, mosques, tribunals, and market places. Births, pairings, sometimes marriages, and family would follow. They would mourn their dead, nurse their sick, and through their tribal forms of due process, punish offenders of social customs. Weeping, laughing, and praying, they waited for an exodus from this bondage that both rescued them from the miseries of their homelands, while imposing new and intense burdens. They yearned to return to a peaceable home land. Many would wait for years.

Roosters crowed each morning, tearing open the still envelope of night. Dawn arrived as the equatorial sun with its rosy fingers of light painted the eastern horizon. I marveled at its rise, a steady vertical ascent through a row of eucalyptus trees in our compound. Charged with promise and dread, the unstoppable, radiating orb would take full charge of the day like a soldier on duty. With it came the precipitous rise in temperature. By noon, I was walking on my own boxy shadow, and realized it was time to hide from the unforgiving rays.

The rainy season came upon us with vehement downpours. The colossal slam-bang thunder claps and spectacular lightning displays were a show well worth writing home about. Due to the heavy rains, our compound blazed with flowers and was visited by a thousand big, golden butterflies. After a drenching, it took no time at all for the penetrating sun and sandy soil to dry everything out. The natives never invented rain gear. They simply got wet, shivered for a while, and then were warmed again by the sun's return.

Sunday, October 8 was my first Mass in the camps. Hot winds blew. I drove to Alere I, about eight miles from the compound. As we traversed a dried streambed that served as our road with huge holes, bumps and dips, I wondered what my white religion from the West could offer these refugees. Would Christian belief sound like mumbo-jumbo to them? Still unanswered was the key question: what do the words "give us this day our daily bread" mean to people whose hunger is always with them like their very limbs? I was told that some mothers had to feed their babies tiny stones to deceive their empty bellies and quiet their cries.

Immediately upon arrival in the camp, our white vehicle was surrounded by a gentle mob of semi-naked children. They came to touch and stroke the shiny car. Our arrival signaled it was time for them to beat their bell, a hanging lorry wheel. The noisy clanging traveled far in the silent air, alerting all that Mass would begin. A roughhewn, small altar rested beneath the shade of three giant trees whose branches and foliage covered an expanse of ground. Seating consisted of gnarled logs in semi-circular rows upon which radiant, thin, children perched and gawked. Their easy presence released my tension, and replaced it with gladness. I walked about offering a hand to shake. Each one shyly reciprocated. Lots of respect for "Father." And also respect for a Mosungo, the Swahili word for white man; it was the Mosungo who had success and means.

By 10:30, morning Mass began. The well-formed choir of men and women captivated me. They sang loudly, strongly, and in harmony. They played eight-stringed, roughhewn harps of graduated sizes. Seven gave seven octaves. Ten delicate girls flowed with ease in front of me. To the cadence of the drum, their small bodies began the entrance dance. There were two other dances that affected me deeply–for the Gospel, and for the offertory. These modest, reserved girls looked me straight in the eyes, unflustered, unperturbed by either my presence or their performance. I was startled by how young were the congregants, and later learned that the average age in the camps was probably no greater than 14 years old. Older folks were forced to remain behind in Sudan and leave the journey of the refugee to the young. So many men had been killed in battle.

Greetings in the refugee camp.

A good number of refugees were Catholic, up to 60 percent in some locations. Twenty-eight settlements had chapels. The next largest denomination in Sudan was Anglican. About one-third of the people embraced their traditional animistic ways, believing that natural physical objects and entities possessed a spiritual essence. Hardly any men came to Mass, and among the women who did, many refrained from communion because of the clash between the laws of church and local custom. The bride-price, or as some called it, bride-wealth, had to be paid for a man and a woman to present themselves at communion as married. The typical price–about ten cows–was to be paid by the groom or his family to the parents of a daughter to confirm marriage. That price was beyond what most men could pay over several years. Legitimacy was determined by a trial to decide whether payment was complete. To find a young couple at communion when the bride-price wasn't fully paid was to stir up trouble. Most marriages were neither tribal nor church approved. Polygamy was also sometimes practiced.

A catechist told me his in-laws alerted him that they were coming to take home his wife, even though she had a five-month-old baby with her husband. Why? Because the husband hadn't paid the full bride-price. He paid $40, but they demanded $75, as well as twelve goats, twelve hoes, a hurricane lantern, and one spear. He didn't have it, nor would 95 percent of the refugees. The catechist had three children by a former wife for whom he'd paid in full. When the third child got sick, the in-laws pressured him for a witch-doctor intervention, but he refused. His wife, loyal to her parents, left him. As for the bride-price for this second wife, he said his brother might be able to help, but he'd gone back to Sudan, looking for a cure for the sick child. These were the ways in Africa.

On October 22, 1993, I turned 66 years old. If I had come to Africa twenty years earlier, I wouldn't have been so tired. Fitting into a diverse, close living community of religious and lay men and women would have been easier when I was younger. However impossible it all seemed to actually be in northern Uganda, I was glad I had come. It felt like fingers were reaching deep into my inner clay and kneading away all the lumps. Grace was working. My outer journey and inner journey were joined in this great land. Externally, I was on the frontier–the Nile, the equator, the heat, lack of amenities, difficulties of community life, being present with refugees, visiting the camps, trying to be a sign of hope. Internally, I was wrestling with many things, but could see that something larger than them all wrestled with me. I trusted that all these forces, harsh or gentle, contributed to changing my inner self. I believed I could do very little for others unless I consciously chose to empty myself of self.

Jack is gifted with a chicken.

Sister Maureen made a cake for my birthday celebration. After a lovely chicken, sweet potato, and carrot supper, I blew out the candles. Our community drank wine, laughed and talked, then retired to our "TV screen"– the wide canopy of stars above. I located the Southern Cross, but felt lonely missing my northern celestial friends–Cassiopeia and the North Star. As I silently gazed in wonder, I realized my life itself had been full of bright stars. But I couldn't get away from the disparity between the abundance I felt in my own life and the almost universal penury and long-suffering of the massive refugee population. ·

Waking to breakfast meant cornmeal mush and coffee. Mike Dorlar, SJ, from the Detroit Province, joined me. I remember his words, "Sometimes I feel like an unappreciated cow. All they want is my milk." It was true. The more we went out to the camps in the role of priest, the more we became known, and the more we were known, the greater the number of needy people asked us for help. They came quietly, with subtle body language and pleading eyes fixed on us. *"I have no milk for my baby. I need food for my sick child. I need medicine. My daughter is unable to get up, please come pray over her. Do you have a pen? Some clothing for my baby, a blanket? Could you get someone in America to sponsor my school fees? Do you have a Bible, a rosary, something to read, chalk for the nursery school, money for transportation?"* Each an individual wave, together a sea of deprivation that I felt could easily drown my heart.

Within the JRS community, we discussed the issue of begging, giving, not giving. At the compound, the policy was to discourage begging. Fr. Celso said we couldn't allow the refugees to turn us into a welfare oasis. And we needed to attend to the twenty-eight grade schools scattered throughout the camps. We couldn't satisfy even a small fraction of the needs of 100,000 refugees to whom we were assigned, who lived in many settlement villages. I tried to remember that our primary mission was to be a sign of hope through our educational and pastoral work. We couldn't address the unending current of need. It was hard to imagine, but sixty-thousand people were still waiting just to be processed. Some twenty-thousand were to be transferred by barge up the Nile to the remote Rhino Camp where they would have a tiny plot of land to till. My role was to take charge of pastoral ministry for these Sudanese refugees who fled the ruthless policies of the Islamic Fundamentalist government of Khartoum, whose aim was to cleanse Africa's largest nation of any non-Islamic influence.

My body regularly felt like a container of anxieties. I couldn't shake off concerns about malaria and disease at Adjumani, among the refugees, and as a threat to JRS workers like myself. Fr. Celso, my companion, had been working for eight or nine months and seemed fearless, but both a sister and a scholastic came down with the fever. The Gospel proved helpful. Jesus reminded me that his glorification was connected to being like the grain of wheat that falls into the ground and dies. This parable challenged me. To go about protecting my life, failing in courage because of doubt and fear, would have caused me to lose my life. I must love my life as Jesus loved it, so I could go into the spiritual battle.

The refugee reality drove me into the deepest reaches of my soul. I often felt marginal, inadequate in my assignment, and struggled against the vast terrain of need. Was it my puny spirit rather than the Holy Spirit? When I finally prayed for humility and openness, I imagined Our Lady holding

Jesus in her lap, and the Christ child holding in his hands the earthly globe with one human race. If I could have a wish fulfilled, it would be that every parish throughout the world would have a central furnishing in its sanctuary–a large globe of planet earth held tight by Jesus–the perfect expression of our universal home and commitment to one another.

Three days before Christmas, 1993, Fr. Celso, Kessi and Margaret journeyed to Koboko. Word came back that their vehicle had been ambushed. Celso was shot in the lower left arm. Much to our surprise, shortly after hearing the ugly news, they showed up. Margaret was driving. Kessi was fine. A sling, fashioned in the hospital in Gulu, held up Celso's arm. Their vehicle bore several bullet holes penetrating the side, seat and headrest, and they were relieved to get home to our compound. Apparently, they were hit by one lone, shirtless assailant, most likely drunk, and willing to kill to take possession of the small four-wheel drive vehicle which was very marketable in Zaire. In spite of these risks, we couldn't dare quit because of danger. Instead, we were to be simple as doves, unafraid, and cunning as serpents on the alert.

January, 1994, a new year, and still I hadn't gone to my main and waiting assignment, Rhino Camp. There were big problems at this campsite: bore holes coming in dry, the tsetse fly, and sleeping sickness. I continued to wait, trying to carve out a space to be involved and productive where I was. So many fears invaded my heart about Rhino. I worried about being sent there all alone. My age and language were barriers. I worried about malaria, sleeping sickness, the long delay in setting up the camp, the difficulties of transporting refugees there. I wondered if I should just pull the plug and move on to other work. Little did I know I would be four more months at Adjumani, waiting for a new beginning.

Luckily at Adjumani, my window faced the east. I observed the sun rising. What is the light of the sun? It drives away darkness so we don't stumble. It creates a world of color and connection. It helps us distinguish between friend and foe, familiar and strange. You, O God, come as new light! In each twenty-four-hour period, God says again, "This is who I am. I come so you can see me for who I am, so that you can be who you are."

CHAPTER 31

Uganda, Africa III:
Lamentations and Inspirations

⊕

"Without babies, death would have reigned.
Without babies, the sun would not rise."

AT THE END OF MAY, 1994, I left for Rhino Camp for my long-awaited assignment, sixty miles up the Nile, on the other side. Within the camp was a large transit settlement, processing and medically screening thousands of refugees. The refugees were promised they could till small plots of land. Before the desecration and poaching during Idi Amin's terror, Rhino had been home to magnificent white rhinos, now extinct. Once it had the reputation of an international tourist spot where even Teddy Roosevelt visited. The place was now hot and forsaken. It harbored scorpions, tsetse flies, and malarial mosquitoes. UNHCR expected to relocate 25,000 refugees here. They planned to give each family six poles and a large sheet of plastic to build a shelter. In contrast, my own house in Rhino was round with two sleeping rooms and a sitting room, indoor plumbing (but no running water), with four hours of electricity in the late evening fueled by a generator.

Rhino Camp was surrounded by rural communities where the unsophisticated ways of an ancient past pushed through, locking in many native tribal languages. Sounds of young children at play, chanting, singing, drumming, and dancing stole the evening. All around me was a lifestyle of subsistence living, going back thousands of years, enfolded by nature and the elements. But I could see that the African spirit—with its commitment to communal, relational identity—offered gifts of insight and human connection that contrasted with our atomized Western world.

A 14-year-old orphan raised her little brother and sister, acting as a mother and father to them. All around, I saw 5-year-olds with small babies strapped to their backs. It was just the way it was. In the cycle of survival, 4-year-olds carried small water containers from the bore-hole. Complaining didn't seem to be a major factor. Life was simply difficult, and no one expected otherwise.

I was impressed and elevated by the inner resources of these people. If laughter was a sign of happiness, there was more happiness among the children and adults in the refugee camps than in Seattle, Portland and San Francisco combined. I studied the symmetry of their faces. There was magic in their smiles. I could go on about what I considered their dignity and beauty, but I'm afraid I would sound beguiled or duped, or that I was merely romanticizing.

By September, despite nets, repellant spray, vitamins and garlic, I was dealing with my second case of malaria. It stole my fire. It made me so weak that I spent my days just sitting, reading, writing letters, and waiting for my body to heal. The saying goes—you're really not in Africa until you experience malaria. Globally, each year, malaria takes the lives of an estimated two to three million, although 300 million contract the disease.

While recuperating, my thoughts would run away from me. This whole business of a preferential option for the poor, while a solid call, wasn't easy to fulfill. My discouraged reveries took me to the millions of dollars in aid from the World Bank and International Monetary Fund, so little of which reached the refugees. Aid organizations contracted for vector eradication, building structures, roads and culverts, and hauling food. Blankets, cooking pots, generators arrived, and bore-holes were sunk into the African earth for water, but at every level, we encountered interference by way of government greed, ruthless politicking, bandits and crooks. So where did hope lie for the refugees? They seemed to possess a preternatural ability to live realistically in the present, and not give up on the future. How? It was that quality of the human spirit that hurls a harpoon into the future, trusting a grand catch. We humans seriously mess things up through our sin, but the reality of a sturdy hope shows we are made to carry God's image in our being, forward through unceasing need.

Christmas 1994. Since coming to the refugee camps, I'd been overwhelmed with the omnipresence of babies. Five young women, strong, attractive, sensual and motherly were walking down the road, four with babies cinched up, riding their hips. Five women occupied a log at Mass, four had suckling babies clutched to them. In every village, at every family compound, babies would pour out the doors to surround me. Women's breasts weren't part of a woman's sexual apparatus, but rather an ingenious milk bottle and pacifier. Many refugee women would have six, seven or eight children.

While the world debated the threat of the population bomb, and opinions swirled around issues of abortion, birth control, and the world's limited resources, my time in the camps shifted my viewpoint. Without babies, death would have reigned. It seemed that without babies, the sun would not rise. Without babies, everyone would give up. Babies were the reason mothers marched single file for twenty hours with heavy loads of wood on their heads, sweat pouring down their faces. Selling the wood would bring them the equivalent of $1 or less. Why would they endure this? Because they had babies to feed.

A refugee I met named Alice showed just such endurance. She had given birth to seven children. Four were with her and three had been lost in Sudan, including one that had been grabbed in a raid and taken off for slave labor. Her husband had been killed. Alice wondered daily how she would feed her remaining family. I asked her, "Do you pray, Alice?" She said, "I pray always. I look at each day for what I have, and I thank God for each day, all day, and all night."

Camp life was grim, harsh, congested, an oppressive beehive. But the children, seemingly oblivious to despair, put gloom on the run. They were like patches of bright wildflowers. I came to see their presence as a sacrament of hope, superior to all others. My message to refugees centered more and more on hope, that essential food for the human spirit. Wordlessly and with abandon, with looks, laughter and upward gestures, the children sang their song, "don't worry, be happy," and endlessly acted out the mystical insight of Juliana of Norwich: "And all is well, all shall be well, and all manner of things shall be well."[52] Babies and children kept these suffering people sane, centered, bold and resilient. The babies in the camps raised up the adults. I came to believe that without them, the men and women were lost.

Jack celebrates the children.

How fortunate was I to take part in the birth of a Sudanese infant? I was driving a pickup to Moyo, five miles from the Sudan border, when my companions and I spied a group of women circled around the trunk of a tree by the road. I slammed on the brakes.

A young woman, dreadfully poor, and in labor for an entire day, needed a hospital. We invited the parents, the birthing mother, and four others to climb into the bed of our truck. Very soon the labor pains, like a high tide, came over the mother. Expectant mothers often carried string and scissors with them so wherever they were at the time of birthing, they could stoop and sever the umbilical cord. Maybe it was the bouncing along the rough road that precipitated the birth, but birth it was going to be. I stopped and got out to watch the hairy top of the head pushed through the stretched portal of the mother. It happened so fast–the baby just shot out. Momentarily I thought, "Oh my God, the head has come loose." Then I beheld the whole baby. With me were two sisters, both midwives. The advent of the tiny, wet, black female body filled the mother and parents with supreme joy. They named her after my mother, Violet Agnes. I cradled her gleaming body, struck by the wonder of this gift from God. Those of us in the circle of her presence were blessed and redeemed by this innocent infant, launched on her life journey in the African bush.

Life and death were joined in the camps. Illness was an ever-present fact of life. James, one of the best church leaders, and a father of five, died suddenly one afternoon. He was only 25-years old. His body was in the ground before noon the next day. By the time I got to Ofogi at four, bamboo poles held up roofs of papyrus, plastic, and canvas to shield people from the rays of the sun. The drumming and wailing (my Irish people call it keening) had commenced. Drumming began with the death, and it was mostly the women who openly wailed and lamented. Thirty feet from where the blanketed body lay, a circle of men supervised the digging of the grave in the shadow of James' family hut. Women warded off flies with their handkerchiefs. A lane parted for me as I moved to the body. I donned a stole, sprinkled holy water, led prayers, and spoke words of comfort through a translator, feeling all the while the incongruities of my presence. I eventually came to see that the Christian faith was as much theirs as mine. In fact, Sudan is mentioned several times in the Bible, and in the first centuries of the faith, there were African popes. They saw the faith not as alien, but as something lost and found.

Early the next morning, while the breeze was still up, I returned for the burial Mass. A table was set up in front of one of the grass huts with three-hundred neighbors and family present. Many were tired, having drummed and lamented all through the night. James' body was placed in a grave, six-foot deep with a narrower trench and logs sufficient to cradle the body. Over the body were carefully laid papyrus mats, fresh grass, mud, and mounded dirt to form an earthen tomb. The family carefully laid out the body and prepared it. The grieving took place right there in their midst where they continued to live. Drumming was continuous, and at Mass they sang in their native Kukou language to the accompaniment of udungus, or native harps: "James lived Jesus' life, and is now gone to paradise." Young women sprinkled blossoms around the site. The men who stomped the mud and pounded the grave washed their feet and sweaty arms as I lifted up the community in Eucharistic prayer. I told them that for Christians, the sadness of death gives way to the bright promise of immortality. James' life was changed, but not ended. After Mass, the feast of maize, beans, and sugared tea began. Following those hours of worship and communion, the people resumed their regular refugee status.

In early 1995, I began a blanket fund in the United States. Seventy-two people contributed $4,500. Fifty blankets were distributed for each chapel. Some, who already had one, received another blanket. Some sold the new blanket for $3, more than they could make in three weeks of work, and bought soap, salt or sugar. I observed exemplary sharing within the clan but this generosity seemed to diminish in the wider tribal group, and disappeared altogether across tribal lines. Wasn't that human nature?

During Easter week, 1995, I traveled from one camp to another. I was astounded by the palpable joy in these people who wouldn't give up. "Father, welcome. He is risen. He is risen!" I baptized from twenty to fifty babies at each place. After the pouring of water, I generously doused the whole congregation as the women with babes in arms followed me in procession, dancing rhythmically, through and around the open-air chapel. The whole congregation extended hands over the newborn babes to bless them, "O baptism, O baptism, we take on the life of Christ and shall live forever."

Our last camp on Easter Day was Eden, where two-thousand refugees had arrived just six weeks earlier. Many people had been without food one or two days. They were given a blue plastic tarp for their shelter, and one or two blankets per family. I worked with an assistant, Kassiano, a native of Lugbara, the tribal area in which we all lived. A few days earlier, we'd spread the word in Eden that we would have Easter Mass there. Refugees cleared a spot under a generous shade tree where a quaint pole and grass chapel were hastily erected. Women appeared with bright dresses, scads of naked babies, and scantily clad children. Many of these people, forced to move over and over in Sudan due to the war, had not seen a priest or been to Mass, for months, even years.[53]

At Mass, the people's spirits lit up. Ululating, they clapped, swayed and smiled. The *Our Father* sounded bold and repetitive in the Kakau language. Ironically, part of my sermon told the story of Jesus, Mary, and Joseph as refugees. I explained that the Bible was the story of a refugee people, whose God was leading His people home. My words were translated for the Bari, Acholi, and Madi into the imposed language of Sudan which was Arabic, the language of the Qur'an. My message: Fear not! Our God is a God who saves. After a few prayers, the young women rhythmically processed to the sound of the udungus, drums and rattles, and full singing. The bearing of gifts followed. Later in the night, I realized keenly that this had been the most extraordinary Easter week of my life. My heart was full of gratitude for the privilege of being with these amazing people who made God's presence and immense love so real.

Jack blesses a child.

In the refugee camps, I saw an image of the whole human race. I saw a people dispossessed, trapped in the midst of war, famine and violence. I realized that what I witnessed was the true condition of the human race. Like the refugees, we had been driven out of our homeland, the Garden of Eden, and now we were trapped in darkness, unable to solve the riddle of life. We, all of us, are refugees, and our only genuine release and liberation is through God's love.

My venture into refugee work proved to be an inward journey. It was God's way of coming to me as a stranger, rapping on my back door. I learned that strangers can bring new light, new revelation into my life. In these people, who have an almost inviolable relationship to the earth, sky and elements, I caught glimpses of the divine. The fragile human vessel I discovered in Africa, is imbued with a great capacity to cradle heaven's beauty. In spite of the immense human suffering, I left full of hope and confidence. Seeing God in these dear people in ways I'd never seen before, was the greatest reward of my life in Africa.

My time in the camps came to a close on June 12, 1995. Some parasite had taken up residence within me. Shortly after Pentecost, I flew out of Kampala to our Jesuit residence in Addis Ababa, Ethiopia, then on to London to check in at the Centre for Tropical Medicine, where I hoped the parasite could be located and eliminated. I shifted my attitude: whatever comes, comes. I felt content and untroubled. The God who works through the flawed and the ordinary was present, and I trusted in his promise to always heal us in our depths.

From London, my health on the mend, I returned to the Pacific Northwest to pastor at St. Francis Parish and work with the Jesuit Volunteer Corps. Around Christmas, 1995, a 20-year-old Sudanese refugee was referred to me when I was in Seattle. Adut Madut was a very tall woman with a refined, serene face and manner. Six years earlier, as a girl, she witnessed her father tortured and killed in front of her, and her family scattered. Adut was seriously injured trying to escape from the killers. She struggled her way to Khartoum, experiencing long months of physical pain, hunger, and fear along the way. From there, she fled to Liberia, where again the madness of war exploded. She was in the place where four nuns (two Americans) were murdered. Again, Adut had to flee, this time to Sierra Leone, where it seemed God opened a door to a refugee resettlement program. Upon arriving in Seattle, she tried to put her life together. What a miracle was my Adut! I was so impressed with her natural refinement. Her faith miraculously intact, she went to daily Mass, convinced that Jesus had saved her life. We became close friends. Adut represents tens of thousands like her. Young, vulnerable, dispossessed refugees looking for a way to reassemble their lives. They lacked education and training in the skills needed for success in the West, and lived on the edge. Many survived, a few prospered, but some did not. Adut symbolized the escape from evil and violent policies, political tyrants, and mob rule. She was the embodiment of God's sorrow and hope.

I had been sending money to help a friend, Doreen Oyella, at the Uganda Spiritual Formation Center. We first met at the Sacred Heart Sisters' community in Adjumani when she was a refugee, running to Uganda. I also sent what I could to Sister Rebecca Abiyo, head-mistress of the Iceme Girls' Secondary School for 450 girls in Lira, Uganda for several years. Sometimes the money was stolen in route. But when it did get to them, it was used for medicine, salt, soap, to build a latrine, to help their most desperate congregants, to furnish school supplies, food, shelter and uniforms for the girls in the school. They had an endless flowing river of worthy needs. It became a "school" without walls or roof when Rebecca, with twenty-six teachers and hundreds of girls had to high-tail it south, running in panic for hours with just the clothes on their backs. They escaped the invading rebels from Sudan who were on a rampage to pillage, burn, profit and rape. When the rebels destroyed their villages, the women and girls could not return to their homes. Instead, they camped next to another school forty miles away, living in make-shift grass huts and classrooms, sleeping on the ground. They could neither grow nor harvest crops because of constant raids. They lived on a ration of pasho, or corn-meal mush, sometimes with rice or beans. What they most wanted was money to purchase a generator so the girls could study at night for two hours. Sister Rebecca wrote me in a letter: "We sing, drum, dance and pray a whole lot to drive our inner darkness away. A priest comes once a week for

Mass. Our spirits remain strong." As long as I might live, I have promised to keep supporting her apostolic work.

I hadn't gotten Africa out of my blood, and my soul was restless. In the summer of 1996, I flew to Guinea and Ivory Coast in West Africa to give retreats, and a course for Mother Teresa's Sisters. I also learned that Holy Cross University was awarding me an honorary doctorate for my role in getting JVC started.

In August 1997, I returned for a second time to Kampala, Uganda to serve as a retreat director and pastoral minister, and to do leadership development with priests, sisters and laity. I was drawn back to the African paradox where the have-nots of the world are really the haves, and the haves of the West, like me, are really the impoverished ones.

I could never have come to feel as much enthusiasm about the Church without living in Africa. Sunday worship was not strictly sacramental. It was a time of communal blessing for the young, the unmarried, and the old. You had to be touched by the faith of catechists who were the heart of the Church in Uganda. Yes, their theological training was poor in some ways, but there was so much spirit. These men and women put aside the chance of making even a little income and instead walked miles and miles to a meeting. They paid for their commitment with blood and energy. Their families suffered, too, because of their devotion to Jesus Christ. Scripture reminds us, "Did not God choose those who are poor in the world to be rich in faith and heirs of the kingdom that he promised to those who love him?"[54]

In spring, 1998, my brother, Rob, visited me in Uganda. He was surprised to learn that 60 percent of the people existed without clean drinking water, 85 percent had no electricity, and 60 percent lived on less than $1 a day. The teen pregnancy rate was the highest of any sub-Saharan African nation. It was hard to fathom that a middle class child in the United States consumes 40 times that of a Ugandan child.

Just like so many adventurous Americans, Rob was most eager to see the famous Ugandan mountain gorillas. I journeyed with him. We rented a four-wheel drive vehicle and found ourselves on the road to the Bwindi Impenetrable Forest National Park in southwest Uganda. Spectacular scenery greeted us on every side. Once into the mountains, we marveled at the myriad slopes terraced right to the sky, a centuries-old mountain culture. Rob went out to tramp the Impenetrable Forest for twelve hours led by guides hacking through the vines and growth. They got caught in the darkness. Rob returned utterly exhausted, but he had seen the gorillas from ten feet away. I was grateful we avoided harm since there were rebel groups active in the mountains as well as on Uganda's borders.

It was Joseph Kony's Lord's Resistance Army in the North that had earned the most malevolent reputation for banditry and mayhem. Kony attacked his own people if he believed they'd cooperated with the Ugandan government. Thousands of school-age girls had been abducted and forced to be "wives" for the bandits. Once captured, the boys and girls were forced to beat one of their school chums to death, or die themselves; it was a tactic of perverse and brutal bonding that turned boys into killers.

All told, I embarked on four trips to Africa–1969 as mission director in Zambia; 1993 with the Jesuit Refugee Service in Uganda; 1996 giving retreats in Guinea and Ivory Coast with the Mother Teresa Sisters; and 1997 in Kampala for retreat work and vocation promotion with Brother Fred. One of the liveliest, most richly textured Masses of all my time in Africa started with a procession of three-hundred people–grandmothers down to children–through the slums of Kampala where they lived. Every beautiful face I saw revealed a deep dignity and solid character. From where did their amazing joy and enthusiasm come in the midst of serious hunger, sickness, and the looming threat of death? They were utterly convinced that God sustained them. Even the children could shut their eyes and sway in prayerful singing, drumming and clapping. They knew how to endure and to wait. Blessed are the poor, the hungry and those who weep, for they shall be the first to inherit and to laugh.

After 2001, I would never return to Africa. I knew I would miss the vast continent. I would miss the brilliance of the sun and the lucid night skies. How I would miss the beauty of the people. I would miss something deeper than it all, something intangible having to do with God's presence with the poor, with the broken-hearted, with those who mourn.

The African lives by experience, testing all with the senses. It rains, and rains hard. The grass gets wet; it dries. The animals get wet; they dry. Why invent an umbrella? The West, it seems, invented the concept of invention. Westerners want to change what is, to shield ourselves from the earth. Africans simply live with what is. For them, it is natural to speak of the famine season, plants, animals and humans longing for rain, yet waiting patiently. To endure, to wait, to adapt to fit into nature, to live simply is their way. At the heart of their culture of survival is hospitality: we're in this together and we need to stick together. It is a culture of sharing and accommodating. Hosting is legendary. Privacy is unimportant. There's always room for another, whether in the home, at a party, or on the bus.

What I witnessed in Africa was a land and culture full of extremes—bounty and deprivation. As a continent, it seemed beyond human management, a place where it was impossible to tame the human fire. Nothing could be controlled, and this led to surrender and humility, or revolt. Africa was a mosaic of tribalism and communalism within the tribes. But these relationships were largely torn and broken in large measure as a result of the domination patterns introduced from the West. It was a place that unleashed unimaginable acts of evil. But overall, the African people had a commitment to their own dignity. I found the society to be filled with people where extraordinary virtue was ordinary.

Africa changed my life. The beautiful African people returned to me the dance and the drum, and gave me back the beat of my heart.

CHAPTER 32

Time Speeds Up

"The best way to hang on is to let go."

As THE YEARS STACKED ONE on top of the other and time sped up, I knew I must get serious about writing my story. I needed to find a place conducive to complete that project. In 2002, the new Oregon Provincial wanted me to go to one of the Native American stations. I would try, I said to myself, but nothing seemed to fit. Finally, I was assigned to be pastor of St. Mary by the Sea parish on the coast in Rockaway, Oregon. I ministered there from 2004 to 2009. Life was relatively simple. I cooked and cleaned for myself, but occasionally accepted a haircut from a parishioner. Each day, I read from a book of saints and heroes of peace and justice. On Sundays, I preached God's love, and told my parishioners that being holy meant doing good works, and creating beauty from within you. I preached: we are all connected to one another and to creation, we are ultimately not in charge, and we need not worry—all will be well. After Mass, we often retired to the parish center for hot cinnamon buns and marvelous conversation. I loved St. Mary's and made such dear, kind friends there. I loved the sea. But I got little writing done, except some poetry:

Rockaway Beach
Here at the seashore waves heave up
Frothing and galloping like mad horses
Colliding, tumbling, racing shoreward...

The sight, the sound, the ceaseless fury
The frenzy of it all here on the shore
Is but the restless edge of something more.

Lift both eyes, tear them from this frayed hem
Scan the vast, seamless plain of blue.
Absolute silence, unbounded serenity
Without fence, road, path or word
With fingertip at the westernmost edge
Trace in wonder earth's confining curvature.
Unzipped, a pellucid sky folds back over us
And all the world, brooding with great wings. (2005)

In a final effort to write, I left Rockaway and came to Portland to live with my fellow Jesuits at the Columbiere community. I struggled to be productive at my task. I had spent hours telling my story to my friend Bennett Comerford. In the late spring of 2011, Mike Merriman, a friend and former Jesuit, suggested I work with writer Barbara Scharff to organize my project. Over many months and get-togethers, she and I became good friends. She tried to motivate me, impose some discipline on my philosophizing and meandering memories, and pull the project together.

Why was it that I wanted to write but I just couldn't sit down and do it? Why did there exist such tensions and opposite pulls in me? What were the divisions and dualities about in my mind? What was up and down about, inside and outside, subject and object, sickness and health, suffering and joy, affliction and triumph, tragedy and comedy, and heaven and hell? No matter what concept I thought of, I could find a split, a differentiation, an opposite. Is everything in the world matched and opposed? Or is it just the peculiar bent of the ego to see this? Why was I so stuck in my own tension?

I'm convinced that paradox addresses this mental system of dualities. Paradox was a primary tool Jesus used to shake up the illusions of the ego, the deceptions that separate us from everyone and everything else. Jesus' own, "The last will be first, and the first will be last," [55] and "Whoever finds his life will lose it; and whoever loses his life for my sake will find it,"[56] are paradoxes that exemplify this. Fullness comes from emptying. The best way to hang on is to let go. God's strength comes to fruition in our weakness. These paradoxes force the human mind out of isolated mirages and the ego's fixation. They stir up, agitate and set loose the preparation for inner spaciousness in search of the truth, in search of union with others, and oneness with God.

Take life and death. In our madness, we fear looking at death, and hence we are unable to really calm down, to embrace and know life. It is absolutely certain that Jesus put a lot of effort into showing us the paradox that to die is to live. Without a keen sense of death, our lives become trivial, mundane and inconsequential. Jesus draws us into wholeness out of our ego selves.

One of the most dramatic and paradoxical ways I was called to equanimity and wholeness was in losing my health, and accepting my illness and disabilities. I got very sick and was hospitalized after Christmas 2011. My Jesuit companions reminded me that when I was released from the hospital, the doctors gave me three days to live. I was skin and bones.

Peter Byrne, SJ, and Brother Fred nursed me to life and took very good care of my needs at the Columbiere Jesuit community in Portland. So many dear friends and family came to commune, to reminisce, to sit quietly, to pray and hold my hand as I rested. I was so grateful to see my brothers, Pat and Rob, and my niece Patricia. Many former JVs, Bethlehem Peace Pilgrims and Jesuits came to be with me. Adut, the lovely refugee from Sudan, stopped by a few times. It was also during that period when I felt released from the writing project. With hope and great relief, I handed over my files, private letters, many of my journals, and photos to Barbara Scharff and asked her to lead the way, to see this project through. Her enthusiasm lifted from me the dread burden of failing to do the writing I had so long felt called to do. I also asked her to seek insight from Peter Byrne, Fred Mercy, JVC Northwest Executive Director Jeanne Haster, my brothers Pat and Rob, and her husband, Gary Scharff.

During this twilight time, I remember a very personal and honest reconciliation with Peter, and with my God. Oh, how it set my soul free! I'll let Peter offer his recollection of those days and that time:

"Bringing Jack home to what we thought were to be his final days was a singular grace for me personally, for our whole community, and, I believe, for Jack himself. It was a privilege to be able to attend to his body, to learn to feel comfortable turning him, washing him, and getting some food and nourishment into him. I spent many hours sitting quietly with Jack while he dozed or slept.

Several in our community gathered with him each day to celebrate the Eucharist, which for Jack became more and more the essence of his faith, his deep surrender into God's love for him. That interlude in our community allowed Jack's family to come and visit together, to assemble the beginnings and fragments of their lives growing up in Anaconda and then dispersed to many parts of the world. Here they all were once again, bringing the strands together. Jack was profoundly grateful for this.

Being with Fred Mercy, Jack's loyal friend and companion, was also a gift for which I am very grateful. Fred showed what it means to be a faithful friend. Fred was a man who followed the Book of Ruth's famous line: "For wherever you go I will go, wherever you lodge I will lodge, your people shall be my people and your God my God."[57]

One powerful memory stands out sharply while I was watching Jack in the night: I was working at a desk, my back to him, and then turned towards him. Lying flat on his back in bed, his arms were raised in silent prayer and surrender to his God.

The time with Jack allowed both of us to ask forgiveness of each other for some hurts and misunderstanding. Reconciliation came late, but then it came in a rush." – Peter Byrne, SJ.

CHAPTER 33

Looking Back, Looking Forward

Life is eternal, love is immortal, and death is only a horizon.[58]

— WILLIAM PENN

WHAT KEPT ME GOING IN life? What kept me looking beyond the horizon? Deep inside and unannounced, I can identify it as the game, the high stakes, the roll of the dice, the adrenalin of venturing beyond my sight and risking all, with my will and entire existence teetering on the edge. I would ask: will I win or lose? Fantastic game! Some do it in Vegas or Monte Carlo. My game seemed wrapped up in daily living, in the ongoing flow of the life of the Spirit. Every day, every decade, I had to cast the dice.

In breaking open the scene at Calvary, there are three rough men beneath a bloody corpse, squatting and shaking the dice for the dead man's cloak. A double scene of gambling. For the guards, the dead man's cloak is at stake; for him on the cross, it was the whole world. Somewhere in between, I fit, we all fit. The dice throwers, card sharks, stock market merchants, real estate magnets, you and me–it's about the game of life, how you see it, how you play it. We are all in it–this game of chance–whether we know it or not. It is for keeps, and for everything we've got.

Jesus was willing to lay his all on the game table. It was a table of holy beginnings and becoming, of danger and risk. I'd have left the Society of Jesus and the priesthood way back if I didn't see Jesus, human like me in all things except sin, risking all on one throw of the dice–his one life for all.

You ask me, what kept me going? It was the wonderful and joyous intimacy of my life. It was so bountiful, with men and women and children, and with families, those I helped, and those who helped me. I shared it with some of my coworkers in the vineyard, those in my Jesuit community, but most of all I walked it with my brother Jesus, the greatest gambler of all. Every time I said Mass, he and I would go to the game table together. Like Him, I tried to lay down my whole fortune the way He did. He showed me how to do it. I lament that I also drew back so many times, worrying that I'd end up losing myself. I was often afraid.

But I was given a great gift—a holy communion with humanity's greatest gambler. Jesus' passion and his desire for me is divine, beyond this world even. When the pain of my losses got high and dread grew intense, I listened a little closer, and I heard, "Fear not, fear not." Jesus' vibrations would sing of peace that no one could steal from me. In spite of my restlessness, my life-long drive towards accomplishment, my confusion and anxiety to become a saint, it was this inner life that kept me going.

I was absolutely sure I was playing the right game. I was sitting at the right table, and was tutored by the right guy. It wasn't about something in my head, but something singular I kept experiencing at my core. It was about a love that sharpened the focus of my life, sounded a trumpet in my blood, and whispered intimacy beyond all telling. The stakes were full of holy insecurity, but Jesus was the one who helped me cross the void that divided me from my true self.

In no way was it possible to totally comprehend the measure of the game or the reality of the passing of time, or to grasp what it meant that 84 years of flowing water had tumbled under the bridge named Jack Morris. Life for me won't end; it will be transformed. I've been more certain of that than anything in my existence. The happiest element in my life has been the adventure, the sheer risk of growing older and closer to God, and my true identity as a spiritual being.

What has my writing journey backwards in time meant? I've been walking toward my future by revisiting my past. In other words, good memories make good guides. Indeed, contemplating old age must be more than imagining a final stage in human growth. Are we supposed to be like old horses in harness, compelled to pull the plow until we drop in the fields? What makes old age different? Isn't there within old age a call to go backwards in time, to gather up all that composes our life, and put it together as something beautiful for God?

For several years, I told people with a smile, and I hope it wasn't prideful, that the single best thing going on in my life was this process we call aging. As strange and countercultural as it may seem, I genuinely appreciated growing old. It felt so personal. I found it mysterious, intriguing, playful, rude, totally unreasonable and challenging. Said differently, I believe I had established a love affair with the irreversible process of life.

So how did that love affair with aging work for me? I believe like this: God is real and God loves me personally and absolutely. Such a God in no way wants to do harm to me. And old age, like life in all phases, comes from God. So old age must be good. My task in writing was to bend over the stream of my life with a gold pan, to dip, sift and wash the sands to uncover the hidden flakes of gold, and to sift in old age what was authentic from what was fool's gold.

I was born, raised, educated, ordained and served my whole adult life under the umbrella of the Catholic Church. Only in the Church did I continually hear the call that each and every individual is stamped with the divine, and is therefore sacred. Does the Church fail? Yes, because the Church is made up of ordinary mortals like you and me. I laughingly would say to people, "Why should we expect religion to work perfectly, nothing else does." My motto: yes, look at the Church's back-side, her shadow, her going to bed with wealth and power, just like you look at your own dark side. We must learn from it and strive to do better. But also walk around and look at her front side. See the prayer, worship, missions, parishes, schools, hospitals and clinics, with the people, often the poorest. Now look at your own light side. We ask others to judge us by what is best in us. With the Church, let's try to do likewise.

After all is said, the Church is at its root about the Holy Spirit. Saint Thomas reminded us that everything and everyone–from Popes, bishops, sacraments, churches, creed–has one purpose, to help us experience the Holy Spirit. She is the giver of wisdom and life. She is the comforter, advocate and friend. We are the people of God, baptized into the life of our Lord on the journey from bondage to freedom.

For the love of serving God and neighbor.

God is a word humans use to name and point to the unfathomable, incomprehensible mystery. We can no more define it than can fish define water, though we, like they, exist and move in it. Yet all peoples of the world experience and name it. Jesus, as fully human as you and I are, felt the presence of the mystery. He renamed the mystery with the word *Abba, Father*, and this made all the difference. He is the mystery in human flesh. We are called to hallow that name, to keep the compass needle of our deepest-self pointed to that brilliance. The mystery has been revealing itself even before the Big Bang. I plant both feet in the Word of God, I believe that the coming of Jesus and unfolding of his agenda is, as Revelation says, about a new heaven and a new earth. The old world is passing away. In this new world, all are one. The lion and the lamb lie down together. Spears are beaten into pruning hooks, and war is no more. It's about changing the water of this world into the wine of the heavenly banquet. This kingdom is already happening wherever people love, suffer for one another, serve, and forgive.

With the passage of my years, I've accepted that I am a pilgrim at heart, finding God through experiences on the road of life. I still see life in this bright, positive way. I don't resist, I know the goal. If anything, joy, gratitude, wonder and anticipation gather richer. I trust in the power of God's mesmerizing love.

Love seems to be the evolutionary goal of our universe. The most comprehensive word we have for the call from one's deepest self is love. God's love is the most mysterious of all cosmic forces. It is huge, ubiquitous and irrepressible, a force that defeats all human efforts to harness it. It runs everywhere beneath our civilization like great streaming rivers. In our timidity, we are conscious only of its edges and ask only to be amused and not undone by it. How much truth and energy is being lost and squandered by neglecting the incredible power of love? We find God in energy, stars, stones, yet more fully in plants, and still more fully realized in animals. But above all, God is most perfectly present in the astonishing love of which humans are capable.

We humans do, however, carry within ourselves a consciousness of the primal tragedy, the seed of our own earthly dissolution as in the "Negro Spiritual" that addresses the sorrows and sufferings of slavery, yet gives the daily bread of hope. The door to the heart of God is the cross of Jesus Christ: "The Lord's so high you can't go over him, the Lord's so low you can't go under him, the Lord's so wide you can't go around him." We've all got to go through the door.

I believe that to be embraced fully by the mystery we name Father-God, I must die. I don't need to live on and on. Death is coming for me on an errand of love to take me to the everlasting wedding. I am unable to reach home, the home every fiber of my being longs for, unless death comes and takes me by the hand. Some may peg my faith as Pollyannaish, as half-baked, but I continually go into my heart and am nourished, warmed, and confirmed with a fulfilling joy. So, is it all crazy and wrong-headed? Well,

I'd sooner live in my faith than die in the dull, vapid secularism that can't see beyond the grave. In the end, if it comes down to pragmatism or fidelity, I'll take fidelity. If it comes down to human worldliness or the foolishness of God, I'll take the side of fools.

Every so often an image of death visited me. I envisioned myself on a train, sitting comfortably at a window seat. I gazed out at the mountains, small towns and running streams, tall trees, and green grasses. I had my coffee, my snooze, and felt loose and relaxed, knowing I was far closer to my destination than to my start. I anticipated a train man or woman entering my car and announcing in a firm, clear voice, "Next stop, Jack Morris!" I'd smile and reach for my luggage, then remember I didn't have a blessed thing. The train would jerk and slow to a halt. I'd float down the aisle to the open door where I noticed a beautiful meadow, birds singing, orchards and hills, lofty mountains and pure blue sky. Many people rushed the train—my family, my brother Jesuits, friends, JVs, even old George Zabelka. Some were singing, dancing, bringing flowers—no one wore clothes, there was nothing to hide, just as in my childhood. The music was out of this world. Only then did I realize it was like paradise and we were all perfectly free!

Sometime before my ordination in 1962, I made a retreat. Let me tell you about it. It was a perfect spring day, a day for a walk. I hiked a narrow trail through the woods and came upon a black thick slug, laboriously dragging his blind body across my path. I bent over him with a twig in my hand, nudged him, and began a conversation. All the while, I wondered what possible use such a glob of cellular matter possessed.

"Good morning Mr. Slug," I teased, "What brings you out today? What are you doing and where are you going?" I condescendingly asked, "Do you feel the gentle breeze, can you hear the birds sing, do you know the sun is moving across the heavens?" The slug surprised me. It humbly replied, "You think you're so smart and better than me as you bend over, annoying me with that stick. I'm alive, and my life is all I know, and precious to me as yours is to you."

I stood up, astounded, and dropped the stick. New insight shook my mind. I had looked on that slug with subtle contempt as if it were closer to non-life than life. Compared to my life, it hardly seemed consequential.

But what about me? Wasn't I in a very like posture when I stopped to compare my sinful, half-asleep life to the blazing, ecstatic life promised to those who surrender to God's ways and truth? Once again, something at the epicenter of my being quivered. How preposterous, a small blob of protoplasm had taught me profound, spiritual truth. That slug was pointing the way to what I longed to achieve.

All spirituality, no matter what tradition, attests to one mystical objective, namely to take the gift of freedom and use it to risk waking up, to find the true, undivided self that slumbers within. We are given clue after clue that all of creation is there at the tips of our senses to set our hearts singing together, to stir, enchant and delight us. It becomes sacrament when we perceive God luminously, lovingly and personally behind it all. To all creation, to all His sons and daughters, God offers a lullaby: "Fear not, for I have redeemed you; I have called you by your name. You are mine."[59]

CHAPTER 34

Last Letter

"I am ready."

JACK LIVED WELL BEYOND THE three days the doctors gave him after releasing him from the hospital in early 2012. After several weeks at Columbiere, in the late winter, Peter Byrne and Fred Mercy drove him to Spokane where Jack received nursing care at the Jesuit infirmary on the Gonzaga campus. He lived for several more months.

Jack wrote a final letter to his family, Jesuit brothers, friends, Bethlehem Peace Pilgrims, former Jesuit Volunteers and Micah friends in the summer, just months before he died:

> *"Dear Family and Friends,*
>
> *Let's face the fact—summer has begun and we are halfway through 2012—so I've decided to send a report on the Jack Morris story. I now weigh 160 pounds, a near thirty-pound weight gain since my "falling apart" when I was near to death (which was news to me) in January.*
>
> *Arriving here at Gonzaga in Spokane at the Jesuit Infirmary in early March 2012, I started gaining weight and mobility. Visitors, cards and letters galore arrived like a wind melting cold snows. I live with about a dozen senior Jesuits, three over 90 years of age, and they are veterans of universities, Alaska and native ministries. I am back in community with my brothers. Across the street at Bea House reside more senior Jesuits. I know them all on this final leg of my journey. It*

is impressive to consider the wide apostolic joy, truth and goodness they have spread through these long years of service. This is considered the most joyful of Jesuit communities.

No doubt you are concerned about my well-being. Our human task, if you like, is to not flee from the ill-being, but to transform it. So let's start there. That is the very substance of our faith in the risen Christ. In other words, this transformative power resides in the human heart.

On the practical level, I am unable to walk. I have taken several falls due to my human conceits. I am thoroughly tired of being an invalid, so I have to keep working at the transformative aspect of this journey.

At the heart of that process is the Biblical insight that all things (I emphasize ALL) no matter how we see them from our human point of view, work for the good of those who keep on loving. So, while my leg pains are rather constant, I have improved in living in this trans-formative zone, and if you can believe it, find joy in the mysterious adventure. I am glad for the ongoing challenge. At present, I am in five days of radiation treatment with some expectation that it will hasten abatement of the pain. Former Jesuit Volunteer, Jan Devlin Charles, accompanies me on these medical journeys and takes notes to help me remember what is going on.

Brother Fred drove over to Vashon Island without me to attend the thirty-year reunion of the Bethlehem Peace Pilgrims. They'll have a grand time and are expecting twenty-five pilgrims. Of course, because the pilgrimage originated with me, I was looking very much forward to this celebration, but I'm quite at peace that they can simply rejoice and I can rejoice with them. There's a stream of humor that flows through my feelings that the greater number of pilgrims were directly out of the Jesuit Volunteer Corps in 1982, and they are therefore now about the age that Brother Fred, Fr. George Zabelka and I were when we began the long walk. They have a whole new respect for the aged contingent at that time! (While writing this letter, the Pilgrims called me via Skype from Vashon Island. We were united in spirit and sang a few

lines with John Drury from his song, "Let There Be Reconciliation."
John flew over from Britain to be with the pilgrims' reunion; for some
things, there is no cost too dear.)

I am battling cancer. The tests show the prostate cancer metasta-
sized to the bones. I am receiving great care, cards, letters, and visits. I
am genuinely happy.

Let's keep praying for one another and trusting in our faith.
Because of a common Father, we are all brothers and sisters. I am in
my 85th year, have lived a full life and am quite happy with my life
and the future.

I suppose the bottom line for me is Jesus Christ's words to the dis-
couraged disciples on the road to Emmaus that spoke through their suf-
fering to the deeper reality: 'Was it not necessary for the Christ to suffer
and so enter into His glory?'

I feel I am on the glory road."

Afterward: Who Was Jack?
– by Barbara Underwood Scharff

"The only true failure is not to love,
not to allow oneself to be loved."

I WAS FAMILIAR WITH MANY legends about Jack Morris from my husband's and my service on the board of the Jesuit Volunteer Corps Northwest. I had shared in his presence sporadically over many years, discovering his many gifts to the world. But, over the last year of Jack's life, I worked with him on his book project. He asked me to finish his writing, and I promised him that I would. Completing Jack's memoir has been a profound honor. I've unearthed the treasures of an intensely personal and philosophical man–and yes, a man of action–from our many conversations together, and from his very transparent journals, honest letters, interviews, articles and homilies. He left traces everywhere of his lyrical Irish soul and his abiding love of Christ.

Jack Morris died September 30, 2012 in Spokane at the Jesuit infirmary after his long struggle with cancer. He was a man of loving energy, excitement, courage and vision. You couldn't miss seeing the glow of hope in his eyes. He was a poet, a prophet, a pilgrim and gypsy. He made a difference in the world by opening the hearts and minds of thousands of people to the Gospel value of caring for your neighbor, and enabling many to participate in the transformative power of service and love. He helped those he encountered see God's intimate and unexpected activity in the world.

He helped us find God's desiring heart for our own life. Jack taught us that however much one wishes to be heroic or saint-like, we are really just lovely signposts of God's love in a world full of billions of other lovely signposts.

Jack had an inventive spirit, and usually attributed what he built to the power of the Holy Spirit. He cofounded, and gave energy, form and structure to the Jesuit Volunteer Corps movement.

Jack tells his stories to new JVs.

Jack, Jeanne Haster, ED of JVC Northwest, Katie Haster,
and Fred Mercy at JVC Northwest Orientation.

When asked if he started the JVC movement, he said, *"I didn't really start it. It was already going...I just saw something worthwhile going on, tried to put some forms together, and got good people to come up to Alaska. I laughed with them and tried to pray with them. I wrote them a letter and told them they were wonderful. I think that's what I did. I told them they were wonderful."*

Jack also instigated the Chore elder program through Catholic Charities in Seattle, the Bethlehem Peace Pilgrimage, the Peace Newspaper in Seattle, a small credit union, and several faith communities.

Jack believed that the knot holding it all together was Jesus, who dwelled at the center of the human quest for community. Only in Christ-centered community could one transcend oneself by creating relationships of love and support. Only in community could one learn humility, and grow toward one's true identity in God. Jack's story is his unending commitment to keep trying community in many forms. He had a capacity for seeing what was needed in the future and addressing it in the now. He wanted to create a new church that opened its arms to the laity–equally women and men—to create new concepts of living together in Christ. In this way, he hoped to transform the very structures of the Catholic Church.

Jack with former JVs: back row left to right David Henry, Charles Bashara, Paul Grubb, SJ, Mark Hoelsken, SJ; front row Joseph Carver, SJ, Jack, Paul Janowiak, SJ, Denis Donoghue, SJ. © Brad Reynolds, SJ.

Jack's wandering spirit sometimes scared him. He feared uselessness, loneliness and rejection. He didn't want to be irrelevant or an outcast. Throughout his vowed life, he thought about leaving the Jesuits in pursuit of individual dreams and idealistic passions. He even thought at one point that he should start a hermitage for peace in the remote New Mexico desert where the first atomic bomb was tested. But those musings were overridden by both his loyalties and his convictions. He loved being a priest, to be Jesus' presence to others, to love, to serve, and to heal. He feared being outside the Society of Jesus, outside the Church, and following the wrong allurement that would interrupt his connection with God.

A man of originality, restlessness and earnest self-direction, Jack chafed at and resisted the normal and the mediocre. Throughout his early life and all through his priesthood, he found it hard to fit in to what others were doing. He was a maverick who had a way of stirring up the waters. He followed God's call farther out into the pounding surf than most of us would dare venture. Jack was a truth-teller. He possessed a radar-like sensibility that tracked the abuse of authority within human institutions. And so Jack never quit scrutinizing and criticizing the powerful male-dominated clericalism within the Church he honored. Deeply egalitarian, he was bothered by the "prestige" of priesthood and the Society. He said at the fifty-year anniversary of JVC Northwest: "Our common baptism, not priestly ordination, is the critical sacrament. Knowing that the Church operates in an increasingly complex, scientific, multicultural world with ever growing numbers of refugees, poor, displaced persons and wars, greater input and wider wisdom are demanded than can be provided by just the clerical governing model."

But whatever the shortcomings of the Church, Jack never quit loving it. He suffered from its falsehood and compromises, yet loved its purity and generosity. It was, after all, Christ's body. At the last Jesuit Volunteer Corps Northwest event he attended at Seattle University in the spring of 2011, he celebrated Mass, and read the words in his homily of Italian spiritual writer, Brother Carlo Carretto, about the Church:

> *"How much I must criticize you, my church, and yet how much I love you!*
> *…Countless times I have felt like slamming the door of my soul*
> *In your face--and yet, every night,*
> *I have prayed that I might die in your arms!"*[60]

I discovered these notes in one of Jack's many journals. They read like a final testament of devotion:

> "These things I believe –
> God loves me profoundly in an unending way, and it is a joyous and excellent love, nourishing and satisfying, always present and

beckoning. O Holy One, gentle and lovely, I adore you and worship you.

The Spirit guides us.

Jesus is the measure of our conduct, our quest and endeavor.

God calls me to a serious engagement with life, and I am given only time once. How I respond has implications for all eternity."

I came upon a late journal passage by Jack: "The sky is gray. Last night it was close in, calm and warm. As I prayed, I saw clearly that I must keep centered in the fact that All Is Well. Nothing can go wrong as everything is in God's hands. I am loved just as much whether I am working or waiting. I am as sacred and precious whether I am successful or a failure. The only true failure is to not love, not to allow oneself to be loved."

Jack believed that every new beginning and every movement of the spirit were identified by a crack, a place of discontinuity, paradox, tension and surprise. He urged us not to fear beginnings or tensions, not to fear the loss of control, but instead to ready ourselves, and search them out. He believed that death would be a surprising and disarming adventure, an entirely new, glorious beginning.

Jack knew he had to cross the threshold of death, but he couldn't wait to meet the Risen Christ, the One who had persistently courted him his entire life with a higher truth and calling. He was confident it would be the ultimate act of surrender, completion and communion.

Jack died just as he had lived, ever romanced by a bigger love.

Appendix

Peter Byrne's Homily at Jack's Funeral Mass
October 6, 2012, St. Aloysius Church, Spokane, Washington

"All Roads lead to Bethlehem and one day all must follow them,
Be ye great or be ye small, may the sweet Lord Jesus
Bless you all upon those roads to Bethlehem—and beyond."

"A cold coming we had of it,
Just the worst time of the year
For a journey, and such a long journey:
The ways deep and the weather sharp...
A hard time we had of it...
With the voices singing in our ears, saying
That this was all folly."

So BEGINS T.S. ELIOT'S MEMORABLE poem, "The Journey of the Magi,"[61] the pilgrimage to Bethlehem of ancient sorcerers, wizards if you will, searching and traversing until they came to the "uncontrollable mystery on the bestial floor."

And of course across field and fountain, moor and mountain, hearing voices singing in their ears saying "this was all folly!" Bethlehem! Jack, Jack Morris, you have got to be crazy! You're going to walk to Bethlehem! I am sure Jack and the many others making that pilgrimage at least once–perhaps many times—heard voices of parents, fellow Jesuits singing in your ears that this was all folly! Wacko! Nuts!

But Bethlehem it was to be, and why? Because there was another song singing—not in Jack's ears but in his heart—that Bethlehem was one of the privileged places of the Divine Folly! The Divine Folly of God in Jesus becoming the ultimate pilgrim, crossing all boundaries.

Why Bethlehem? Because Bethlehem was where God became homeless so we could all be at home. Bethlehem: where God, in Jesus, disappeared into the mess of humanity, became totally vulnerable. Bethlehem: where the Wonder Counselor, God-Hero, and most important the Prince of Peace would also become a pilgrim, and become the Way. Yes, Bethlehem it was to be, though as one writer said of the whole Middle East: "it is an unstable destination through unfamiliar territory, on an uneven road and, critically, having already used its spare tire."

In his heart, Jack was a pilgrim—he once told me he had a "gypsy soul," his lyrical, poetic Irish soul haunted by God, haunted by the beauty, searching always for this beauty, wandering, a modern day Augustine knowing that his heart was made for God and he would not rest until he rested in his Origin, his sources, his destiny.

Ruined for Life! Of course Ruined for Life became Jack's mantra to countless young people and older ones as well—to live a life of risk, of service to the poor, to ruin their lives as a Jesuit Volunteer—to take the risk of the Gospel even if their parents' and friends' voices would be singing in their ears saying that this was all folly. Who in the hell is this Jesuit putting these hare-brained ideas into your head?

Like Paul of Tarsus, the early pilgrim who constantly kept in touch by letters with the little communities he had started—Jack wrote numerous letters to Jesuit Volunteers and former JVs to encourage, to goad, to challenge, and to express his affection. An anthology of letters—a collection, edited and shared. Jack would resonate with Paul's letter to the Philippians:

My dear sisters and brothers:
I thank my God whenever I think of you,
And every time I pray for you all,

I always pray with joy for your partnership
In the gospel from the very first day up until the present.

I am quite confident that the One who began
A good work in you will go on completing it
Until the day of Christ Jesus comes.

It is only right that I should feel like this towards
You all, because you have a place in my heart, since
You have all shared together in the grace that has
Been mine, both my chains and my work defending
And establishing the gospel.

For God will testify for me how much I long for
You all with the warm longing of Christ Jesus;
It is my prayer that your love for one another
May grow more and more with the knowledge and
The complete understanding that will help you come
To true discernment, so that you will be innocent
And entirely filled with the fruits of uprightness
Through Jesus Christ, for the glory and praise of God.[62]

Returning to Eliot's poem, "Journey of the Magi," an important line:

"All this was a long time ago, I remember,
And I would do it again, but set down,
This set down
This: were we led all that way for
Birth or Death?"

Jack always knew the ultimate pilgrimage to God led to death. Jack knew the ultimate pilgrimage of Jesus led him to a hillside outside of Jerusalem, the place of Roman execution, led him to a beggar's grave where the story seemed to come to such an abrupt end—where Jesus on the cross certainly heard all sorts of voices saying that his whole life, his insistence on loving our enemies, of resisting evil and violence, with compassion and love was sheer folly, utter nonsense.

But we are here today to proclaim that the pilgrimage of Jesus did not end either at Bethlehem or at Calvary or a cold-stone tomb. We are here to proclaim with as much faith as we can muster that Jesus heard another voice—a voice stronger than death, the voice that always called him My Beloved Son!

And that voice sang a song so new—never heard before—so sweet, so strong, so creative and fanciful that it summoned Jesus, not back to life, but into a whole new life. And, after Jesus, every song is possible.

We are here to proclaim with as much gumption and trust and faith that Jack's pilgrimage is not ending up at St. Michael's cemetery where we will entrust him to the earth next to his Jesuit companions. But a Band of Angels will come after him to take him home.

Like Jesus, we believe, that because of the voice of the relentlessly faithful and fiercely loving heart of God: that for Jack too and all of us—all will be changed, changed utterly, and a terrible beauty will be born.

To Jack's two brothers Robert and Pat: When we brought Jack home to die last winter, you need to know how profoundly Jack appreciated the time that he had with you two, to tie up loose ends, to remember with such affection and gratitude your Montana roots, your heritage, your family. When we sat with him at night after you had to return home, he would comment.

To my Jesuit brothers: It meant so much to Jack that we could bring him home to Colombiere Community to be with us, his companions, on this Jesuit journey, and to gather to pray with him.

Fred Mercy: you were Jack's ever loyal friend and companion.

Pat Lee: you remind us we're not here to canonize Jack. We'll avoid naming buildings after him…it's not really our way.

> *"All Roads lead to Bethlehem and one day all must follow them,*
> *Be ye great or be ye small, may the sweet Lord Jesus bless*
> *You all upon those roads to Bethlehem—and beyond."*

Now Jack is "circling the deepest forest
Then turning into the last red campfire burning in the final hills
Where saints and heroes Rise and make him welcome,
Recognizing, under the shambles of his body,
A brother who has walked his thousand miles."

Yes, his pilgrimage is over. He is home.

Jack's Acknowledgments

THANK YOU TO MY FAMILY, my dear friends, my fellow Jesuits, the Jesuit Refugee Service, the faithful who served the Church in Africa, and all past, present and future Jesuit Volunteer Corps and Jesuit Volunteer Corps Northwest members, staff and supporters.

Thank you to my fellow **Bethlehem Peace Pilgrims**, both the core group and the many guest walkers who numbered in the hundreds who joined us on the way:

Core Walkers: Maureen Casey, Mary Frazel, Anne Galisky, Bookda Gheisar, Laurie Hasbrook, Rev. Janet Horman, Bill Ingalls-Cox, Pam Ingalls-Cox, Fr. Kevin Lafey, Sr. Genevieve Masuo, Fred Mercy, SJ, Dean McFalls, Alice McGarey, Mimi McKinley-Ward, Steve McKinley-Ward, Jack Morris, SJ, Bob Patten, Mary Jude Postel, Jim Thomas, Fr. George Zabelka.

Guest Walkers (a sampling): Anna Bianchi-Janetti, Elaine Caroll, Fr. Benoit Charlemagne, Joan Clough, Aideen Collins, Zvonko Curkic, Gerard Daechsel, Tony & Bert Daigle, Jim Doherty, John Drury, Nancy Faberge (aka Lhojaz Hidalgo), Georgette Goldman, Fr. Larry Gooley, Marcus Groffman, Olaf Guttler, Jerry Hartigan, Susann & William Holmes, Nick Jackson, Jack Jones, Nancy Kiehl, Yvette Naal, Paddy Martin, Jerry Malloy, Niall & Betty McElwaine, Sister Nina, Sister Nicodema, Sr. Christina O'Neill, CSTP, Danny Postel, Catherine Peck, Annie Plane, Chip Postem, Al Sagadelli, Hedi Vaccaro.

Thanks to the special folks I was with at **Bethlehem Farm:**

Alice McGarey, Paddy Martin, Mary Jude Postel, Fred Mercy, Larry Gooley, Maureen Casey, Bill & Pam Ingalls-Cox.

Thank you to Bennett Comerford for his friendship and interviews many summers ago. Heartfelt thanks to Barbara Underwood Scharff for agreeing to compile, research, edit, co-write and complete this holy mess of a writing project.

Barbara extends her gratitude to: Mary Doherty and Brittany Wilmes for their editing suggestions; Peter Byrne, SJ, Gary Smith, SJ, Fred Mercy, SJ, Larry Gooley, SJ, Pat and Rob Morris, Pam Ingalls, Gary Scharff, Jim Thomas, Joanne Bovey, Char Collora, and Nancy Haught for commenting on the manuscript and/or fact-checking; Peter Byrne and Joe Rastatter for their stories of Jack; Brad Reynolds, SJ, for permission to use his photographic images of Jack and former Jesuit Volunteers; Bill Cox for permission to use his BPP photos; the Jesuit Volunteer Corps Northwest media archives for the use of their photographic images; Pat and Rob Morris, and Fred Mercy for their photo images; and June Cooley for designing the book cover and helping with interior photos. Thank you to Rob Morris, and to the Foundation of Mercy, Yakima, Washington for their material support to bring this memoir to press.

Authors

Jack Morris, SJ, was born in Anaconda, Montana in 1927, served in the U.S. Navy before attending Georgetown University and Regis College (Denver). Jack entered the Jesuit Novitiate at Sheridan, Oregon in 1950 and was ordained a priest in 1962. Jack is most remembered for co-founding and organizing the Jesuit Volunteer Corps movement, founding the Senior Chore Services in Seattle, instigating the Bethlehem Peace Pilgrimage, an almost 7,000 mile walk from Bangor Naval Base, Washington, to Bethlehem, Israel in the early 1980s, and working for the Jesuit Refugee Service in the 1990s in Uganda, Africa. Jack started several intentional communities for peace, and lovingly pastored a number of parishes in the Oregon Province of Jesuits.

Editor/co-author **Barbara Underwood Scharff** graduated from the University of California, Berkeley in 1979, and authored with her mother *Hostage To Heaven* (Crown/Potter, NY, 1979). Barbara was an NBC radio producer in San Francisco in the 1980s, a founding board member of Friends of Trees in Portland, and a political staffer for schools, parks, and candidate campaigns. She and her husband Gary served many years on the Board of the Jesuit Volunteer Corps Northwest. Barbara is the mother of three children, one of whom served as a Jesuit Volunteer in Tacna, Peru.

Scriptural quotations are from the *New American Bible*, Saint Joseph Edition, The Old Testament 1970, Revised New Testament 1986, by the Confraternity of Christian Doctrine (CCD), Catholic Book Publishing Co., New York, NY.

CHAPTER 1. EXPLORING MY LIFE–WHY I MUST WRITE

1. T.S. Eliot, "Little Gidding" from FOUR QUARTETS. Copyright 1942 by T.S. Eliot; Copyright © renewed 1970 by Esme Valerie Eliot. Reprinted by permission of Houghton Mifflin Harcourt Publishing Company. All rights reserved.

2. T.S. Eliot, "East Coker" from FOUR QUARTETS. Copyright 1940 by T.S. Eliot. Copyright © renewed 1968 by Esme Valerie Eliot. Reprinted by permission of Houghton Mifflin Harcourt Publishing Company. All rights reserved.

CHAPTER 2. BEGINNINGS

3. St. Paul's Catholic Church was torn down in the urban renewal of Anaconda in the 1970's. A new church complex was built called Holy Family located on Pennsylvania Avenue.

CHAPTER 4. MY INTERIOR WORLD

4. William Wordsworth, "Ode. Intimations of Immortality" from *Recollections of Early Childhood,* The Oxford Book of English Verse: 1250-1900, edited 1919 by Arthur Quiller-Couch, Oxford: Clarendon.

Chapter 7. Meeting Maureen

5. Frank J. Sheed, *Theology and Sanity*, 1993, Ignatius Press. (Fifty years after Maureen had given Jack his first copy of the book, Maureen sent him another copy for his birthday in 2003, with a note that read: "Jack, I thought you might be interested to review this, since it made all the difference." signed–M.)

Chapter 9. Jesuit Formation Begins

6. Jean Vanier, *Community and Growth*. Reprinted by permission of Darton, Longman and Todd and Paulist Press publishers, revised edition, 1989, NY, p. 43.

7. Thomas Merton (translator), *The Wisdom of the Desert–Sayings from the Desert Fathers of the Fourth Century*, 1970 by New Directions Publishing, New York, NY; original copyright ©1960 by The Abbey of Gethsemani, Inc.

8. Philippians 3:8-10.

Chapter 10. Mount St. Michael

9. Romans 7:6.

10. Jack earned his Master's degree in economics from Gonzaga which provided the background for his work in establishing Toronto's Italian-Canadian Catholic Credit Union for the benefit of 160,000 immigrants. He continued studies in economics with summer work at the University of Detroit.

11. John 8:32.

12. John 9:39.

Chapter 11. My Father Dies

13. Matthew 8:22.

Chapter 12. The Far North

14. It has been estimated that from its founding in 1540, Jesuits worldwide set up a new school every three months for 250 years.

15. The six lay college women who answered the call: Ann Kent, Marge Mannix, Jacqueline Langlois, Rosemary Bobka, Jeannette Rageotte and Shirley Richard. Among the five St. Ann Sisters: Mary George Edmond, Alice LeGualt, Mary Eulalia, Mary Ida Brasseur and Jeannete LaRose. In the 1992 book *North To Share* (published by Sisters of St. Ann, British Columbia, Canada), authors Sr. Mary George Edmond, SSA, and Sr. Margaret Cantwell, SSA, named the five with their vocation names: Superior George Edmond, Agatha of the Angels, Freda, Alice Therese, and Edward of Jesus. The brigade of men consisted of: Fr. Jake Spils, Brother Hess, Steve Jankowski, Tony Sipary, Aldor Rageotte, Jim Poore, Tim Boardwell, Joe Newman, Larry Douville, and Al Gyllenhammer.

Chapter 13. Memories from Copper Valley

16. Martin Buber, *"Daniel: Dialogues on Realization,"* Translated by Maurice Friedman, Holt Rinehart & Winston, 1964, New York, NY, p. 95.

17. Sister Lou Ella Hickman is with the Sisters of the Incarnate Word & Blessed Sacrament (I.W.B.S.). She has been a member of the Incarnate Word and Blessed Sacrament congregation in Corpus Christi, Texas since 1970. She is a teacher, librarian and parish minister as well as a freelance writer with some 200 articles and 200 poems published including "she: robed and wordless," Press 53, 2015. "Gypsy Music"

is reprinted by permission from the author, originally published in National Catholic Reporter May 12, 2006.

18. John 3:8.

Chapter 14. Toronto and Theology
19. Pope John XXIII, Opening speech, Council of Vatican II, October 11, 1962, delivered in St. Peter's Basilica.

20. *Ibid.*

Chapter 16. Jesuit Volunteer Corps Movement Is Born
21. Dom Helder Camara, Letter from Dom Helder Camera to Mons. Jeronimo Podesta, Oct 1981, quoted from the blogspot of Iglesia Descalza – a voice from the margins of the Catholic Church, July 4, 2011, "Worlds of Worlds: Dom Helder Camara's Three Dreams."

Chapter 17. Tertianship
22. Romans 7:18-19.

23. Simone Weil, *Gravity and Grace*, London: Routledge and Kegan Paul, 1963, p. 53.

24. 1 Peter 5:8.

Chapter 18. Ruined For Life
25. Jack visited the Jesuits for three weeks in Zambia as a mission director in 1969.

26. The Jesuit Volunteer Corps (JVC) movement began in 1956, under the auspices of the Oregon Province of the Society of Jesus. A few committed volunteers helped build and teach in the new Copper Valley School in Copper Valley, Alaska, a boarding school for Native Alaskan and European-descent Alaskan students. The first volunteers were recruited and supported by the Jesuits of the Oregon Province and the Sisters of St. Ann. The Jesuit Volunteer program expanded out of Alaska in the 1960s to work with Native American communities throughout the Northwest. Jesuit Jack Morris was the first director. By the early 70s, Jesuit Bill Davis became director, and with JV Denny Duffell, opened placements for volunteers to serve in inner cities in the Pacific Northwest and throughout the U.S. and other countries around the world. Beginning in 1974, overseen by Jesuit Larry Gooley, JVC in the Northwest inspired the opening of five domestic regions of JVC in the Midwest, East, Southwest, and South, and one international region (JVI), each an independent non-profit office. JVC Northwest has been the catalyst for many other faith-based volunteer organizations, and served as a model for the U.S. Peace Corps. In JVC Northwest's 60 year history, over 6,800 persons have served in placements in the northwest and a similar number have served in JVC/JVI. In 2006, JVC Northwest discerned to remain independent and locally based to better serve the urgent needs of vulnerable people and places in local and regional communities in the Northwest including Alaska, Idaho, Montana, Washington and Oregon. At that time, the East, Midwest, South, and Southwest regions of JVC, along with JVI, made a decision to form one centralized structure based in Baltimore, Maryland. JVC Northwest continues to collaborate with JVC, united in the shared four foundational values of Jesuit Volunteers – social and ecological justice, simple living, community, and spirituality. Jesuit Volunteers (JVs) are committed to serving full time for at least one year in shelters, schools, health, and social and ecological service organizations in inner cities, rural areas and Native American and Native Alaskan communities providing essential skills, willing hands and great idealism for a better world.

27. Thirty-Fourth Congregation of the Jesuits.

28. The Jesuit priestly abuse scandals of children from the 1950s to the 1990s primarily took place or were alleged to have primarily taken place in Jesuit-operated mission schools on Indian reservations in the Pacific Northwest and Alaska. Father John Morse was named as one of the abusing priests as part of a $166.1 million settlement in March 2011 between the Oregon Province Society of Jesus and hundreds of abuse victims. Morse had served at St. Mary's Mission, Colville Reservation, near Omak, Washington in the 1960s. John Morse died in 2015, still asserting his innocence. John Morse is no relation to Fr. John "Jack" Morris. None of Fr. Jack Morris' writings indicates he was aware of any priestly abuse complaints while he was Director of the Jesuit Volunteer Corps in the 1960s. The Department of Health Services, State of Washington, did not keep records on complaints in the 1960s.

CHAPTER 19. ROUNDTABLE
29. 1 Corinthians 13:12.

30. One of Jack's efforts during this time: Writing from the Oregon Province of the Society of Jesus, Jack fired off a series of letters to his colleagues and superiors serving in Alaska, spurring them to take action on a new permanent Native Diaconate Program. His letters found a receptive audience in the Fairbanks diocese. Jesuit Bishop Francis Gleeson played a key role behind the scenes urging Vatican II leaders to restore the permanent Native Diaconate in anticipation of a time when there would be fewer priests to minister to the people of the region.

31. A lasting connection that developed was through Micah, a Washington State non-profit that is a network of people, families, and individuals of all ages, joined together to live out the values of community, prayer, social justice, and simple lifestyle. It began in 1991-1992 with monthly planning meetings in Seattle, Yakima, and Nestucca with founding

board members: Jack Morris, SJ, Mary Medved, Patty Houts-Hussey, Fred Mercy, SJ, Julie Burns-Christensen, Joe Orlando, Laura Cryan, Kate Kremer, Greg Kremer, Joe Hastings, Carol Donohue, Patrick Hussey, and John Christensen. The first Micah retreat was held in 1993, and Micah annual meetings and retreats have continued ever since. Not solely a JVC alumni organization, it embraces all organizations with values of Micah. "This is what Yahweh asks of you, only this: to act justly, to love tenderly, and to walk humbly with your God." Micah 6:8.

CHAPTER 20. TAKING CARE OF MA
32. Tobit 4:3.

CHAPTER 21. BETHLEHEM PEACE PILGRIMAGE I
33. Father George Zabelka served as Chaplain to the 509th Bombing Squadron that dropped the Hiroshima and Nagasaki bombs.

34. Archbishop Raymond Hunthausen speech, June 12, 1981, "Faith and Disarmament," Northwest Synod of the Lutheran Church; web post March 23, 2011 by Disarm Now Plowshares.

35. The U.S. Catholic Bishops 1983 pastoral letter, *The Challenge of Peace*.

36. "An Interview with a military chaplain who served the Hiroshima and Nagasaki bomb squadrons," August 1980 issue. Reprinted with permission from *Sojourners*, (800) 714-7474, www.sojo.net.

37. Jim Wallis and Joyce Hollyday later featured the story of George Zabelka in "Cloud of Witnesses," Orbis Books, 2005, p. 231.

38. J. Oppenheimer Media Gallery, atomicarchive.com.

39. On December 23, 1953, in what it claims were the "interests of national security," the Atomic Energy Commission (AEC) temporarily suspended Robert Oppenheimer's security clearance. Ultimately he was found to be a loyal citizen, but his security clearance was taken away.

CHAPTER 22. BETHLEHEM PEACE PILGRIMAGE II

40. John 17:21.

41. Martin Luther as quoted on MinistryHealth.net; "Preaching the Gospel–More Ministry Health Snippets," Wayne Dobratz, M.Div., Number 92.

42. Thomas Merton,*"Conjectures of a Guilty Bystander,"* Doubleday Religion, division of Random House, Inc., NY, ©1965, 1966 by The Abbey of Gethsemani, p. 21.

43. Matthew, 14:14-21.

CHAPTER 23. BETHLEHEM PEACE PILGRIMAGE III

44. *Gods of Metal* is a short 28-minute documentary film produced by Maryknoll Fathers Roy Bourgeois and Paul Newpower and directed by Robert Richter in 1982. It was nominated for an Academy Award for Best Documentary Short. It can be rented or ordered from Maryknoll Films, Pinesbridge Road, Maryknoll, N.Y.

45. Thomas Merton, "Cold War Letters," edited by Christine M. Bochen and Williams H. Shannon, 2006, Orbis Books, Maryknoll, NY.

CHAPTER 24. BETHLEHEM PEACE PILGRIMAGE IV

46. Hebrews, 11:16.

47. This prayer is found in A New Zealand Prayer Book/He Karakia Mihinare o Aotearoa (p.164). Although it has also been credited as an adaptation by the Hindu Swami Chidananda Saraswati, it is a well-known adaptation of the famous mantra from the Hindu Upanishads by Satish Kumar, a former Jain monk.

Chapter 25. Bethlehem Peace Pilgrimage V

48. Luke 23:34.

Chapter 26. Examining My Affections

49. Philippians 3:8-12.

Chapter 28. Bethlehem Peace Farm

50. Jean Vanier, *Community and Growth*. Reprinted by permission of Darton, Longman and Todd and Paulist Press, revised edition, 1989, NY, p. 109.

51. This prayer was composed by Bishop Ken Untener of Saginaw, drafted for a homily by Card. John Dearden in Nov. 1979 for a celebration of departed priests. As a reflection on the anniversary of the martyrdom of Bishop Romero, Bishop Untener included in a reflection book a passage titled "The mystery of the Romero Prayer." One mystery is that the words of the prayer are attributed to Oscar Romero, but they were never spoken directly by him.

Chapter 31. Uganda, Africa III

52. Juliana of Norwich, *Revelations of Divine Love*, 14th Revelation, Chapter 63, c. 1393.

53. Nor had their children been to school for six years. JRS set up a school in Eden, with 800 students in grades 1 through 8. Six-hundred

children, up to age ten, were placed in the first grade due to this long period without schooling.

54. James 2:5.

CHAPTER 32. TIME SPEEDS UP

55. Matthew 20:16.

56. Matthew 10:39.

57. Book of Ruth 1:16.

CHAPTER 33. LOOKING BACK–LOOKING FORWARD

58. William Penn, prayer originally attributed to him (1644-1718).

59. Isaiah 43:1.

AFTERWARD: WHO WAS JACK?

60. Carlo Carretto, *I Sought and I Found*. Reprinted with permission from Darton, Longmann and Todd, London, England, 1984.

APPENDIX–PETER BYRNE'S HOMILY AT JACK'S FUNERAL MASS

61. T.S. Eliot, "Journey of the Magi" from COLLECTED POEMS 1909-1962. Copyright 1936 by Houghton Mifflin Harcourt Publishing Company. Copyright © renewed 1964 by Thomas Stearns Eliot. Reprinted by permission of Houghton Mifflin Harcourt Publishing Company. All rights reserved.

62. Philippians 1:3-11 (as paraphrased by Peter Byrne, in his funeral homily).

Made in the USA
Monee, IL
07 May 2022

96047558R00156